THE

Afterlife Chronicles

EXPLORING THE CONNECTION BETWEEN
LIFE, DEATH, AND BEYOND

Nicole Strickland

KAYLI MAX BOOKS

Interior layout by Rachel Newhouse for elfinpen designs
Cover design by Abby Simmons of AbbyDesignsIt.

ISBN: 979-8-9880654-0-1

Published by Kayli Max Books
www.authornicolestrickland.com

Once again, Nicole Strickland has done humanity a great favor: she has combined her diligent research and editing with a seasoned writer's panache in order to gently nudge the veil separating this world from the next to one side. In doing so, she presents readers with a hopeful glimpse into eternity and fosters hope, the kindest gift of all.

Gary Mantz: Alternative Talk AM 1150 Seattle

Death takes many forms but often a certain serenity comes over people as they near passing. Having witnessed many people who have transitioned from this life, there are many unknowns that are faced. Author Nicole Strickland has included many experiences and ideas in her new book *The Afterlife Chronicles: Exploring the Connection Between Life, Death, and Beyond.* It provides an interesting coverage of perspectives from many different sources. It is a worthwhile read for anyone interested in learning more about this often-overlooked subject. I recommend it highly.

James Brandmueller: Retired Hospice Chaplain

If you're like others, you've wondered what happens to our soul after we die. Is there some sort of intelligent 'life' after death? Does our conscious mind end or continue on in some fashion?

For the sake of argument, let's state that there is some undying consciousness that lingers on. How do we communicate with that consciousness? Is there a way to intelligently interact with those who have passed on? Can we do that on our own or do we need a psychic medium to give us whatever messages are out there?

So very many questions surround this topic. While we don't definitively know the answers, Nicole's book will touch on these very subjects in a thoughtful, concise, and straightforward manner so that after read *The Afterlife Chronicles,* you can make your own informed decisions regarding the afterlife and the paranormal. Interspersed with Nicole's narrative are stories from contributors who have encountered beings from beyond the grave.

This is a fantastic, informative, and entertaining read. I very highly recommend it.

Lisa Krick – Ghostly Voices

Hope for the soul, an eye-opener! This book is a must-read for those curious about life after death. Let's face it: we all think about the existence of an afterlife and this book not only sheds much-needed light on the subject but also helps prepare the soul.

Todd Bates – WLTK-db Owner, Founder of Haunted Voices

The Afterlife Chronicles delves into some of life's most mysterious subjects, including what happens to us after we die, why spirits communicate with the living, and why everyone has psychic potential. Nicole Strickland engages, educates and entertains the reader with subjects that include the different types of spirit communication, the power of crystals and chakras, the influence of our thoughts on the world, and much more. The collection of personal paranormal experiences shared in the book is also extremely compelling and thought-provoking.

Cheryl Knight – Editor of Paranormal Underground Magazine

The Afterlife Chronicles explores what all of us wonder about at some point in our lives: life, death, and beyond. With exemplary writing skills, and with a wealth of research and knowledge, including many stories from those who are blessed to experience the afterlife, Nicole Strickland has created a bridge, connecting life, death, and beyond, through the wisdom of her words. A must-read for those who have experienced the loss of loved ones, and for everyone who wonders about life and just what there may be beyond.

Helen Margaret: RN, BSN

I have had the opportunity to work with Nicole for over 15 years exploring the paranormal in a variety of settings. Nicole is always looking to explore the unknown and examine the connection between life, death, and beyond. It is a topic that piques the interest of many individuals. Nicole can bring topics to life and present information in a thoughtful manner that lets readers immerse themselves in new ideas and think beyond. Nicole is not afraid to challenge the status quo and provide a new thought process about a topic. She wants her readers to use her research and experience to gain a better understanding of the afterlife in their own lives. This is a must-read book crafted by a well-known member of the paranormal community.

Nicole Tito: Ghostly Voices

Dillon Martinez – Friend and Beloved RMS *Queen Mary* Tour Guide

I first met Dillon onboard the legendary RMS *Queen Mary*, an iconic ship that both he and I revere. With his infectious personality and devotion to the ship, Dillon brought about the best in all those around him. On my many visits to the liner, I would often see Dillon with his natural enthusiasm, giving memorable tours to guests. He had an innate gift of connecting with visitors as he shared enriching historical accounts from the *Queen Mary's* prodigious career on the seas.

It's been almost seven years since Dillon and I first met. He has touched the hearts of his fellow crew and many from around the world. He was an exceptional tour guide and a remarkable individual who now knows the secrets of the universe. Indeed, the stately *Queen Mary* called Dillon over and forever wrapped her arms around him. His zest for life continues to infuse all those who knew him and have had the opportunity to be graced by his presence. Rest in eternal love and peace.

Rosemary Ellen Guiley – A Guiding Light and True Pioneer

The beauty of paranormal phenomena lies in their ability to be vague and mysterious. As researchers of the unknown, we should be open to all possibilities and possess an optimistic skepticism while remaining objective. As a foremost researcher and prolific author in all the key branches of supernatural phenomena, Rosemary Ellen Guiley was able to accomplish that optimistic skepticism with grace, honor, and dignity. She wasn't afraid to step outside the proverbial box and experiment with various methodologies. Her keen ability and confidence in doing this, along with her heartfelt passion for the unknown realm, made her a standout scholar in the field of paranormal study. With her countless years of devotion, she helped pave the way for newcomer and veteran researchers alike by braving the challenges that often come with investigating the supernatural.

I was blessed beyond words to have the opportunity to work with Rosemary. It was an honor to witness her seamless agility in combining learned knowledge, creative investigation, and unique research methodologies. Rosemary was a true mentor to all and a leading pioneer on so many levels. I will cherish the times I spent with her and other members of the Ghost Research Society at renowned places like Waverly Hills Sanatorium and the RMS *Queen Mary*. In a way, paranormal research is a form of art. Watching Rosemary's work was synonymous with witnessing any other notable artist in the creative process.

Rosemary now knows the secrets of the universe; she's unlocking the keys to understanding what she hypothesized, tested, and researched for so many years. As in life, she will continue her quest in spirit, offering guidance and expertise from beyond the ethers. The paranormal community is truly saddened by her loss. Let's honor Rosemary by continuing her legacy. Shared knowledge leads to brightened horizons, and this is something she deeply understood.

We love you, Rosemary, and will be reunited with you someday. Until then, we are just across the veil on the other side, continuing down the path that you've paved for so many. Rest in eternal love and peace.

"I know beyond a shadow of a doubt that there is no death the way we understood it. The body dies, but not the soul."

ELISABETH KÜBLER-ROSS

Contents

Foreword I

Acknowledgments III

A Note to the Reader VII

Studying the Afterlife: Personal Implications VII

CHAPTER 1 | 1

What is an Afterlife, Anyway?

The Distinction Between Ghosts and Spirits 2

Why Does the Spirit World Communicate with the Living? 6

Encountering My Grandmother's Spirit.............................7

The Loss of a Brother 11

The Loss of a Best Friend 13

Jessie's Warning..15

The Afterlife According to Various Cultures......................22

The Influence of the Spiritualist Movement on Modern-Day Spirit Communication and Paranormal Research 24

CHAPTER 2 | 29

Spirit Connection with the Living: Recognizing the Signs

An Ethereal Hug..36

Dream Visitations with Kayli..38

Norma's Dream Visitation 41

Ali's Dream Visitation..43

Not a Fan of Snakes 48

Edinburgh Terror...50

Spirits Reaching Out..54

CHAPTER 3 | 59

The Role of Intuition and Mind/Body/Spirit in Connecting with the Afterlife

What is Intuition? 59

The Role of Intuition in the Mind / Body / Spirit Nexus 63

The Connection Between Mind/Body/Spirit and the Afterlife 65

Exercise to Hone Your Intuition 66

Utilizing the Six Intuitive Modalities 67

The Chakras: The Body's Energy Fields 74

Exercises to Balance the Chakras 78

Exercises and Tips for Strengthening Your Psychic Potential 81

Meditation is Integral to the Connection Between the Living and the Afterlife 84

CHAPTER 4 | 87

Examining the Profound Connectedness Between the Living World and the Afterlife

Aunt Lydie Appears 92

Aaron's First Paranormal Experience 95

Dawn's Visions 96

The Role of Psychokinesis in Communication with the Afterlife 98

Bob Encounters His Grandmother's Spirit 100

The Living Soul Hypothesis 103

Do Near-Death Experiences Hold the Key to Understanding Life after Death? 105

Benje's NDE 111

Could Einstein's Theory Shed Light on the Afterlife? 112

Quantum Theories and Life After Death 112

The Orange Balloon 114

CHAPTER 5 | 119

Common Misconceptions of the Spirit World

Do Ghosts and/or Spirits Harm the Living? 120

The Influence of Thought Projections and Tulpas on the Spirit Realm 122

The Misconception of Paranormal Television 127

CHAPTER 6 | 129

Communicating with the Spirit Realm— Standard Techniques

The Scientific Method: Stepping Outside of the Shadows of Pseudoscience 130

Audio Communication Methods: Electronic Voice Phenomena (EVP) and Instrumental Trans Communication (ITC) 132

Spirit Photography 144

The Relationship Between the Afterlife and the Environment 147

Paranormal Vigils 151

CHAPTER 7 | 153

Communicating with the Spirit Realm: Alternative and Divination Techniques

The Power of Crystals and Gemstones 154

Divining (Dowsing) Rods 158

Pendulums 160

Automatic Writing (Channeled Writing) 163

Séances 164

Talking (Ouija) Boards 166

Scrying 168

CHAPTER 8 | 171

Fostering the Connection: The Power of Spirit Guides

Spirit Guide Awareness 171

Types of Spirit Guides 173

Perception is Key: Spirit Guide Contact 177

Ways to Get in Touch with Your Spirit Guide(s) 184

Kathie Guetzko's Story 187

Pete Orbea's Story 192

Auriel Grace's Story 197

CHAPTER 9 | 201

Fostering the Connection: How Moving Through Grief and Loss
Can Help You Further Connect with the Spirit Realm

Universal Experiences: The Five Stages of Grief and Loss 201

Bereavement   Hallucinations: Visits   and   Messages   from   the
    Dearly Departed 207

Healing Your Loss While Honoring Your Loved One 209

Healing from the Loss of a Beloved Sister 214

A Profound Experience at Pomerado Hospital 217

A Healing Message in Numbers 219

A Symbolic Message After My Grandfather's Transition 221

Healing from the Loss of a Beloved Friend's Son 225

Endless Love: Max Transitions to the Afterlife 231

Epilogue 239

Bibliography 243

About the Author 249

Foreword

The afterlife is real. It is as real as the chair you are sitting on or the book you hold in your hands. It is all around you—not in some faraway place or beyond the clouds in the sky. The magical wonder of the afterlife envelopes you from the moment you leave your physical body behind.

How do I know this? Because I've been there. Well, sort of. Not in the sense of a near-death experience, but through the afterlife communication sessions I've conducted over the last two decades. I've witnessed countless images and descriptions of the afterlife from thousands of souls who stepped forward through the veil that separates our worlds. While their sole purpose was to send messages to the loved ones they left behind, they opened a portal that allowed me to glimpse into their spiritual world with amazement and wonder.

Nicole Strickland is about to take you on a fascinating journey to explore this spiritual realm and the bonds of love that connect you with your departed loved ones. The factual stories within these chapters reveal tantalizing insight into how connected we are to our loved ones and the creative and unexpected ways they let us know they are near and still very much a part of our lives.

There is a synchronicity in their messages that can be so powerful that it impacts the very core of your belief system in profound and life-changing ways. If you are already open to the idea of life after life, you'll find comfort and validation in the unique and loving ways spirits reach out to help us throughout our lives.

Perhaps you have had an afterlife experience, and that is what brought you here today. A desire to discover more about the strong connection between this world and the one beyond the veil. But even if the idea of the afterlife is new to you, the chapters within this book will undoubtedly fill your mind with a new perspective and many uplifting stories to ponder.

I have no doubt that your departed loved ones gently guided you to this thought-provoking book and fueled your thirst for knowledge about the afterlife. They want you to know that you are more than just a physical body of flesh and blood. You are an eternal soul, a being of light, and one day when your time here on Earth is complete, you will thrive with your loved ones in the shimmering glory of the afterlife.

Karen A. Anderson - Afterlife Specialist & Medium
#1 National and International Bestselling and Award-Winning Author of
The Amazing Afterlife of Animals and *Hear All Creatures*

Acknowledgments

The actual writing of this book didn't take long at all to complete. In reality, however, the creation of this manuscript has taken around forty years of my life thus far. In that time, my experience as a paranormal researcher, coupled with countless encounters with the spirit realm, has allowed me to develop my own perspectives regarding the afterlife. In other words, my views regarding the supernatural didn't just develop over a year or two; the combination of my childhood and adulthood has contributed to my attitude about ghosts, spirits, and the ethereal domain. I am happy to share with you my opinions regarding the beauty of the spirit world. I realize that not everyone will agree; that's completely understandable, as this topic is highly controversial and subjective. As such, I want to thank all my readers for taking the time to read this book. It is my hope that it can bring you comfort in times of grief and/or a new way of looking at those who dwell in the spirit world.

In addition to my own shared incorporeal experiences, many individuals opted to impart to me their unique encounters with the afterlife. This manuscript would not be complete without these profound stories, as they help shape the overall foundation of this book. Therefore, much gratitude goes to all contributors as their accounts will be forever memorialized in this written work. A huge thank you to Norma Strickland, Ali Schreiber, Marie D. Jones, Elizabeth Wise Mazak, Pete Orbea, Kathie Guetzko, Auriel Grace, Dawn Gaudette, Benje, Bob Fountain, Denise A. Agnew, JC Rositas, Linda Myers, Scott Oates, Angela Wallace, William Brower, Lon Strickler, Aaron Collins, and Joanne Yates. I am very indebted to these individuals for taking the time to share their stories.

The foreword is an integral part of a book. With that said, an author needs to apply careful thought as to who writes it. I am more than honored and grateful to have Karen Anderson, bestselling author and afterlife expert, write this manuscript's foreword. She has a humble and genuine understanding of the spirit realm and a knowledge of what it takes to connect with those who've departed the earthly plane.

I also want to acknowledge all of the loved ones who are no longer here but remain with us in spirit. We love you and will be reunited with you someday. As you've moved through the ranks of spirithood, you've gained a deeper understanding of the cosmos and the greater good for all. We thank you for imparting this profound knowledge to those of us still residing in the mortal realm. Andrew F. Lopinto, M.D., Helen Lopinto, Marion Strickland, Max, Merlin, Simba, and Kayli, you are always in my heart. I also want to thank my own spirit guides for helping to assist me along the way. I am forever grateful for your genuine love and wisdom.

Thank you to my family and friends for believing in me and my work. I am grateful for my parents' (Byron Strickland and Norma Strickland) love and encouragement throughout the years. I am honored to be your daughter. Aeries and Kayli, your support hasn't gone unnoticed; I have cherished the times you sat by me and purred as I typed for hours on my Macbook Pro. To all of my paranormal research friends and colleagues, keep delving into the unknown and conducting great research.

I am thankful for all the ghosts and spirits I've come across throughout my life. Through my experiences with each and every one of you, I have gained a deeper awareness of the afterlife and a greater understanding of physical death.

A Note to the Reader

The concept of life after death can be a difficult topic to talk about. Although this book addresses various aspects in relation to the afterlife, please understand that its purpose isn't to persuade you to have beliefs in the spirit world. Whether you do or not, this book is meant to open your heart to the wondrous possibilities that exist when we pass from the mortal plane and, most importantly, to emphasize that the bonds of love between us and our departed loved ones remain eternally. Everyone experiences the loss of a loved one. It is my hope that this book offers you comfort and guidance when that day comes.

Studying the Afterlife: Personal Implications

I first opened my eyes in the delivery room on May 21, 1979, at precisely 8:02 a.m. At that moment, I was saturated with an infinite sense of wonder and curiosity. Yes, I actually remember being born and hearing the doctor say, "Quick, close the lights; she's opening her eyes." Instead of belting out a cry to exercise my brand-new lungs, I laid on my back with eyes wide open, possessing an almost infinite awareness that has penetrated my life ever since.

Perhaps it was at that moment that I met my divine maker. Is this possible with birth just as it is with death? I was born into this world feeling an overpowering sense of love and peace.

Even in my infancy, I had a great interest in the paranormal and spiritual realms. Being the creative and innately intuitive youth that I was, I often stared up at the stars at night, yearning to discover more about our galaxies beyond. As a young child, I began to experience the paranormal and communicate with the spirit realm while living in Las Vegas, Nevada. On a particular summer night, my parents and I had just finished swimming in our backyard pool when I had the most unusual encounter: As the sun made way for the celestial stars, I noticed this mass swiftly move right past us. It almost resembled a wide-open cape, minus the physical body inside it. I wasn't scared at all. I was mainly encased with sheer curiosity.

Quickly realizing that my mom and dad were oblivious to the anomaly and my reactions to it, I assertively exclaimed, "Look at that draft. What is it?" My parents looked at me dumbfounded, not entirely cognizant of what I was asking or referring to. Of course, with my limited learned vocabulary at just five years, I tried my best to explain what my eyes saw. Yet, they were still confused, and rightly so. It was then that my seed of intrigue was planted in the ever-elusive soil of the supernatural.

As I sit at my desk now typing these words, I look back and wonder why I referred to what I saw on that one summer evening many years ago as "a draft." Noun, verb, or adjective definitions of the word don't explain why I chose it as a marker for what I witnessed. Perhaps I felt a cold draft of air rush by my parents when I saw the mass gliding by. Honestly, I don't quite remember. There has to be some sort of universal reason why I chose to describe my occurrence using the word "draft." The answer will either come to me one day or remain elusive until I am granted the keys to unlocking the secrets of the universe when I reach those pearly gates.

While residing in Nevada, I was at the age when children create imaginary friends; however, the alleged make-believe individual I talked with almost on a daily basis wasn't all that made up. Yes, in addition to the aforementioned encounter, I was able to communicate with an ethereal specter. You see, he was an earthbound spirit from the 1800s who made a point to visit me. Of course, my parents must have thought, "There goes Nicole playing with her imaginary friends," when they heard me talk to thin air in my bedroom. The specter and I instantly became friends; as an adult, I surmise that he originated from the Gold Rush days and desired to share his life stories with me. Maybe this particular entity chose to communicate with me because he knew I could sense his energy. As a young child, I possessed a keen awareness, sensitivity, and imagination beyond my years; perhaps all of these combined to help me develop abilities to communicate with the spirit realm.

As I grew older, I made a point to research the paranormal realm during my middle and high school years. Prior to the Internet commencing, I relied heavily on books and articles written on the subject. However, it was an experience during my senior year of undergraduate college that catapulted my interest in investigating the paranormal field as an adult. Many ghost researchers can relay a life-changing encounter that propelled them into the field of the supernatural. For me, this particular occurrence involved the spirit of my maternal grandmother, Helen Lopinto, who you will read about in the coming chapters.

This singular yet powerful experience with the spirit of my grandmother sealed my quest in learning more about the unknown. Honestly, I don't know if I would be where I am today as a paranormal researcher and spirit advocate if it wasn't for this encounter. Perhaps her decision to appear before me in ethereal form was her way of letting me know the eventual path I was supposed to be on. That or I was merely projecting her ghostly form in the physical due to my sadness over her demise.

After spending twenty-plus years as a paranormal researcher and gathering compelling data on the spirit world, I have realized that there is something else to the equation. There is something greater involved in any given encounter than just capturing audio or photographs of the afterlife. After reviewing paranormal evidence from each case project, I am now left with various questions. "What, now?" "What can I offer the spirits in this particular case?" "Are they seeking my help and, if so, how should I approach assisting them?" "Or are they making their presence known, so to speak, to give me a profound message or to help further my understanding of their existence?" In essence, my list of questions goes on; however, I am now aware of the fact that there is a duty among all paranormal researchers besides just data collection and historical research. It entails delving more into the reasons behind our specific personal encounters with the afterlife and trying to ascertain why we've encountered certain spiritual entities.

This may seem strange to some and totally relatable to others. My study of the unknown has further molded me into the person I am today. It has helped to provide an understanding of my unique makeup, behavior, personality, hopes and dreams, etc. Studying the paranormal realm is my ultimate passion, and it has extended a helping hand when I've had to endure grief and loss. For that alone, I am forever indebted to the field of supernatural study.

In this book, you will read about various unexpected encounters with the paranormal and spiritual realm. These stories have a positive, everlasting effect on the storytellers. There's a common theme running throughout each submission, in that each of the events discussed has a profound, life-changing impact on those that experienced it. Whether these shared occurrences brought about belief in the survival of consciousness after death or changed someone's destined path for the better, it is my hope that you will learn from and relate to each person who opted to share his or her story in this manuscript.

Other discussed topics include universal consciousness; the human soul and its purpose(s); the connections between mind, body, and spirit; and potential reasons for and explanations of spirit communication. This book focuses on the potential intrinsic yet cosmic motivations between the living and afterlife's desire to communicate with each other. The stories and information contained within this manuscript will impact your heart and further showcase that life continues after we physically pass on. In essence, this book demonstrates the beauty and authenticity of the spirit world.

It is my hope that this book will enlighten you in one way or another. Perhaps it and others like it can plant a seed of curiosity within your soul, one that eventually becomes a beautiful tree of unconditional guidance and shared knowledge. I also hope that this manuscript can provide healing for those who've experienced the tremendous loss of a loved one by sharing that life goes on after physical death. It is my aspiration that you, after reading this book, become aware that your departed loved ones are not forgotten. They are always here with you, albeit on the other side of the veil.

"And it is you, spirit—with will and energy, and virtue and purity—that I want, not alone with your brittle frame."

JANE EYRE

CHAPTER 1

What is an Afterlife, Anyway?

Where do we go and what happens to us when we die? For millions of people, belief in life after death provides comfort in knowing that we don't reduce to nothingness after our bodies cease to function. A recent increase in the speculation of life after death is also due to certain trends, such as developments in neuroscience that have ignited new ideas about human consciousness, theology, paranormal research, and the aging population's questions of, "What will happen to me when I die?"

There are similarities and differences regarding the many beliefs in the afterlife. There is a growing faith in the existence of some form of survival after the physical body ceases to function. As a paranormal researcher of many years, I wholeheartedly believe in life after death. The soul, or the very essence of a human being, has evolved from previous lives into life on earth. From that point, it continues on its journey to evolve and grow; this cycle continues on, quite possibly, for eternity. Thus, I don't think of those in the spirit world as being "dead" at all. When we physically die from the world we presently live in, our soul continues on as it advances and progresses to the next. The spirit world is just the next destination in the soul's perpetual journey to the divine.

While there, it has evolved towards greater consciousness and unlocking of the secrets to the universe. This is the main impetus for why the spirit world reaches out to the living. It desires to educate and guide humanity in reaching its full potential. Elaborated on in the pages to come, afterlife descriptions can be quite similar across the board for visual, auditory, and/or tactile experiences. The more open we are to recognizing them, the more likely we are to benefit from a spirit's presence and communication.

The Distinction Between Ghosts and Spirits

Prior to delving into the goals for why ghosts, spirits, and those dwelling in the afterlife choose to communicate with the living, let's discuss what the spirit world consists of. It's quite hard to definitively answer this inquiry, as the afterlife is not clearly defined by scientific standards. However, individuals who devote time and study to the paranormal and life after death have established their own theories for what it is. Even various cultures and religions have their own description of what the afterlife entails.

There are many classifications of supernatural energies, each complete with its own set of characteristics and mannerisms. The list is broad, ranging from ghosts (earthbound spirits), wholly evolved spirits, ethereal guides, elementals, angels, demons, extraterrestrials, ultra-terrestrials, etc. Not all of these types fit into the same category, nor are they all a part of the afterlife. Even though alien species may have a knowledge base similar to an evolved spirit, their type of life form(s) and origins vary. Angels, demons, and elementals differ from departed human beings because they never lived in a human body. They are considered separate species. You will read more about spirit guides in Chapter Eight; however, I want to mention now that there are several types of afterlife guides. Certain types of angels and other higher-evolved beings can be guides. Furthermore, deceased human souls, upon mastering the governing principles of what it takes to be a guide, can also be included in this category. You often hear people say that their departed relatives or close friends are now their "guardian angels." As you can glean, one can devote an entire book to discussing the similarities and differences among these groupings. For the purpose of this manuscript, I am going to concentrate on the specific beings that encompass the afterlife, according to my own convictions.

While often used synonymously, ghosts and spirits are considered two separate types of energies. Intelligent ghosts are considered earthbound—entities still tied to the mortal realm for whatever reason(s). Residual energy isn't considered a ghost at all, but rather the psychic impressions left over from an emotional or traumatic event. This is commonly seen with natural disasters, places of mass casualty, or events associated with large amounts of collective joy and amusement. Residual paranormal activity can be found on battlefields, other areas of hallowed ground, hospitals, theaters, amusement parks, airports, iconic locations, etc.

An intelligent ghost's silver cord remains connected to the living either voluntarily or involuntarily. Most researchers believe that earthbound specters have some sort of unfinished business to take care of prior to further evolving to spirit; they may be attached to a person, place, or item; or they may exhibit apprehension of what awaits them in the ethereal world. Ghosts still retain many of the behaviors and characteristics they had while of body. As such, it may be difficult for them to let go of the familiarity of how they were while alive. In this case, it may be challenging for an earthbound to endure the progressive steps needed to transition to spirithood. Surviving loved ones can also contribute to a ghost's remaining attachment to the mortal realm through grief, sadness, and/or longing for its physical presence. An earthbound may decide to stick around and remain close to a particular family member as a way to assuage anguish and heartache. When decisive timing permits, these entities can fully transition to the level of an evolved spirit and gain a deeper soul awareness of their place in the universe and galaxies beyond.

The spiritual realm is one of purity, enlightenment, and soul advancement. When the silver cord connecting a spirit to its physical body is completely severed, it can permit the expansion of universal knowledge and understanding of the soul's true purpose. This occurs when these energies meet the celestial "white light." They understand their previous life, have come to terms with it, and are ready to proceed to the next level. Therefore, they aren't bound by the traits, mannerisms, and memories they had in the mortal realm. Those who progress to this higher level can choose to come back and either assist or visit the living realm. Spiritual beings are discarnate entities not bound to any one place in particular. They can freely travel from one dimension to the next, gaining further insight and awareness of the divine. Spirits are educated by their angels and/or guides and proceed through the gates of higher knowledge.

So, what types of spiritual beings comprise the world of the afterlife? Honestly, there has never been a definitive answer to this question in black-or-white, scientific terms. However, those studying the paranormal and those who've briefly shaken hands with life after death due to a near-death encounter have collectively painted a picture of what encompasses the spirit realm. It is agreed upon by many, including myself, that there are various levels to the afterlife. I believe that the departed immediately enters eternal paradise along with loved ones there to greet them. Some believe that Earthbound ghosts inhabit the transient phase of limbo; this is similar to a waiting room of souls who are in between mortal life and evolved spirits. During this period, entities are in a tug-of-war between staying connected to their physical bodies or progressing to spirit. Since time may not exist in the afterlife, it's hard to measure how long this will typically take as it's an individual spiritual process.

One can't discuss theories and rationales regarding the afterlife without mentioning the influential convictions of Emanuel Swedenborg, a Swedish scientist and statesman. Born in 1688, he thrived during the Enlightenment period, where academics preferred logic and reason as opposed to dictatorial religious teachings. Swedenborg spent much time attempting to discern the intricacies of the spirit realm via exploration of the physical world. He claims that his sixth sense was opened; thus, he began to directly interact with various residents of the ethereal spectrum through nightly dreams of angels and saints ascending divine staircases.

In his book *Heaven and Hell*, Swedenborg claims that he was permitted to endure the dying process and be awakened in spirit. He discusses how angels accompanied him throughout the entire transition. It was after this poignant experience that he was able to perceive the spiritual realm and understand what happens to the soul after death, in many cases convincing people of his ability to contact the deceased. In fact, upon the demise of his former instructor, engineer Christopher Polhem, Swedenborg wrote the following in his diary:

> *Polhem died on Monday. He spoke with me on Thursday, and when I was invited to his funeral he saw his coffin, and those who were there, and the whole procession, and also when his body was laid in the grave; and in the meantime he spoke with me, asking why he was buried when he was still alive: and he heard also when the priest said that he would be resuscitated at the Last Judgement and yet he had been resuscitated for some time; and he marveled that such a belief should exist, as that men should be resuscitated at the Last Judgement when he was still alive; and that the body should rise again when yet he himself was sensible of being a body* (Swedenborg, 2007).

This portion of Swedenborg's diary is interesting as it highlights Polhem's beliefs that he is still alive and in the body. Those who study the afterlife strongly believe that deceased individuals attend their funerals. Obviously, this diary passage supports this widespread conviction.

Some of my personal ideologies regarding the spirit world align with those of Emanuel Swedenborg. I agree with him that those in the ethereal domain reside in landscapes similar to those on earth. They have a spiritual body, live in dwellings, and experience community just like the living. However, the incorporeal realm is much more vibrant, vivid, and alive. Wholesomeness and the sense of celestial love permeate the world of the ethereal. I contend with Swedenborg's convictions that in the afterlife, one's inner state of being is mirrored in his or her surroundings. What spiritual beings see directly correlates to what they are feeling and thinking. When one crosses over to the other side, he or she will be met with other loved ones who've also transitioned. With the assistance of angels and guides, newly arrived spiritual beings will, through a variety of lessons, become fully acquainted with their authentic selves. They live according to their soul's innate values. As such, egotistical mannerisms and materialistic predispositions common to life on earth completely vanish.

Why Does the Spirit World Communicate with the Living?

Asking someone why the spirit world connects with the living will undoubtedly reveal a broad number of answers. Since no two ethereal entities are alike, their reasons for interacting with the living remain varied and unique. In addition to the two domains offering reciprocal guidance, there are many motivations as to why the mortal and spirit worlds commune with each other. Some motives are quite obvious and others vague. Regardless, the coalescing of these two parties remains a beautiful universal event.

In my supernatural research and conducted case studies, I have worked with numerous spiritual energies in private residences, businesses, and historical abodes throughout the United States. Although there may be motives not elaborated on in this book, I have found that the majority of afterlife members choose to interact with the living for one or more of the following reasons:

Offering Assistance During the Mortal Grieving Process: Losing a loved one is one of the most difficult life events to endure. When transitioning to the next world, those treasured individuals we've lost go through a process of soul maturity and evolution. As such, the spirit world is more capable of sensing mortality's grief and sadness over the loss of a close friend or family member. Thus, it offers guidance to the living through visitations, coming through in dreams, or instilling a sense of warmth and comfort. This invaluable support enables the mortal world to understand that there is welcoming solace and further life to live in the ethereal realm.

Encountering My Grandmother's Spirit

You will hear many paranormal researchers talk about that one unexplained encounter that propelled their intrigue in the supernatural and, as a result, catapulted them into the active investigation of the unknown. For some, it may entail a culmination of unsuspecting experiences. Regardless of the number, they all share one aspect: commencing one's path in studying the concept of survival after death. Even though I possessed an innate fascination with the unknown since birth, my path was firmly initiated in 2001 when I encountered the spirit of my beloved grandmother, Helen Lopinto, during my senior year of college at the University of Arizona. It's quite intriguing as the campus is known for its studies in parapsychology.

Helen called me from San Diego, California, the day prior to her passing. It was in the afternoon when I answered her call and heard her lovingly familiar voice say, "Hi, sweetheart. It's Grandma." Being sidetracked with schoolwork and intense studying for my courses, I elected to have a quick conversation with her; today, it's something that I still regret, as I was obviously unaware that it would be my last discussion with her. The last discussion with her in the corporeal realm, that is.

While we were on the phone, she proceeded to ask me if I was okay, an odd question that didn't quite seem to fit the overall tone of our talk. In fact, I remember asking myself, "Why did my grandmother ask me this question, as it seems odd?" However, when the next day dawned, the answer became glaringly clear as my mom, Norma Strickland, called me with the heartbreaking news that Helen passed away in the early morning hours. She knew she was about to transition and made sure that her family was okay.

The author with her grandparents, Andrew F. Lopinto M.D. and Helen Lopinto, in Las Vegas, Nevada. Author's Private Collection

"Hi, sweetheart," my mom calmly said as I picked up the receiver. As she echoed the following words, "I want you to know how much I love you..." I instinctively knew that I was about to hear some tragic news. As I heard the remaining words, "...but I want you to know that grandma passed away early this morning," sadness, anger, and shock permeated through my body. After I finished talking with my mom, I sat in my bedroom as tears ran down my face—a cathartic release from my soul.

When I regained my composure, I made airline reservations to travel back home to San Diego to be with family and attend Helen's private viewing. As she lay peacefully in her casket, I couldn't help but notice the three-part picture frame displaying the photos of her three grandchildren, a piece that for years sat on top of her bedroom vanity. But at that moment, it took on a different journey as it eternally comforted Helen's earthly remains in her beautifully adorned casket. Silence remained as our family convened; no words needed to be relayed as we all interconnected with each other's sadness and grief. I stared at Helen's serene face and restful body as she lay peacefully. As I touched her hand, I thanked her for many years of love and memories. I wished her well and told her to come back and visit in ethereal form.

After an exhausting few days in San Diego, I flew back to Tucson, Arizona, and continued on with my studies. It took my entire mind, body, and spirit to glide back into the swing of things as grief and sorrow followed me around like my own shadow. As par for the course, I was plagued with fatigue and exhaustion for a few days; however, I started to notice a shift in my individual stages of grief. I accepted my grandmother's death, as in all reality, she was 96 years old when she passed on from this mortal plane. She lived a happy, thorough life complete with lasting memories of those who adored her.

One night while I was studying, I distinctly heard my bedroom's doorknob rattle of its own volition. My logical senses kicked in, and I immediately examined the door to see if I could come up with any rational explanations for the event. I chalked this odd experience up as some random event that I couldn't naturally justify. The following day, I heard my apartment's front doorknob move in motion as if someone was trying to open the door. With my spiny senses now at full force, I then asked myself, "Okay, what is going on here?" as these incidents had never before occurred. A few days and nights went by, and I still came into contact with my doorknobs moving by themselves.

A few evenings later as I was lying in bed studying for an exam, I felt the disembodied caress of a hand touching my face. The sensation felt eerily familiar, as if it came from someone I deeply loved. These encounters culminated in something beautifully unexpected the following night as I again lay in my bed studying for my courses. Out of my left peripheral vision, I noticed someone standing in front of my closet doors. I saw Helen as she appeared about ten years younger, adorned in her favorite blue and white house dress. With a glowing light behind her, she appeared rather peaceful, with a slight smile across her face. My eyes stared at her for what seemed like an eternity. After her spirit form slowly disappeared, I was engulfed in an extreme sense of stillness and tranquility. Perhaps I was tapping into how her spirit felt at that exact moment. Needless to say, Helen's ethereal being appeared before me for the next few nights, a profound yet life-changing encounter that many people go a lifetime without experiencing.

I immediately called my mom up on the phone and told her that Helen was getting in touch with me from the spirit realm. After a lengthy discussion, both Norma and I agreed to openly talk with my grandmother and let her know that she was free to move on. In other words, she didn't need to carry any more worry about the family, and she was free from any earthly anxieties. It was then that my otherworldly occurrences with my grandmother's ethereal form completely stopped.

Since my chance encounters with the spirit form of my beloved grandmother, I have been actively researching and investigating the unknown, with a chosen focus on ghosts, spirits, and hauntings. I have often paused to look back at the very moment my eyes met Helen's ethereal energy and thanked her for paving the pathway for me as a paranormal researcher. It's as if she knew all along that I was destined to step foot on this trail.

Having empathic tendencies, I often sense Helen when she travels from the stars to pay her mortal loved ones a visit. She stops by often, typically around holidays and/or special anniversaries. I do believe that my grandmother has evolved fully to the spirit realm as opposed to remaining earthbound. Perhaps she needed a little reassurance from her daughter and granddaughter that it was permissible to journey on to the divine.

The Loss of a Brother

My friend and colleague Linda Myers shares a heartfelt experience after the passing of her brother. She alludes to how her view regarding life and death has changed since losing her sibling. After this profound encounter, Linda developed a healthier attitude toward the concept of life after death.

A little bit of history before I tell you what happened. I was 19 at the time of my brother's death. We were very close and kind of different for our ages. I used to lie out in the pastures and sing to the cloud people, and my brother used to go around rescuing wild animals. I believe we were, even then, very in touch with our spiritual/intuitive nature. My brother was killed in a motorcycle accident at the age of 17. I was devastated; he was my best friend and adventure pal. The strange events began after his death.

I was at home and working two jobs. I was taking a short nap before going to my second job. I was lying on the couch in the living room. Suddenly, I felt my arm grabbed and, without thinking, told my brother to stop. I then realized that he couldn't have done that... he was dead. I couldn't rest, so I decided to go to work early. When I went out to get into my car, I found that both of my front tires had been flattened. I had just driven on them a few hours earlier. I later found that they had been purposely flattened. Did my brother warn me of danger? I think so.

Two months later, I went to visit friends in Colorado. It was a very snowy/stormy night, and we had lost power. I had spent the evening entertaining their two young girls with shadow people on the candle-lit walls. We went to bed at about 2:00 a.m.

I woke up from this dream: I am in a cavern or cave. It is very old. The floor is dirt and the furniture is made from old tree limbs. There is a table and two chairs. I am wondering why I am there. I hear a sound and look across the room. There across from me stands my brother just as he looked the day he died. He is there with a bow and arrow in his hands. He lifts the bow and arrow and points at me. He says, 'I can shoot you in the heart and your heart would stop, but you would not die. Do you understand?' He looks at me and says he loves me, then disappeared. I woke up crying.

I believe he came to me in the dream because I had been so angry since he died. I hated that he was no longer here. After thinking about the dream, I began to feel an overwhelming sense of peace. I have to say, that dream totally changed how I felt about death and dying.

Since then, I've never been afraid of dying. This has been with me all my life; now, when a loved one has passed, I don't feel angry, because I know that they are just there on the other side. It is such a gift to me from my brother.

I, too, know the immense pain that comes with the physical loss of a cherished individual. The experience with my grandmother's spirit form in my college apartment some years ago not only catapulted me on the path of paranormal research but also further blessed me with an understanding that life goes on after we pass from the corporeal realm. Most importantly, that profound encounter gave me the same lingering sense of peace Linda alluded to after the tragic loss of her beloved brother.

The Loss of a Best Friend

My friend Joanne Yates shares about the painful time she lost her best friend, Monique, to illness. At a time when grief dominated her heart, Joanne received the ultimate healing gift of comfort and peace from her departed friend. Spirits utilize symbolism as a way to communicate with the living. In this case, Monique chose an angel as a way to let Joanne know that she will eternally watch over her and the family. This experience also demonstrates that physical death cannot separate the bond between two people who care deeply for one another.

In October 1997, my best friend, Monique, was hospitalized. She was in a coma and on life support. She was taken off life support after four days. The night before, I had a dream of her. She smiled and waved goodbye. The day she was taken off life support, a pastor showed up and asked all of us to form a circle in the hospital lobby. As he started to recite a prayer, I felt a warm sensation starting at my toes and moving swiftly upward through my head. I had never felt anything like it in my life before or since.

When I got home, I was crying in the bathroom and felt a gentle touch on my left shoulder. I think it was Monique comforting me and maybe giving me a sign that she was okay. Two years later in 1999, I had my daughter, Monique (named after my friend), who was born in the same hospital where my friend had died. After Monique was born, we moved into a new home, and I noticed a tiny piece of confetti on the carpet leading to the upstairs. It was a white piece of confetti shaped like an angel. My friend used to put confetti in all of my birthday cards, so I looked at it as a sign that my friend was there and looking out for us and her god-daughter.

Years later, my daughter and I visited my friend at the Eternal Hills Memory Garden and placed flowers and balloons for her 40th birthday. When we arrived home, my daughter and I turned on the computer screen to play a game together, and it made a pop sound. It stopped working, and a minute later it came back on by itself. We both thought that was weird, but then I told my daughter, 'It's your Auntie Mo saying thank you for the flowers and balloons.'

To Demonstrate that They are at Peace: It is universally common for people to wonder if their deceased loved ones or close friends are at peace. It is for this reason that the spirit world elects to deliver messages to us as a way to alleviate our concerns. This type of communication, whether large or small, can come in various forms. In my experience, these messages mainly come via symbols or signs, dreams, music and song, or by way of a warm sense of touch. Meaningful items (coins, feathers, talismans) can mysteriously show up in random places. When an event like this occurs, it is considered therapy in its own right for those residing in the mortal realm.

To Keep in Touch: The title says it all: Our loved ones who've departed earth's plane may miss us just as much as we do them. It is for this reason that they find interesting and uncanny ways to let us know of their presence even from afar. A person may receive a random message or thought that serves as a reminder of his or her deceased family member, friend, or furry companion. The reason for this is as varied as the methods they may use to keep in touch. We may feel and sense their disembodied presence, which is reassuring in its own right. When this happens, there's no doubt and no denying the strong and familiar presence of someone we revere.

To Warn of Potential Danger: Since the spirit world has access to the secrets of the universe, it makes complete sense that it can sense potential and/or imminent peril in the living realm. Many living individuals will disclose their foresight of danger or disaster. Of course, this can be due to one's innate intuition, or it can be the result of the other side offering assistance. One of the most common ways the afterlife accomplishes this task is by communicating with mortals via their dreams or meditative sessions. Furthermore, spirits can repetitiously deliver messages of impending disaster to the living in creative ways. Remember that Linda Myers felt that it was her departed brother who notified her of the flattened tires. Those in the mortal realm need to pay close attention to the warnings delivered from the other side.

Jessie's Warning

On a summer evening in 2019, I decided to interview Angela Wallace about the unexplained encounters that she'd experienced. Since Angela is a member of the Spectral Tech Paranormal Research Team, she's no stranger to the supernatural. The following encounters with the spirit of her grandfather are among the most profound she's ever endured. These occurrences highlight the rather unique ways spirits utilize to awaken our knowledge of their presence and to further warn us of forthcoming threats to our safety and well-being.

Angela first learned about Spectral Tech when she took over management of an antique mall plagued with various ghostly events. In fact, she shared with me how she, her mom, and a customer witnessed a particular apparition on differing days. It was then that Angela phoned Bob Fountain, the team's founder, as he had previously conducted a paranormal research project at the location. After discussion, they agreed to have a second and third case study done with Angela and her daughter present.

Paranormal research training classes were held at Angela's antique store. During these courses, attendees were instructed on proper investigative procedures, methodologies, and types of equipment employed in supernatural research practices. Three different spiritual entities were discovered during this time, which included a territorial male who seemingly enjoyed breaking items; an older, very sweet lady at the store's front; and another male energy who walked around.

Looking back on her childhood, Angela shared that she didn't really possess strong feelings about the paranormal. She further discussed how she grew up in a household that believed in the unexplained but didn't actively go out and pursue it, nor conversed about it. This is surprising considering her mom's adamant claims of being abducted by a UFO. Angela's grandparents were instrumental in raising her; her beloved grandfather, Jessie ("Paw"), was diagnosed with stage IV terminal cancer in the cold months of January when Angela was just 19 years old. Due to his declining health, Angela moved in with her grandparents to assist in taking care of him. The disease rapidly invaded his physical body, and Jessie sadly passed away on March 1st.

"My grandfather was a creature of habit, and he had the daily routine he did," Angela relayed. Every single morning after waking, he went around to every room to make sure all the clocks in the home were in-sync. According to Angela, he had one clock that ran slow and one that ran fast, and he made sure they were also running in line with the others. Jessie's night routine was equally habitual. Since Angela's grandparents never slept in the same room, Jessie occupied the bedroom at the end of the hall. The guest room was in the middle, with her grandmother's bedroom at the opposite end across from the bathroom. With a precise routine, Angela's grandfather emerged from his bed at midnight, opened the door, and proceeded toward his wife's room to check in on her as she was also in declining health. After looking in on his beloved wife, Lela, he retreated back to his room and shut the door.

Angela occupied the middle bedroom while she stayed with her grandparents. The week after her grandfather's demise, she realized that all the clocks but one in the home stopped functioning. She inspected the batteries and placed new ones in each clock. None of them continued to operate even after she tried to unplug and plug them back in. Angela took the broken ones out to the carport, where they operated beautifully; however, they ceased to function after thirty minutes of being brought back inside. She even shared how they performed appropriately in family members' residences. An interesting backstory to this is that her grandparents were given a special clock on their 50th wedding anniversary. Oddly, it was this specific timepiece that continued to function. Angela feels that this particular oddity was her grandfather's way of letting her know that he was okay. She further disclosed that she has since spoken to the new owners of her grandparents' former abode and they relayed that they, too, had problems with the clocks working properly at the location.

Paw was a smoker but only enjoyed an occasional cigarette outside. The new owners of her grandparents' home asked Angela if anyone previously smoked in the home, as they picked up the residual scent of cigarettes in Jessie's bedroom. She told them that no one did so inside the home, only outside.

Tragically, Angela was given the news of Lela's breast cancer diagnosis just six weeks after Jessie's departure to the stars. During this time, she drove her grandmother to medical appointments in Memphis, Tennessee. Of course, Angela continued to reside with her grandmother due to her declining health. At times when the two sat in their living room, a wall picture would seemingly move of its own volition, thus appearing crooked. This uncanny event occurred multiple times, each with a random photo. "I would go straighten the picture after it turned and it would move again," Angela imparted. What is intriguing is that this eerie happening occurred with various pictures everywhere in the home, but never the same one!

Another unusual encounter after the passing of Angela's grandfather occurred in the kitchen. A particular utensil drawer on rollers would move on its own accord. Other people besides her witnessed this odd happening. Of course, she inspected it to make sure there wasn't a natural explanation for its opening; however, she couldn't find any real reason. People would be talking in the kitchen area and become startled when this mysterious drawer moved. As a way to assuage her company's anxiousness, Angela told them, "Oh, that's Papa; it happens all the time."

Furthermore, Angela went on to discuss how she trained herself to sleep lightly, which allowed her to easily hear her grandmother should she need any assistance in the middle of the night. A bell was positioned on the doorknob of her grandmother's room mainly as a way to help alert Angela. Angela completely shut the door to her grandfather's quarters after his passing until family members were emotionally ready to go through his belongings. One night, precisely at midnight, she heard the sound of a bedroom door opening. Thinking that it was her grandmother's, she wondered why the bell didn't make any noise. Almost immediately after, Angela heard whistling and the sound of popping knees. She then told me that Jessie's knees popped when he walked and he had one tooth in his mouth; as a result, he would typically make a distinct whistling sound. Frozen in shock, she then heard the sound of the bell and the door to her grandmother's room opening up. After a few moments, she heard the noise of someone walking back down the hallway and closing the door to Jessie's room. Angela went into his room, only to find it empty. She then proceeded to check on her grandmother, only to find her fast asleep. Once back in her bed, Angela pondered whether this odd occurrence was all a dream. Attempting to get some sleep, she kept waking up, perseverating on the aforementioned encounter with the spirit of her grandfather.

Angela heard Jessie's bedroom door creak open yet again at midnight the following night. The events from the evening prior continued to replay themselves with exact precision. In fact, she shared with me that these occurrences happened every single night at 12:00 a.m. for almost a year. She confided in her family members after she became quite accustomed to the events. Angela's consensus was that her grandfather continued to check in on his wife just as he did when he was of body. Her cousin spent the night and he, too, experienced Jessie's spirit. Her cousin actually stood in the hallway and visually witnessed the doors opening and closing as well as the whistling and knee-popping noises. After the fact, he rapidly put on his shoes and slept the rest of the night in his car.

Jessie was extremely protective of his belongings. After about six months, Angela had to go back to work. She was eventually hired to work in the evenings so she could be with her grandmother during the day. To help assist her, Angela's siblings came over to help care for her grandmother. Her aunt invited Lela to stay with her one weekend a month. After coming home from work on a particular Saturday night, showering, and getting comfortable in bed, Angela heard the sound of a kitchen chair. Her grandmother utilized a walker, so Angela always made sure the chairs were tucked in to avoid any accidents. Since Angela was the only one home at the time, she logically thought that either an intruder was inside or one of her relatives stopped by for a visit. She turned the kitchen light on and noticed that her grandfather's chair was moved out a bit. She pushed the chair back toward the table and went back to bed. Then, all of a sudden, she heard it move again. Like she did previously, Angela proceeded to the kitchen and visually saw it out of place.

Thinking of the possibility that this may be a prank by one of her cousins, she turned off the kitchen light. Then, she quietly tip-toed to the pantry, opened the door, and placed her arm inside. To her surprise, it was completely devoid of anyone. Quite perplexed this time around, Angela, once again, walked down the hallway. Before she even arrived at her bedroom, she heard the kitchen chair scoot out again! She bolted to the kitchen, turned on the light, and exclaimed, "Jessie, I am trying to go to bed. Please leave the chair alone." Believe it or not, after she turned the light off yet again, the same chair slid out before she even took four steps.

However, something was different this time: Angela noticed flashlights outside. With the kitchen lights in the off position, she glanced out the window and noticed two men attempting to cut the lock off her grandfather's shed where his belongings were held. She retrieved her shotgun as a scare tactic, stepped foot outside the back door, and fired two bullets toward the sky. Caught off guard, the two guys took off running. In retrospect, Angela truly believes that her grandfather was trying to turn her attention to this attempted burglary by moving the chair he used to sit in. After thanking Jessie for alerting her, she changed the locks to his shed the following day. She even went into his bedroom and verbally told him that the compartment was protected now that it was more secure.

Angela said that she would love to help her grandfather move on because, in her opinion, she feels he is still tied to the house. Whether that's by voluntary choice or not, it's difficult to tell. With that said, Angela does feel that his experiences are synonymous with a time loop; as he was so ingrained in taking care of his wife while alive, he continues to do so in spirit. When she and the family placed Lela in a nursing home, Angela sat on Jessie's bed and told him that his work here was done, as his wife wouldn't physically be in the house any longer. "Grandpa, you've done all you can do; you're free to move on," she said.

As our telephone conversation neared the end, Angela told me that all of these unexpected encounters made her a firm believer in the afterlife. She accepted and was at ease with the experiences, even though she didn't have a complete comprehension of them. That's the beauty of spiritual occurrences: They are sometimes meant to be elusive.

To Assist a Mortal with Transitioning to the Other Side: There are numerous stories of individuals recounting instances of the deceased making appearances when someone near and dear is about to transition to the other side. Although near-death experiences are detailed in Chapter Four, I do want to highlight that those who've come close to shaking hands with physical death have reported seeing the spirits of loved ones waiting for them. Those who've graduated to the spirit world have endured this ephemeral process; thus, they desire to assist their fellow comrades' journeys to the heavens. Many individuals who have departed and then been brought back to physical life have relayed a sense of peace and comfort when experiencing this transition. Nonetheless, spiritual residents show up to encourage a smooth, seamless crossing.

To Demonstrate that There is Life in the Spirit World: This is a simple reason, but it is extremely essential and important to the mortal world's understanding of the afterlife. It's not uncommon for people to imagine that life literally stops forever once the physical body ceases to function. For thousands of years, the ethereal kingdom has convincingly showcased to the living that life continues after we make our exodus from the corporeal realm to the spirit world. Through paranormal occurrences and spirit communication sessions across the globe, we've grasped what may go on in the spiritual landscape. My personal belief is that life beyond the stars mirrors that of life on Earth except for a few distinctions: 1) Once we enter the incorporeal fields, we are given a greater knowledge; 2) Once we arrive at the gates of the afterlife, our soul evolves and matures to a greater understanding of ourselves and the universes around us; and 3) We are bestowed with the knowledge of how to better infiltrate love and good intention to all galaxies and life forms.

The Afterlife According to Various Cultures

Examined since the dawning of man, the concepts of spirituality, survival after death, and higher consciousness have only become even more interesting topics to study in recent years. With society's growing intrigue in the paranormal realm, individuals are becoming more aware of life after death and the possibility that the human soul can survive it. Each year, more people are coming forward to share how they've witnessed or communicated with the spirit form of a deceased relative, co-worker, friend, or furry companion. Many of these reports from all over the world describe coming into contact with an ethereal entity in similar ways, even though various cultures exhibit their own individual beliefs about life after death.

Some believe that a person's soul is reincarnated with no memory of a previous life; this process happens continuously until that person is granted entry into the ethereal world. Certain creeds hold that the departed may travel to a specific point of existence, one that God determines based on how that individual lived his or her life. Even though certain religions have differing views on exactly what life after death entails, one aspect remains consistent: the universal belief in eternal life.

Early compositions, such as Homer's *Odyssey* and the biblical book of Samuel, discuss life after death. In the northwestern section of Greece, for example, near the river Acheron (or "River of the Dead"), exists the ruins of an ancient religious group called the Nekromanteion (or "Place for the Oracle of the Dead"). Here is where pilgrims gathered to communicate with their deceased relatives.

People started to exhibit different attitudes toward life and death around the twelfth century; many cultures during this time started to contemplate what happens to the soul after physical death. This was the basis for *The Divine Comedy,* an Italian long-narrative poem conceptualized and written by Dante Alighieri in 1320, one year prior to his death. Thought to be one of the most paramount pieces of literature, the poem showcases a visionary view of the afterlife characteristic of the Western Church's Middle Age philosophy, specifically its theological viewpoints. In particular, this narrative allegorically represents the soul's expedition toward the divine. In the past and present, *The Divine Comedy* has been a solid inspiration to artists from all walks of life (Alighieri, 2016).

Buddhist culture believes in rebirth and that, upon physical death, a person will be reborn again to achieve a state of absolute peace. Buddhists hold to the conviction that the spirit immediately leaves the body upon death but may linger in limbo near it. Therefore, it's vital to treat the body with reverence so that the spirit can carry on its expedition to happiness. Believing in reincarnation, Hindus feel that when a person succumbs, his or her soul transitions to a new body on its way to Nirvana. Interestingly, those of Hindu culture are cremated upon death as they believe the spirit will be released upon the burning of the body.

Ancient Egyptian culture believed in immortality. They regarded physical death as a temporary interlude, as opposed to the complete ending of life. Paying homage to the gods during and after life ensured this immortality for them. When someone passed, he or she was mummified so the soul could return to the body. To provide for afterlife necessities, family and friends placed household items, food, and drinks on offering tables outside the tomb's burial space. Egyptians believed that those who passed on would go through a certain unique journey to the afterworld.

The Greek Orthodox religion believes that the deceased are eternally alive with God. With death comes the separation of the soul from the physical body; with the coming of the Last Judgement, the two will be rejoined. Those of the Jewish faith hold to the conviction that they will go to Heaven to join with God upon death. After the body ceases to function, the spirit evolves into the "world of truth." Muslims assert that the soul continues to thrive after the death of the physical body. They feel that a person can positively or negatively shape his or her soul depending on the life he or she lived.

Catholics believe an afterlife exists and decedents will come face-to-face with God. People adhering to the Christian religion trust they will enter Heaven's gates to be with their maker. This is also true with the Jewish religion, where death is thought to be a part of God's plan. Mormons, on the other hand, assert that the physical body and spirit separate when one physically dies. The spirit thus travels to the ethereal world prior to reuniting with the body. Scientology holds onto the notion that humans are immortal beings called Thetans who live several lives. Upon death, a person transitions to a new life.

Although some of the specifics vary from one religion to the next, you can see how different theologies all believe in some sort of life after death. It's also easy to see how a person's convictions on life after death may be shaped according to his or her religious following.

The Influence of the Spiritualist Movement on Modern-Day Spirit Communication and Paranormal Research

Even though people have tried to communicate with the dearly departed, the number of people doing so reached exponential proportions during the Spiritualist movement. This religious crusade reached its high point between 1840 and 1920 and holds beliefs not only in the existence of spirits but also in how ethereal entities can communicate with the living. Attracting many to psychic mediumship and introducing various methods to communicate with the spirit world, this movement's credibility dramatically diminished by the late 1880s due to indictments of fraud and dishonesty. However, denominational Spiritualist churches continue to practice today, especially in Canada, the United Kingdom, and the United States.

Those following Spiritualist dogmas made contact with the departed typically through the use of a medium, or person believed to possess the aptitude of directly contacting the dead. Some mediums opted to work in a trance-like state, whereas others claimed to be the mechanism whereby psychokinetic (PK) energy was created by the human mind. You will hear more about psychokinesis in the coming paragraphs.

Spiritualists maintain that it's highly possible for the living to communicate with the spirits of deceased people. They also insist that spirit mediums are innately gifted to facilitate such interaction, even though anyone can learn to do so with study and exposure. Along the lines of ethereal world evolution, Spiritualists believe that astral beings are capable of perfection as they move through higher planes in the afterlife. Furthermore, another conviction holds that those in the celestial atmosphere can offer advice and knowledge on moral and ethical issues, mirroring the concept of spirit guides. I truly believe in the afterlife's uncanny ability to act as an honorable compass for the living with almost daily assistance and guidance.

One cannot hear the word "Spiritualism" without thinking about the Fox sisters. On March 31, 1848, Kate and Margaret "Maggie" Fox of Hydesville, New York, claimed that they had communicated with the spirit of a peddler who was murdered. Even though no forensic documentation of this individual was ever discovered, the sisters reported that he interacted with them via rapping noises. Soon afterward, the Fox siblings became a wonderous phenomenon, recruiting many people to attempt spirit communication. As the premiere celebrity psychic mediums, Kate and Margaret claimed notoriety for their public séances in New York and elsewhere. Sadly, and rather exploitatively, the sisters admitted in 1888 that their contact with the deceased merchant was fraudulent, but after some time, they retracted their confession.

The Fox sisters were gauged by many qualified scientists and skeptics alike after claiming they could talk to the dead. Physician E.P. Longworthy appraised the siblings and took note of how the knockings or raps typically came from under their feet or when their dresses touched the table. He, therefore, determined that they produced the sounds. Reverend John M. Austin later asserted that the noises could be produced by cracking joints in the toes, with Reverend D. Potts demonstrating this to a curious audience. However, between 1871 and 1874, noted physicist William Crookes determined that the rapping noises were authentic, even though some mediums he examined were exposed as fakes. The smoking gun came to fruition in 1851 as Mrs. Norman Culver, a relative of the Fox family, openly disclosed via a signed affidavit that she had assisted Kate and Margaret during their séances by touching them to signify when to produce the rapping sounds. Additionally, she also admitted that the siblings told her how they made the sounds: by cracking their toes while using their ankles and knees.

Accomplished magician Harry Houdini became enthralled with the idea of spirit communication after the death of his beloved mother. Although fascinated with the concept of spiritualist mediums, he spent the last thirteen years of his life exposing them. Whether this was due to gaining publicity or because he simply could not condone the exploitation of the dead (most likely the reason why), Houdini utilized his magic skills to reveal fakery and trickery. With the aid of illusion, Houdini successfully duplicated alleged ghostly apparitions, noises, and unusual levitations produced by mediums and their spiritual aides. He eventually became known as the most celebrated Spiritualist after having been instructed by famous psychic Anna Eva Fay. All in all, he helped expose many of the well-known mediums and channelers of his time. Houdini, via the writing of his book *A Magician Among the Spirits*, narrated his debunking achievements, which cost him his friendship with Sir Arthur Conan Doyle, a staunch supporter of the Spiritualist movement.

Houdini and his wife, Bess, decided that if he found it feasible to communicate from the other side he would do so with the coded message

"Rosabelle believe." As it turned out, they both shared a love for the song "Rosabelle." Bess held annual séances on Halloween for a decade following her husband's passing. Bess patiently waited for ten years but never got the secret words from beyond the veil. Although we will never know for sure, maybe Houdini chose other ways to communicate with his wife (Houdini, 2002).

Even though Spiritualism led to the uncovering of many fraudulent mediums, it further perpetuated a curiosity and intrigue in the supernatural and life after death. Perhaps those who possess a desire to learn about and communicate with the spirit realm in today's society had ancestors who were also interested in the subject. Even with its undesirable events, Spiritualism has demonstrated the viable notion that life exists after physical death. Furthermore, it goes to show that death does not free a person from mortal world consequences; as in the afterlife, the soul continues to evolve and make amends with life's corollaries. By all accounts, studying concepts of an afterlife should eradicate the fear of eventual mortality.

The Spiritualist movement created the need for paranormal research and investigation. Its claims of life after death virtually crafted the desire to scientifically study what goes on after the human body dies. Many individuals during the era were cited for fraudulence; as such, the movement caused people to objectively look at the practices of Spiritualists and develop a gold standard for honest, constructive examining of paranormal events. This led to the birth of the Society for Psychical Research in 1882, the premiere organization formed to scientifically study claims of psychic phenomena and paranormal occurrences. Modern-day supernatural researchers utilize the methodical framework initiated by the society's numerous intellectuals and scientists.

In the following chapter, you will read about the various signs of spirit presence and communication. To this day, it is not proven how ethereal energies manifest and converse in the way that they do, but it's exciting when it does occur. By recognizing the signs, you will be better prepared when you encounter a ghost or spirit. Adopting creative ways to engage with the afterlife can add to the entire spirit communication process.

> "The desire for connection with the Divine and our formless inner self is at the foundation of all desire for human connection."
>
> DONNA GODDARD

CHAPTER 2

Spirit Connection with the Living: Recognizing the Signs

It is normal to feel anger, sadness, confusion, and hopelessness with the death of a departed loved one or friend. Your heart may feel bruised and your soul devoid of any feeling. This is an absolutely normal human response when we physically say goodbye to those we knew and loved. You will learn that it is quite customary to experience a wide range of intermittent emotions and feelings when someone dies. When a person moves through this inevitable process, he or she will learn to cope and come to terms with the loss of a departed relative, friend, coworker, etc. With death, it's common to feel that a person may be gone from your life forever, but in actuality, that person is always with you, albeit in spirit form. Of course, you may miss seeing a person's physical attributes or hearing an individual's contagious laugh, but know that the true essence of that person lives eternally.

We are all alike in that we are born into the mortal realm only to experience our physical demise at some point and eventual journey to the next world of life. The living and dearly departed are really no different, as they both occupy a soul that lives eternally. The only main difference is that with death, a person's soul is no longer attached to the human body. It's free to roam the universe in an unconfined fashion. As mentioned, the soul often grows stronger once it reaches the full heights of spirit. It is then when powerful spirit communication between the living and departed can occur.

Just as the mortal realm grieves over the passing of a beloved individual, understand that said individual, albeit in spirit form, can sense the living's heartache and sorrow. As previously mentioned, it's for that reason that many of our departed loved ones attempt to communicate with us from beyond the veil. They may want to let us know that they're okay and no longer suffering or in pain. They may also be attempting to provide us endless comfort as they guide us through our grief. Death can never interfere with love, and it may be that the spirit of your beloved desires to pay you a visit now and then, especially around important dates, holidays, and/or anniversaries.

The following consensus is based on a general culmination of people's experiences with the spirits of their departed friends or loved ones. It is normal for deceased persons to make visitations immediately following their physical death. Then, there may be a stagnant period where the living doesn't encounter their departed loved ones for some time. This is normal. Please realize that they need to get accustomed to existing in spirit form; thus, we need to grant them as much time as they need to acclimate to ethereal life. For them, there are lessons to be learned and experiences to be had in order to be fully comfortable as astral beings. This path may take longer for some depending on life retrospection and/or when they transitioned from earthbound to spirit.

The messages we receive from celestial beings can occur on any day and at any given time. These encounters tend to happen when you are in solitude, without distraction from others, ego, or day-to-day trials and tribulations. When you are alone, you are more prone to sensing a spirit's presence, whether it be a change in your energy, the energy of the room, or wispy movements. You may feel the disembodied caress of an invisible hand touch your face, stroke your hair, or hold your hand; regardless of the sensation, it can provide lots of serenity.

The physical body may cease to function; however, it's the energy comprising the soul, the true essence of an individual person, that survives death and lives eternally. When someone passes, this unique energy remains and disperses throughout the universe. In my opinion, it's the surviving soul that is responsible for communicating with the living. To allow for easier identification, it may show itself along with the physical body that it once inhabited. Either way, here are some of the indications that someone is communicating with you from beyond the grave:

Compelling Vocalizations: Whether it's a disembodied voice that you hear or an electronic voice phenomenon captured on a recording device, ethereal entities can speak to us to impart a message or to let us know of their presence. You will hear more about electronic voice phenomena (EVP) and Instrumental Trans Communication (ITC) in Chapter Six. Since spirits are in the astral plane and no longer confined to a body, how is it that they can retain the same intonation in their voice? This remains a mystery and is something we mortals may never entirely comprehend. I believe this is purposefully accomplished to add a dose of familiarity. In other words, if the grandmother chooses to retain her unique voice in spirit form, then family and friends will be better equipped to recognize it during attempted communication sessions. In my paranormal research work and in everyday life, I have experienced compelling spirit voices on a number of occasions.

Shortly after my paternal grandmother, Marion Strickland, passed away, I believe I encountered her in ethereal form. At the time, I was staying at my family's timeshare at the Welk Resort in Escondido, California. One morning as I was making my much-needed cup of coffee, I distinctly sensed Marion's presence. A few seconds later, I heard her say my name; the vocalization identically matched her voice, so I instantly recognized it. I even responded by saying, "Grandma, I hear you." I then heard a response but could not quite decipher what was said. Most important was the wave of peace that came over me at that exact moment. I felt comforted and knew in that instant that Marion was "okay" and was where she needed to be.

The author with her grandmother, Marion Strickland,
in Las Vegas, Nevada. Author's Private Collection

In July of 2019, I traveled up to Alameda, California, to attend the "History and Mystery" overnight paranormal event at the USS *Hornet.* Visiting this aircraft carrier has always been on my bucket list, so I was truly excited to attend the event and even be a VIP speaker and guest. After a delicious dinner and prior to dividing into investigation groups for the evening's research project, I gave a presentation about the RMS *Queen Mary,* which was well received by the other guests and ship volunteers. As many know, the *Queen*

Mary is another iconic vessel known for its history and supernatural phenomena. Having written three books about the ship, I have spent numerous years researching *Queen Mary's* prodigious history and spiritual occurrences.

Around 10:00 p.m., our investigation cohort went to the engine room to conduct some audio experiments. This is when the docent told us about the suicide that took place there in 2007. Out of respect for this spirit and his surviving family members, I will not reveal his name. As our volunteer guide proceeded to tell us what happened, an overwhelming sense of sadness came over me; this was not a surprise, as I am quite empathic. We asked, "Do you need any help?" A response of "No" was captured on our recording devices. It's vitally important to keep your emotions and feelings in check when conducting paranormal case studies; however, that didn't stop me from shedding some tears. Communicating with the departed is so much more than just attaining data of the paranormal; it allows for a rapport to be made between the two realms.

Coming Through in Our Dreams: This type of ethereal communication is one of the most influential methods a spirit can utilize when communicating with the mortal realm. The Society for Psychical Research (SPR) began the scientific study of paranormal dreams. It was in 1886 that SPR published a two-volume manuscript titled *Phantasms of the Living*, written by Edmund Gurney, Frederic Myers, and Frank Podmore, which discussed and analyzed 149 unique cases of documented telepathic dream encounters. In many of the cases, the authors found that both agent and recipient were interconnected either as friends or family members. Even today, many of the characteristics regarding psychic dreams as unearthed by SPR continue to be replicated in modern-day studies. This demonstrates a substantial similarity among such experiences (Gurney, 1886).

Louisa Rhine, wife and associate of modern experimental parapsychologist Joseph Banks Rhine, amassed more than 10,000 spontaneous events of possible PSI experiences (psychic phenomena), which became the subjects of many articles and books. In her conclusive review, Rhine deduced that 65% of all extrasensory perception (ESP) encounters occurred within dreams, a statistic that's been approved by various smaller-scale inquiries.

Almost everyone has dreamed of a deceased loved one or pet. In fact, it's very common to receive messages from the spirit world during this unconscious state of slumber, as our inhibitions and preoccupations are lowered. The veil between the living realm and the afterlife is at its thinnest when we sleep. As a leading psychic medium, James Van Praagh believes that when we fall asleep, our soul leaves its human shell and travels to the spirit world. While there, it can visit loved ones, spirit guides, or other dimensions.

When you meet up with a beloved spirit in your dreams, it's common to wake up feeling fulfilled and refreshed. Trust your feelings should you wake up from sleep with a renewed sense of information about a certain person, place, or event. If one of your departed relatives appears a certain way in your dream, understand that he or she has manifested that way for your comfort. Not needing a physical body to impart messages to the living, the spirit world sometimes instead delivers an imprint of energy into our corporeal mind.

If you desire to communicate with someone close to you who now belongs to the ethereal kingdom, make sure you set that intention prior to falling asleep. Envision that spirit appearing before you in your dreams and imagine a visitation. Once you get used to practicing this objective, you will be amazed at the profound meetings you will have with other realms and with those who've passed on.

Spirit communication can occur via imagery or messages, or it can act like a movie scene playing out in a certain order. It's especially comforting when your dearly departed talks to you in your lucid dream state; this occurs often when he or she wants to pass on a message to you, one that will provide comfort and solace. In my experience with these types of lucid dreams, I have awakened with a profound stillness and harmony within my heart. You may want to consult a dream analysis expert should you not be able to fully decipher the reason(s) behind spirit visitation during slumber. Either way, don't rush when trying to unlock the reasons behind these messages; allow the understanding of them to flow naturally.

A Note on Sleep Paralysis

Authentic visitation from the astral plane should not be confused with sleep paralysis, which is more or less a physical phenomenon. Simply put, sleep paralysis is a feeling of being awake but unable to move your body. It usually occurs during one of two states: the hypnagogic phase, when you are falling asleep (predormital sleep paralysis), or the hypnopompic state, when you are waking up (postdormital sleep paralysis). The dreamer is typically not aware that he or she is dreaming but instead thinks he or she is awake in bed. During this time, you may be unable to move your body for several seconds or even up to a minute. Other symptoms may include a sense of pressure, a feeling of choking, and/or seeing a presence standing over you. You may not be able to speak; however, you are fully aware of what's happening. During an episode, a person may also experience the sensation of falling, floating, flying, or leaving their body (out-of-body experience, or OBE).

Sleep paralysis will usually end on its own terms when someone touches you or you make a conscious effort to move. It may accompany other sleep disorders, such as narcolepsy, disturbed night sleep, slumbering during the day, etc. Sleep paralysis may also be caused by certain medications, substance abuse, medical condition(s), and/or mental health disorders, such as bipolar disorder or schizophrenia. Sleep deprivation or times of intense physical and emotional stress may trigger an episode.

Many sleep researchers believe that this condition may be a sign that someone is not adequately moving through the stages of sleep. For hundreds of years, people have described sleep paralysis as experiencing some evil force or entity; in fact, almost every culture has reported this phenomenon in conjunction with the belief that someone is being attacked by some shadowy, malevolent specter. Although it may seem that a supernatural force is attacking you during this stage of sleep, a paranormal origin is quite unlikely. Reality and fantasy mesh together during an episode, with lucid dreaming potentially intensifying. Some people will mistake sleep paralysis for alien abductions, as its identifying symptoms often mimic abductee reports. It often affects people in their 20s or 30s.

Is it possible to have a true paranormal encounter or visitation from the other side during sleep paralysis? It's feasible and certainly should not be ruled out. This is especially the case with the aforementioned predormital and postdormital states of sleep, mainly because our inhibitions are lowered while in these phases. The following accounts demonstrate how the spirit realm can communicate with us while we are sleeping. These are not considered sleep paralysis episodes, but rather the natural way we can connect with the ethereal while dreaming.

An Ethereal Hug

Ali Schreiber married her first husband at the age of 27 while living in Utah. On their wedding day in September, her mom called her at their hotel room. The phone call was a devastating one, as Ali found out her dad was diagnosed with cancer and was only given about six months to live. Her father was receiving hospice care around the clock at his residence. The family knew that he was going to pass soon, but they weren't sure when. Ali's first husband was an air-traffic controller and worked evenings; while he was at work one night,

Ali could not fall asleep. She felt anxious, uneasy, and fearful but could not ascertain why.

Eventually falling asleep, Ali recalls getting out of bed and walking down the hallway toward the kitchen. When she arrived at the end of the hall, there at the top of the stairs stood her father in ethereal form. With similar looks to Elvis Presley, Ali's father had black hair and beautiful olive-colored skin. Ali said that he looked vibrant and healthy in her dream. He wore a plaid flannel shirt and looked freshly shaven, with hair neatly brushed. As was the case with the spirit of my grandmother Helen when I first saw her, Ali's dad looked about ten years younger, without a wrinkle on his face.

Ali felt not one ounce of fear upon seeing her dad's glowing apparition. While standing there in spirit form, her father didn't communicate any words; however, she knew in her heart that he was saying "goodbye" and that he loved her. She then felt him give her a huge hug. "I wasn't watching the hug from somewhere else as if you were watching a movie; he gave me a real, warm hug," Ali went on to say.

The next thing she remembers was hearing the loud sound of her alarm going off at 5:00 a.m. When she opened her eyes, she felt an overwhelming sense of calm and peace. Her mom then phoned Ali and told her that her dad passed away during the night. Ali and I truly believe that her father came to her in spirit at the exact time he departed the physical plane.

It took Ali years to share the aforementioned experience, as it was, and remains, a deeply personal and profound occurrence. As a paranormal researcher, she now knows that there isn't anything foreboding about encountering and/or communicating with those who've transitioned to the stars. As an investigator, she looks forward to building a rapport with the spirit world and heeding the messages it duly imparts.

Dream Visitations with Kayli

Kayli crossed the Rainbow Bridge on December 19, 2021, to reunite with her brother, Max. Inserted is an excerpt from my book, *Max and Kayli: Two Remarkable Felines Forever Imprinted On My Heart*, which documents how I connected with Kayli's spirit via dreaming. Since publishing that book, I have continued to meet up with Kayli while asleep. She quickly became accustomed to her role in the afterlife, and this is one of the reasons why I'm able to encounter her so profoundly in this fashion. In other words, she helps me do so.

Kayli Strickland. Author's private collection

When you become in tune with life's synchronicities, it's hard to ignore them. One of the first universal signs of Kayli's journey to the afterlife was showcased in a billboard advertisement. While turning the corner onto Balboa Avenue after exiting In n Out, I glanced right at a sign that displayed a finger touching a bright orb of light. I talked with my mom the following day, and she said that she heard two ethereal meows the following morning. Immediately, I knew this message was signifying that Kayli and Max were reunited once again. Later that same day, I made a trip to Starbucks for some much-needed caffeine. While at a stoplight, I looked up into the blue sky and saw two birds dancing together—another surefire sign that demonstrated their togetherness.

About two nights after Kayli's passing, I had a profound dream—not the typical variety that stems from our subconscious, but rather a spiritual type of communication. In the dream, I was standing in my bedroom and noticed Kayli lying on my desk. I said, 'Kayli, you're here. Can I feel you?' I motioned toward her as she intently looked at me. I touched her warm fur, embraced her, and then woke up with utter peace. Max came to me in this fashion shortly after his transition, so it was no surprise that Kayli did as well—after all, like brother, like sister. They both mastered the ability to come to me during sleep.

Since Kayli passed in the days before Christmas, I made a promise to dedicate the holiday to her legacy and memory. With that said, Christmas 2021 just wasn't the same, and with good reason. I preferred to have a quiet Yuletide and stay at home. It allowed me to mourn with ease. I've never been one to cater to the materialism of Christmas, as buying gifts isn't nearly as important as the memories shared between loved ones and friends. Nonetheless, I was utterly amazed at the tribute gifts people sent me in regards to Kayli's passing. It perfectly epitomizes that the love between her and me is palpable to many people. Each trinket is placed throughout my home, representing my girl's memory and celebration of life.

As the days ventured on, I occasionally heard their distinct meows. They essentially sound the same as they did in life but more distant, which is often the case with auditory spiritual accounts. About three days before

New Year's Eve, I was intently watching some television when I noticed movement out of my left peripheral vision. There Kayli was in ethereal form, walking down the stairs and onto the entryway.

Additionally, I had another profound dream in the early morning hours of New Year's Eve. This was a unique experience as I was either in between an awake/sleep state or I astrally traveled to meet Kayli. During the dream, I was resting in bed when I heard some ruffling at the foot of it. I said 'Kayli' out loud and then felt her pawprints walking up to meet me. When she arrived, I embraced her and felt her warm fur and heartbeat. She was even purring, which she loved to do when alive in the physical. This dream lasted for a while as if it moved in slow motion. The symbolism in this was quite palpable: Sensing the heartbeat represented new life, and experiencing this dream the day prior to 2022 signified a fresh slate.

I went to bed somewhat early on Saturday, January 8th, and had another amazing dream. In the dream, I was lying on my back in my bed, the same position I was in when I fell asleep. The dream commenced with me intently looking at a bulletin board situated right in front of me. The board was essentially bare, with the exception of an 8x10 photo in the upper left-hand corner. It displayed a picture of a mug with an attachment that read, 'Hope you enjoy the mug.' By the way, I had designed a mug on Shutterfly for my mom with photos of Max and Kayli and the text 'All you need is love and a cat' and 'We love you, Grandma.'

Max and Kayli also had a brother. I was told at their adoption that he was sick and was being cared for at another facility. Sadly, I never got the chance to meet their sibling. The 8x10 picture referenced in my dream showed three kittens positioned next to each other looking up toward the sky. This was the universe's way of letting me know that Max and Kayli had been reunited with their brother.

While dreaming, I do believe I astrally traveled slightly from my body to meet Kayli's ethereal form. I felt her jump up on my bed and motion toward me. When I sat up in bed, I swiftly extended my arms, hoping to feel her. When I did, I felt the upper part of her tail. I then sensed her plop down and sit against my left leg. She was purring. I said, 'Kayli, I love you. You're here.' Our eyes met as she looked up at me with endearing intent. I caressed her ears, face, and back, a gesture of love she craved when alive. This entire dream seemed to play out in slow motion, and I cherished every moment. I then woke up with such a pervading layer of peace.

Kayli joined me in an adventure dream I had a couple of nights later. One of my friends and I decided to take a trip to the mountains to go hiking. I typically recall descriptive details of my dreams, so I remember taking Kayli with me in one of those kitty backpacks. Right before awakening, I was holding her in my arms as I gazed at the beautiful scenery the mountain pinnacle bestowed on the eyes. Perhaps the higher altitude in this dream represented her ascent to the afterlife and the paradise it's often described as from those encountering NDEs (near-death experiences).

Norma's Dream Visitation

My mom, Norma Strickland, shares the dreams she's experienced with our beloved cats, Simba and Merlin, who are now over the Rainbow Bridge. She says, "The most recent dream I had was early in the morning before it was time for me to get up. I felt that I wasn't quite in a dream but was in a dream, if that's understandable. So, I was lying on my back, and Little Girl (Aeries), my other living cat, was on the right side of me. Then all of a sudden, my hand moved to the left side of me, and I felt what I believe was Simba. I felt him there. I even saw him. He was a little lighter in color and I said, 'Oh, Simba is here with Aeries because she misses him.' Then, the dream switched to where I was standing by my closet, facing my bed, and Simba jumped down to come toward me. He had a glow to him; he looked healthier."

Norma also shares the following: "In another dream, one in which I felt sadness, I wanted to know where Merlin was because I don't see him in my dreams that much. Again, I was in a state where I was dreaming but not quite sure that I was, and little Merlin was over in the other bedroom, lying in a little ball. He didn't come to me but was sleeping between us. I missed him and wanted him to be closer."

Simba Strickland, also known as "Bubba." Author's Private Collection

Merlin Strickland. Author's Private Collection

       THE AFTERLIFE CHRONICLES

For Norma, coming into contact with Simba and Merlin while dreaming has allowed her to feel close to them even though they are no longer physically with her. She says, "The impact is that they are alive and well; one day, when it is my time to transition, I believe that they both will be there to greet me. I truly believe that." My mom offers salient advice for those who've had to say goodbye to beloved animals. She says to have trust in the love you have for your animal and in how the strength of that love will enable your pet to return to you in some form, whether it's via a dream or symbolic message. It's important to feel the bond you have with your pet in your heart; as long as we live on, they live on within us.

Ali's Dream Visitation

My dear friend, Ali Schreiber, grew up with her beloved dog, Chewie. The two had a special bond; in fact, Ali could not sneak out of the house without Chewie alerting her parents. It was during her high school years that she experienced his traumatic passing. One afternoon as she was cleaning the horse stalls, Ali's neighbor walked up to say something to her dad. It was then that her father motioned her to come over. Shockwaves pulsated through her body as she heard her neighbor say, "I am sorry, but I shot your dog." You see, he also had a dog that Chewie would go visit, especially when she was in heat. Her neighbor went on to explain that he was shooting at Chewie only to scare him away, but tragically missed and accidentally killed him. Ali was extremely distraught, and it took her a while to get through the tragedy.

Chewie always slept at the foot of Ali's bed at night. About a week after his passing, Ali was asleep in her bed when she felt him jump up on the end of it near her feet. Startled, she was too afraid to open her eyes and take a look; instead, with her foot, she nudged Chewie off the bed. Unsurprisingly, Ali had a hard time falling back asleep for the rest of the night. In retrospect, she feels that Chewie made himself known in spirit form to comfort her and let her know that he was okay. Ali discloses her guilt over bumping Chewie off the bed; she now realizes that she was anxious at the time and didn't know how to immediately process coming into contact with him in ethereal form. It took many years for her to finally share this experience. She mentions that all the other animals she's had since Chewie have been extremely close to her. Perhaps parts of Chewie are channeled through her other animals. It took Ali a while to realize that her encounter with his spirit was his way of spreading his love beyond the veil.

Ali was by her mother's side as she passed away a few years ago. At the time, she wanted to have a spiritual encounter as she did with her dog. While she didn't have an experience at that exact moment, her mother came to her in a dream about two months later. In the early morning hours after getting up to fetch a glass of water, Ali went back to sleep and had a vivid dream of her mom. Ali said that her mother sat right next to her with a recognizable look on her face. Her mom chose her to be the trustee of her estate; as such, she feels that the look on her mother's face was to tell her to "Be the bigger person and take care of what needs to be done." That, and she wanted to let her daughter know that she will always be with her.

Messages in Numbers: Spirits and angels are often responsible for showing us certain number patterns that may have significance to our lives. Oftentimes, a person will randomly see the same numbers repeatedly until he or she understands the message. Sometimes, coming into contact with a sequence of numbers is the spirit of your beloved letting you know they are with you. For example, my grandmother passed away at 4:44 a.m. and my cat, Max, at 4:44 p.m., and it's often those exact digits that I see throughout my day. I see this sequence in various locations, whether it be on license plates, billboards, or via clocks in my house. When it happens, I instinctively know that both my grandmother and cat are with me in spirit form. In fact, the sequence of "444" is often attributed to angelic symbolism. When you see this particular number structure, you may feel a sense of peace and contentment in the present moment. These digits represent purity, love, and the notion that "all is okay."

Signs Through Animals and Insects: Have you ever seen the most beautiful butterfly or birds fly by you at the time you are experiencing grief or recollecting the life of a beloved family member or friend? Oftentimes, the dearly departed communicate to us through various animal life or insects. This reminds me of the scene in the movie *Patch Adams* when Robin Williams' character sees the butterfly at the exact moment he is drenched in utter pain and sorrow from the loss of his significant other. For him, seeing the life in that butterfly commenced his grieving process so he could go on and flourish in the medical field. These encounters have occurred to me many times. In fact, after my cat Max transitioned in 2016, a beautiful monarch butterfly appeared before me the following day and flew around me for several minutes. The comfort that ensued during and after was priceless.

A similar scene is evident in the movie *Dragonfly*, starring Kevin Costner. Costner's character repeatedly encountered sightings of dragonflies, bewildering him into studying the reasons why. Of course, it is that poignant scene at the end of the film when he fully comprehends why he kept seeing the insects. He realized that his deceased wife utilized the symbolism of dragonflies to guide him to his son. Indeed, the afterlife is creative in its attempt to communicate with the living via symbolism.

The sixth sense is developed in our furry companions. As a result, they are able to alert us to the appearance of a spiritual entity. It's for this reason that my paranormal research team always includes a question about animal behavior on its client interview form. In order to let us know about spirit activity, animals may stay fixated on a certain portion of the house or try to get our attention when a presence is near. They may be very vocal, almost as if they are talking with an unseen part of the home. It's up to us to pay attention to their behavior and deduce whether or not a spirit could be around.

Animals have a sixth sense of knowing when other animals have passed on. Take this scenario regarding my friend Kathie Guetzko's two Siamese cats. When her cat Molly passed away, she buried her beloved pet in the yard. A year in a half later, she got a new Siamese kitten in the middle of January. This male kitten was the runt of the litter and had an eye condition. When springtime came, Kathie acquainted him with the backyard, where he wandered around. Not surprisingly, he went up to the exact spot where Molly was buried and laid down with a peaceful look on his face. To put this in better perspective, the family has two acres of land, so he could have sat anywhere. He instinctively knew where Molly's resting place was. Perhaps finding the spot was due to some divine knowledge, or maybe Molly somehow communicated to him. Animals are in many ways more in tune than humans, so this comes as no surprise.

Unexplained Noises: When a departed loved one or friend is trying to get your attention, he or she may do so by making odd noises or sounds. These can include knocking on doors or windows, moving items around in the home, closing or opening doors, turning on or off lights and/or electronic devices, etc. There may be a pattern to these events where a spirited entity may try to replicate any noises he or she made while of body. Think back to Angela's story and the whistling and knee-popping sound her deceased grandfather made. These occurrences happen mainly as a way to alert the living that a ghost or spirit is near.

Speaking of knocking sounds, is it possible that ethereal entities utilize the making of certain sounds as an alternative way of communicating with the living? In the case of rhythmic knocking, a sound often heard during paranormal investigations, perhaps it's some spiritual messaging code for talking with those who are still in the body. As Morse code is used for ships, maybe knocking is a type of protocol applied by the afterlife. Depending on the level and/or strength in manifestation, maybe it's easier for certain energies to make noises as opposed to vocalizing certain words or phrases.

Odd or Familiar Smells: One of the conventional tactics spirits use to get the attention of the living is to somehow appear with a familiar scent, one that their surviving loved ones will easily recognize. I have heard many people, including several paranormal research colleagues, talk about instances of smelling phantom pipes or cigarette smoke, cologne, and perfume. Shortly after my paternal grandmother passed away, I traveled down to her house in Chula Vista, California, to visit one of her daughters who happened to be staying there. I remember standing in the kitchen when, all of a sudden, I distinctly smelled the strong sense of her unique perfume. Perhaps my grandmother came through to comfort me as I was stricken with grief from saying goodbye to her.

Disappearance and/or Reappearance of Items: There are instances when someone may suddenly find a misplaced object has reappeared in a random place or find a beloved item or gadget from a deceased loved one. In this case, the ethereal energy instinctively knows that the living will recognize its importance. Be cognizant of when this occurs, as it could be a sign that the spirit realm is desiring to communicate. Certain items that are known to offer spiritual messages—such as coins, feathers, or rocks—may appear seemingly for no reason. Also, the emergence of certain objects may intensify if the living is ignoring their significance.

This happened to me after I saw feathers appear several days in a row. At first, my logical mind considered it to be a pure coincidence. For the rest of the week, I was seeing feathers everywhere. Once I paid close attention, I examined the various reasons behind this. That is when I researched the symbolism of feathers and learned that it is often associated with angelic communication. If you see feathers, it could be a sign from the ethereal realm that you are on the correct path in life. It's also a sign of honor and a connection between all living entities.

Not a Fan of Snakes

In life, there are people we meet who leave an everlasting impression. With her innate intuitive ability and heartfelt humble demeanor, Elizabeth Wise Mazak is one of these individuals. When I approached her about potentially sharing a story for this project, she responded with, "Well, I am not sure my particular account is exactly what you're looking for." I reassured her and said that her contribution will definitely fit the overall theme of this book. It even has a drop of humor, which is a sure delight, as many inspirational stories about the afterlife are saturated with intensity.

At the beginning of our conversation, Elizabeth imparted that some of her family members are intuitively inclined; thus, she believes her psychic aptitudes are hereditarily based. We discussed that one of the biggest lessons for us is to have a strong faith in our abilities; in doing so, we are able to set the appropriate intentions and parameters when communicating with the ethereal realm.

Sometimes, spirits may use creative ways to communicate with us to let us know that they either like or dislike something. Elizabeth's father, who passed away many years ago, was a soldier in World War II. Elizabeth strongly feels that he is present in spirit form, as he always looked out for his family and beloved wife. Her father's service medals and photographs are cherished family mementos. When Elizabeth moved into her new residence, she decided to place her father's items in the room that houses her 14 pythons, as opposed to in the hallway outside her mother's room. She even announced out loud, "Oh, I bet my dad is going to be mad at me for doing this to him."

Having appropriately dubbed that room the "Snake Room," Elizabeth conveyed how these reptiles terrified her father. This inherent fear obviously didn't pass on to Elizabeth or her daughter, as both revere the animals. She relayed with a slight humorous edge the time when she awakened around 3:00 or 4:00 a.m. in the morning to find her dad slicing and dicing a tiny snake that had inconspicuously snuck into the family home. "My dad used to be a truck driver, which required him to wake up really early; I heard this loud noise, ran out, and saw my father hitting the snake with his shovel."

Shortly after her father's prized keepsakes were placed in the "Snake Room," Elizabeth encountered a sheer surprise upon entering the space on the first or second full day. When she went inside, she noticed that it was completely trashed, with garbage everywhere, a knocked-over broom, and tipped-over water bowls. Elizabeth first thought that perhaps her daughter had something to do with this. Her daughter hadn't been inside that room on those specific days, prompting Elizabeth's mind to further think about this seemingly odd phenomenon.

Elizabeth spent some time cleaning up the room, only to find it in the same condition the following day and the day after that, with trash spewed everywhere, a tipped broom, and displaced snake water bowls. This was when she had a full-fledged epiphany, strongly suspecting her dad was behind the mess. "Okay Dad, I am getting the impression that you don't want your items in here, so I will move your things out," Elizabeth conveyed out loud.

She decided to create a permanent home for her dad's mementos on the wall just outside her mom's bedroom. As you can surmise, the "Snake Room" has remained quiet ever since. Nothing else happened. Since his duties as a soldier during the Second World War were extremely meaningful to him, Elizabeth believes her dad's spirit was behind these strange events. In fact, when she asked her dad in his elder years as to the most significant event in his life, his words were, "Being a soldier." He considered his time as a serviceman the biggest accomplishment of his life. It makes sense that he remains attached to his military keepsakes.

Feelings of Uneasiness or Being Watched: In this case, the spirit form of a departed loved one or friend may follow living people around and/or hover over them as a way to try and get their attention. Maybe this is done in an attempt to get the living to understand a particular situation, or as a way for spiritual energies to share the manner in which they passed on. Typically, this may be done when the living person is alone, not distracted by others or in everyday life situations. A person may feel like he or she is being watched in a particular part of the home and may also encounter extreme cold or hot sensations isolated to a certain area. Certain fragrances connected to a once-living person may appear and disappear in addition to disembodied vocalizations accompanying the sensations.

Edinburgh Terror

The following experience by the accomplished author Denise A. Agnew may indicate the lengths ethereal energies go to let us know of their presence. In her own words, she describes what she calls the "Edinburgh Terror."

Since I was a little kid, I've been fascinated with the paranormal in real life, movies, and books. While I can't say I've ever seen a full-body apparition, I am an empath, and I believe that I've experienced other types of paranormal activity. My fascination with things that go bump in the night has included a burning desire to investigate haunted places, which I've been able to do off and on for several years now.

But long before I became a paranormal investigator, a powerful experience in Edinburgh, Scotland, started me on the path of wanting to explore the paranormal in a deeper fashion.

My hubby and I lived in England for three years from '96 to '99. It was a dream come true, because since I was a little kid, I have always wanted to visit Britain. My ancestry is mainly from England, Ireland, Scotland, and Wales, and you could say I was fascinated with Scotland from an early age. My husband and I adored Edinburgh in particular, and it became our favorite city in the United Kingdom.

One year we took a Hogmanay tour (New Year's Eve in Scotland). The night before the Hogmanay celebrations, we decided to take a ghost tour. Quite a few tour companies visit Mary King's Close and the South Bridge Vaults in Edinburgh all year round.

When we reached the South Bridge Vaults (we didn't tour Mary King's Close), the tour guide opened a door on the side of a building, then took us down a winding staircase illuminated by candles. He'd flipped the electric light switch and it didn't work. Whether it was set up that way to add to the atmosphere, I don't know, but it certainly gave the place a spooky ambiance. I am not claustrophobic, and I'm not scared of things underground. I didn't feel particularly spooked, just curious about the history and ghost stories. Everything was peachy...until it wasn't.

We reached a barrel vault room with a somewhat high ceiling, and everything changed for me in the blink of an eye. The air felt too close. At first, I figured thirty people in relative proximity to each other might be getting to me. I stayed close to my husband. The feeling that I couldn't get a full breath became worse. Much, much worse. Even though it was very cold down there, all of a sudden I started to feel very warm and my hands started to sweat. Dread and apprehension overwhelmed me until I couldn't wait to leave. The idea of running obsessed me. In my head, I could hear, 'Let me out, let me out, let me out.' I couldn't believe how I felt, and it disturbed me like nothing else I'd ever experienced. I'd never had a panic attack before, but this felt like what people described as a panic attack.

I don't recall now how long we stood in that room, but by the time we left, I realized I hadn't heard a word the tour guide said about ghosts or history. If I thought I'd escape the feeling by leaving that room, I was partially right. When we left the tour sometime later, the relief was enormous. I told my husband about my experience and asked him if he'd felt anything. He hadn't.

Ever the skeptical believer, I thought maybe I'd developed claustrophobia. When we visited the wartime tunnels at Dover Castle, which are also underground, I thought the same thing might happen. It didn't. Nothing like it has happened to me since. For months afterward I was eager to learn if anyone else had the same experience. There wasn't too much on the Internet at that time about experiences in the tunnels, but once we returned to the United States, I found more articles alluding to others who'd felt exactly the same way in the tunnels.

Mediums and psychics I've talked to since then have told me that perhaps, I'd been 'jumped' by a spirit that was trying to make me feel/understand something that happened to him or her in the vaults. Perhaps at that moment, I'd become a physical medium.

My craving to experience and understand the paranormal may have always been high, but after the terror I felt that night in the vaults, my desire to learn more about the paranormal shot sky high. Maybe I picked up a small part of the trauma that occurred in those rooms many centuries ago. Who knows, but the paranormal investigator in me would like to go back someday and see if it happens again.

I wholeheartedly believe that Denise empathically felt the torment and suffering that occurred in that particular location. One of the hallmark gifts of clairsentient (empathic) individuals is to feel someone's (even a spirit's) pain as if it was their own. After researching the history of the South Bridge Vaults, I learned that they were initially utilized as houses and workspaces for shopkeepers. As time went by, the history of this abode took a darker turn. When the vaults deteriorated, the poorest citizens of Edinburgh resided there. Many of them died. The site became stricken with illness, poverty, prostitution, and violence. After learning about its past, I realize it is no wonder why Denise experienced what she did.

Spirit Form Sightings: Spirited entities may choose to show themselves in unique ways, whether they are fully or partially manifested. Some may desire to appear as misty, translucent masses or shadow forms. They may also appear as light anomalies or self-illuminated moving orbs. Either way, pay attention to these sightings and try to discern a pattern. If there is a pattern associated with their appearance, are they trying to show you something or give you some sort of message? Intelligent spiritual energies may choose to appear in a form that allows the observer to easily recognize them. This could be why some ethereal residents choose to appear younger than when they departed. Or they may decide to show up wearing a favorite set of clothing, especially a garment known to the surviving family, as was the case with Helen Lopinto's spirit form being adorned in her blue and white house dress.

Random Phone Calls: I can tell you from my own experience that this has occurred. After the sudden passing of my maternal grandmother, my mom and I received random phone calls, only to hear static on the other end of the line upon picking up the receiver. I have talked with many other individuals who have experienced the same phenomenon. It is often theorized that the deceased can easily manipulate electrical objects and use the medium of electricity to manifest communication. This is potentially one way how spirited entities can communicate with us using a variety of electronic gadgets, including audio recorders, televisions, answering machines, two-way radios, telephones, etc.

The following account is provided by best-selling author and researcher Marie D. Jones. This story is interesting as both she and other relatives received an uncanny phone call around the time her "Nana" passed away. She also experienced something unusual when her father passed. Since I don't believe in coincidences, I find that the two instances are intrinsically relatable. Synchronistic events, as is the case with Marie's experience with the death of her father, often play out to showcase signs of ethereal communication. Indeed, spirits often use ingeniously creative ways to converse with the living world. The messages are there, but the mortal realm must know and sense these patterns to take notice.

Spirits Reaching Out

I've written and researched paranormal phenomena for several decades and never truly experienced a direct encounter with a ghost or spirit of a beloved relative. I did hear my grandfather, Poppy, call out my nickname a few times after he passed away, but how easy is it to pass off something like that as my imagination? Maybe I just wanted to hear his voice, to be comforted in my grief? I was a skeptic and never considered that type of experience 'paranormal' right off the bat. Surely there were other common-sense explanations.

Even though I never saw a ghost of a past relative, I may very well have gotten a phone call from one of them after she died. I believe I received a phone call the moment just after the death of my father's mother, my Nana. Not a phone call before death, or in the hospital bed at the moment of death to say goodbye. I'm talking about at the recorded time of death according to hospital records and the death certificate.

The call from the other side came from our family matriarch, a formidable woman who carried a lot of weight in all of our lives. Though we lived all the way across the country, she still managed to be a big presence even in her absence. This was over 15 years ago and long before cell phones and caller ID, so when the call came a bit past 11:00 at night, I had no way of knowing who it was. Because only family called that late, and usually only if something was wrong, I answered in a panic, only to find static on the other end. I stayed on the line for at least a minute, saying 'Hello' over and over again. But to no avail. I hung up and passed it off as either a wrong number or a prank call.

About an hour later, my sister called to tell me our father had contacted her about Nana's passing. The weird thing was that she, too, got a phone call around the same time as I did. So did my father, who lived in another state and time zone. We later found out that, according to the recorded time of death, our phones all rang simultaneously.

Because it only happened once, I passed it off as a weird coincidence, but I did some research and found out that these phone calls from the other side at or around the moment of death are incredibly common, and it seemed that everyone I mentioned it to had an experience of their own to report.

When my father died years later, I had an experience that even defied the phone call from the dead. At the moment of my father's death (which I did not yet know about), a very close friend texted me and asked if I was doing okay. I replied, 'Yeah, why?' He said he felt as though something bad had happened. I assured him I was okay, but about an hour later, I got a call from my sister that my father had died while in hospice. We had just been out to visit him, so it was quite a shock. The time of his death?

At the same exact moment my friend had texted asking if I was doing all right. He knew something bad had happened even before I did. When his own father died, I had a similar feeling of something being off—a disturbance in the force, if you will.

Despite my never seeing a full-bodied apparition of my Poppy, my Nana, or my father, these experiences were eerie and surreal enough for me to believe that loved ones can find ways to reach out to us when they want to let us know they will be, and are, okay on the other side.

Repeated Messages: If a particular spiritual entity knows you will benefit from a certain message, then it will go to great lengths to get you to listen. Obviously, messages to the living can be sent in a variety of fashions, with some of the most obvious being relayed via the written word. You may be going about your day and come into contact with the same words or phrases, whether they occur at home or at work. Perhaps you've encountered these while you're pondering making a significant change in your life but are not sure how to go about it. It's extremely possible that spiritual beings may be guiding you through worded imagery; if so, pay very careful attention.

It is possible that some of the above signs of ethereal energy may in fact be due to residual phenomena or some sort of psychic imprint on the environment, which replays itself over and over at certain time intervals. Think of phantom cannons booming in the distance over Gettysburg battlefields when reenactments are not taking place. Or a certain appearance of an apparition that appears at the same time and in the same place. Typically, with intelligent spirit communication, the living will acquire feelings of peace and harmony with the departed presence of someone they knew and loved. Then again, someone may get anxious around a spirited entity that perhaps caused them grief or hardships in life.

Messages in Song: Have you ever heard a song on the radio play at the exact moment of a special event or anniversary? There are numerous accounts of correlations between certain musical numbers and specific individuals. One personal example is evident in the song "Unchained Melody" by The Righteous Brothers. As we were driving home after my grandfather's military funeral in 1993, this particular musical number appropriately played on the radio. To this day, I often hear this song, or I'm switching between channels when it suddenly plays. Could this be my grandfather's unique way of communicating with me? Another salient case in point revolves around the song "Endless Love" by Diana Ross and Lionel Richie, which you will hear more about later on in this book, as it centers on the passing of my cat Max.

A person doesn't need to have scientific proof of the afterlife to experience and/or encounter deceased loved ones. The love and bonds we have with those who are close to us cannot be explained by science. In a way, the elusiveness of the spirit world is what makes ethereal encounters with the departed so beautiful at times. When we respond to such events, we must do so with the heart as opposed to the ego, as this is the only surefire way of heeding the benefits and having an everlasting impression. Each experience I have had with the afterlife has taught me something special; there's an inherent message in every single encounter I have had with those who've transitioned to the ethers.

The mortal and spiritual worlds are not far from each other. In fact, they interconnect in so many unique ways. We owe much gratitude to our predecessors who, via their teachings and writings, have given us a glimpse of what happens when we die. In light of their work, we have developed an understanding that life does exist after the human body stops functioning. Through continued paranormal research and humanity's desire to connect with the ethereal, we are seeing the beautiful conjoining of these two worlds. As you will read in the next chapter, utilizing innate intuition as a way to communicate with the spiritual domain is vitally important to connect with the other side.

> "The two most important days in your life are the day you are born and the day you find out why."
>
> MARK TWAIN

CHAPTER 3

The Role of Intuition and Mind/Body/Spirit in Connecting with the Afterlife

What is Intuition?

T he concept of intuition can't be defined in just a sentence or two. It's a topic that carries a lot of subjective opinions, depending on upbringing, cultural preference, or religious predisposition. As such, you will hear a slightly different synopsis of what it entails depending on whom you are talking to. Nonetheless, the whole idea of intuition is something that needs further exploration in order to fully understand its benefits, not just for life in general but also for strengthening the parallel connection between the living and the afterlife. Innate perception is deeply ingrained in every living creature. However, some are more adept than others at tapping into and utilizing it. Think of it like an athletic sport; the more one practices and increases the various skills needed for that game, the better he or she will be at playing it. The same principle can be applied to utilizing intuition. It's important to not just acknowledge it but to also comprehend how to infuse it into our daily lives to coalesce mind, body, and spirit.

Intuition is that little wisdom-packed voice that acts as our emotional, physical, and spiritual survival compass. It's the divine knowledge of what's best for each of us at any given moment in time. Intuition is an instantaneous intelligence that operates separately from intellect and analysis. There's a delicate thread running through the core of intuition which is often overruled by our egotistical criticisms and doubt. It wants to stand on its own and not befriend sheer intelligence. It peaks its head at seemingly random intervals as a way to say, "Hey, why don't you incorporate me into this very moment because I am trying to help you with…"

Neuroscience agrees that intuition is connected to the unconscious. Even renowned transpersonal psychologist, Carl Jung, defined intuition as the unconscious perception that accesses embedded processes and knowledge contained in the body and brain. Penney Peirce is a foremost expert and author on the focus of intuition. She feels that when an intuitive moment emanates from our unconscious, it's typically via the physical body or our five senses. She also believes that when our innate perception surfaces from our higher selves, it is usually experienced like a major all-knowing epiphany or a genuine rush of global awareness.

We've all had "gut feelings" at times, feelings that suggest we do or not do something. These intuitive hunches appear quickly without any apparent reasoning. Through experience, we've found that these internal premonitory voices will continue to scream at us if we ignore their signals. Intuition typically rears its head through impressions, metaphors, and symbols. Practicing the incorporation of intuition in your daily life involves gathering what it's telling you and then interpreting its message(s). It takes courage and diligence on your part in desiring to make sense of what an intuitive moment is trying to assist you with, as it doesn't operate in a literal fashion.

In her book, *Practical Intuition,* author Laura Day discusses common misconceptions about intuition. As mentioned, any person on this planet can utilize it to his or her benefit. Day outlines that intuitive impressions must be decoded and understood in order to make true sense. Since they come in symbolic, nonlinear fragments, there's much room for error in comprehension (Day, 1996). To many, an intuitive moment can look something like the following: A parent suddenly gets an anxious sensation that her daughter was involved in a car accident. Just a few minutes later, she receives a phone call that her daughter was, in fact, involved in a vehicular accident and subsequently hospitalized.

Of course, aligning with our innate wisdom permits us access to the truth and all-knowing aspects of the universe. When we tap into this divine knowledge, we follow its path, as opposed to one that we've learned or been taught. Listening to our intuitive instincts helps us with achieving life endeavors, whether they be for health, relationships, career choice, etc. Just to clarify, the process of implementing intuition in our daily lives should not be done to exploit others or read people's minds, nor should it be used for materialism and greed, as in the case of going to a casino and attempting to win the progressive payout. Using our innate compass is merely for our positive growth and safety as human beings, as well as for humanity at large. As it's divinely pure, so should its uses be.

As a society, we've been taught to abide by logical and rational thinking. Intuition transcends these and allows us to be in touch with our primal instincts, which are infinitely more aware. With that said, there should be a healthy balance between listening to our intuitive compass and applying sound reasoning. Here's an analogy: There is a fast-moving stream before you. You need to cross it in order to get to the other side, but you have no idea how to accomplish the task. Allow your primal instincts (intuition) to be the invisible bridge that connects you to the other side of the stream. At the same time, you apply reasoning to find various methods to help you achieve your goal, whether that be to find a second person to assist or a long piece of rope you can hold on to, or deciding to swim across if you're a solid swimmer. Your gut feeling as to what method you should choose is your intuition coming forward and collaborating with your logical and rational mind.

As elaborated on later in this chapter, there are various exercises one can incorporate to further recognize and apply intuition. To get the process flowing, here are a couple of easy assignments to help you connect with your innate intuition:

1. As you go about your daily routine, pay attention to and keep a journal of your "gut feelings and hunches" and when they occur. Without overanalyzing them, examine at what point in your day they occur. Write down your thoughts and feelings associated with your intuitive voice and what exactly you were doing the moment they came forward. Take some private time to reflect on these experiences; as mentioned, try not to intellectually scrutinize them. Pay attention to what your heart is saying as opposed to your mind. When we overanalyze something with our mind, we negate our inner intuitive dialogue and prevent it from coming forward.

2. Take some time out each day to concentrate on an emotional connection you have with an object, place, color, piece of art, or person. Then, via meditation or plain solitude, listen to your heart as opposed to the logical mind as to why you have that bond. Allow your inner emotions to flow; through journaling or voicing out loud, focus on the feelings and sensations that emanate from deep within.

As you incorporate these exercises, you will commence the process of becoming more aligned with your innate intuition. Furthermore, you will open the door to becoming one with yourself as you allow your intuitive awareness to develop and come to the forefront.

The Role of Intuition in the Mind / Body / Spirit Nexus

The art of acknowledging and practicing intuition in daily life is a needed prerequisite to the balancing of the mind/body/spirit (soul) nexus. Integrating our innate perceptive compass in all aspects of our lives gives us a greater knowledge of the connection between these three interrelated pillars. One is no greater than the other, as a healthy balance between all three combines to produce the true individual that we are. For thousands of years, indigenous populations have comprehended the unity of mind/body/spirit within each of us, as well as the reality of an individual being linked to all that is divine.

A philosopher named Descartes propagated the notion of mind-body dualism in the 1600s, suggesting that the mind and body are separate units. This belief further influenced religion and medicine. To this day, many physicians and medical personnel practice allopathic medicine—or treating the body in parts as opposed to treating the body as a whole. Modern society is starting to veer from the tendency to separate these three integrated components. Instead, there seems to be a collective understanding regarding the existence of a mind/body/spirit nexus and the importance of balancing it in order to lead holistic lives. There seems to be a greater belief that consciousness belongs not just to the brain/mind, but also to our body and spirit as well.

There are many examples across the board that showcase the unification of the mind/body/spirit relationship. We have all had anxious moments in life which produce an increase in breathing, heart rate, muscle tension, and sweating. This would not happen if the mind and body were disconnected from one another. Experts now believe that our minds are present in our bodies. Our emotions can affect our physical and spiritual state(s). Depression, for example, can affect the mind/body/spirit nexus. It can cause weight gain or loss, skin pallor, sleep issues, and fatigue while also dampening our emotional status as we feel sadness, loss of hope, and alienation. Additionally, it can affect our minds by causing forgetfulness, lack of concentration, and inability to effectively deal with everyday challenges.

Another way to examine how these three pillars are linked is to study how animals and babies behave. Very young children have not yet learned how to shield their emotions; as such, their faces and other parts of their bodies exhibit various emotional states. For example, when a baby cries, his or her face turns bright red, and arms and legs flash. When excited, they will exhibit happy eyes and clap their hands with enjoyment. In contrast, when babies are calm, their bodies will be relaxed. When my cat hears a loud noise outside, her ears go back and her eyes widen as she exhibits signs of heightened anxiety. Another example is how dogs behave when their owners come home from a long day of work. The dog hears the car coming into the garage and the keys being inserted in the front door. He or she will display happiness by wagging his or her tail or vocalizing with excitement.

Author Val Silver, in the article "The Mind-Body-Spirit Connection," discusses how even the microscopic elements that make up the human body have a connection to the mind/body/spirit unison. Bruce Lipton, PhD., a renowned cell biologist, equates our body's cells to small people. A cell's ecosystem is influenced by nutrients, toxins, and an individual's perceptions. They are in constant communication with each other through photons of light in the human energy field that exists just outside of the body. As such, they comprehend the energy from this layer and justly respond. Our cells endure the same emotions that we do via energy vibrations and body chemistry alterations. Just as each individual operates independently and as a member of society, so, too, do our cells (Silver, 2020). For example, it is not at all surprising that the cells in our hearts and brains communicate with each other through the vagus nerve. Both of these organs are responsible for receiving, interpreting, and processing intuitive information, with the heart obtaining the information first.

The Connection Between Mind/Body/Spirit and the Afterlife

You don't necessarily need a complete balance of mind/body/spirit in order to communicate with the spirit world. Without a balance, though, one's connection with the afterlife will be limited and lack a deeper understanding. When people are in touch with their own intuition while at the same time balancing these three pillars, they will be able to further access divine information and comprehend coded messages from the spirit realm. This, in turn, creates a more profound rapport between the mortal world and the afterlife. You will have a more soulful relationship with the afterlife if you are being true to yourself and ascribing to intuitive awareness and equilibrium of mind/body/spirit.

As mortal individuals, we are comprised of energy fields. These energy fields make up the unique individuals that we are. Upon death, they are no longer affiliated with the human body but instead disperse out into the universe. The forces that encompass our mind/body/spirit while alive continue to exist when we die. When someone transitions to the afterlife, he or she may retain the same behavioral patterns and beliefs he or she had when of body. Cells hold memories, whether they are alive or dead. Through memories, a spirit may continue to experience a health issue he or she had while alive. A person's mind/body/spirit nexus at the time of physical death may continue on as it was or become even more balanced as one successfully evolves to the higher ranks of spirithood. This interconnects to previous and future lives and how the core of our individual being evolves through each life we live. In a way, we are all a part of the greater spiritual domain.

Before I delve into discussing the five intuitive "clairs" used to communicate with the spirit realm, I want to highlight that their uses will be more developed when one incorporates intuitive awareness and balance of mind/body/spirit.

Exercise to Hone Your Intuition

Before getting into this favored exercise, I want to point out some prerequisites to practicing intuition. Before the successful practice of soulful perception can be included, one has to establish trust, live an authentic life, and not engage in anything that contradicts the mind/body/spirit connection. We have to clear ourselves from living in an egotistical state full of fear, negativity, and judgment. If an undesired thought or any form of negativity appears, thank it and kindly state that "Only that serving my highest good is welcome." We've all heard the saying that "Love conquers all." Living life with love and compassion at the forefront will provide the essential building blocks to reaching our divine potential. Since intuition allows us to look through the window of truth, we must be ready to heed its messages.

Individual Symbol Meditation

Many people have found Penney Peirce's meditation exercise beneficial to assist with intuitive development. Inserted here is the reminder that intuition surfaces through various signs or symbols, typically the ones that you've interconnected with throughout your life. Symbols have been incorporated for thousands of years. They have been utilized for art, psychology, prayer, religious or nonreligious rituals, business, and health. There are many examples of symbols and their attached meanings; for me, both butterflies and feathers often find their way into my life. In my experience, these signs have been more elusive, as it's up to me to find the meaning or message in them.

The following is an adaptation of Peirce's Personal Symbol Meditation as highlighted in Dr. Cate Howell's article "Developing Intuition: An In-Depth Guide to Accessing and Decoding the Language of Your Soul" (Howell, 2020). I have personally found this exercise to be quite beneficial; after going through it a number of times, I have found myself more cognizant of the intuitive moments and the role they play in my life.

Get in a comfortable, peaceful position and close your eyes.

1. Concentrate on your breathing as you physically and mentally relax.
2. At this moment, ask your body and mind to bring you a personal symbol to help grow your intuitive development.
3. Pay close attention to the specific symbol that communicates with you and give permission for it to enter your mind. This may not happen right away; it could occur over the next several minutes.
4. Stay in your relaxed state as long as you need.
5. When the time is right, slowly open your eyes as you become aware of the present.

Utilizing the Six Intuitive Modalities

Everyone has the capacity to be intuitive and psychic to some degree. When extrasensory talents are developed and properly used, one is merely paying attention to and honing his or her intuitive faculties. In other words, implementing psychical work is a consciously focused use of instinctual perception. Those who've mastered the art of integrating psychic awareness have worked hard to cultivate their gifts, whether it be via divination, tarot, astrology, mediumship, etc. After trauma or a specific life event, some individuals have found that they are suddenly "psychic." What this means is that they have located and adequately tuned into their intuition. Think of intuition as the foundational building block to strengthening psychic proficiencies.

Here are some examples of using intuition versus psychic skills:

Intuition

You are driving on a crowded interstate and suddenly get the notion that you should exit as an accident, that you are as of yet unaware of, is two miles ahead of you.

Psychic Skills

Through psychometry, you are attempting to feel any emotions associated with an antique you are holding in your hand. After concentrating on the item, you pick up a sense of attached sadness.

Intuition

You and your significant other want to go see a movie. However, you have a strong inclination that your favorite theater isn't playing that particular film.

Psychic Skills

A paranormal researcher is investigating a private residence. As she enters the master bedroom, images flash in her head related to the physical attributes of one of the resident spirits. She begins to see in her mind's eye an older lady with curly hair who's dressed in a vintage nightgown. This is an example of utilizing clairvoyance.

Developing our intuitive and psychic compasses can be beneficial in various ways. As mentioned, it can be of assistance when we choose to connect and communicate with the afterlife. Just as the mortal realm is constantly learning and evolving, so are those in the spirit world. Our soul continues its expedition through various lives as a way to keep progressing until it's reached the ultimate celestial state. Upon balancing the mind/body/spirit, refining intuition, and developing psychic awareness, a living individual can have access to the deeper layers of those in the afterlife. They will be better prepared to zero in on imparted messages from the ethereal world. They will be able to channel the various tiers of what comprises a particular spirit or hone into the specific assistance and/or teachings offered.

The Akashic Records is a past-present-future anthology of all the occurring human events, thoughts, words, emotions, and intentions. In other words, it's a completed book of our past lives; by examining them, we will have a greater understanding of our true purpose and our soul's ultimate potential. Accessing the chronicle can permit divine healing of past traumatic events as one aligns with celestial love and truth. It can permit an understanding of the reasons why certain convictions, behaviors, and limitations are problematic. Both the living and spiritual worlds can have access to this complete compilation. This occurs when there's a balance of mind/body/spirit and the development of extrasensory perception and intuition.

There are six specific modalities psychics and "intuitives" use when connecting with the spirit world and/or accessing the all-knowing compendium of the Akashic Records. Some individuals are trained in all six, whereas others prefer to utilize just one or two methods. As a paranormal researcher who's spent twenty-plus years investigating the unknown, I have incidentally cultivated my clairvoyant, clairaudient, and clairsentient abilities. This goes to show that mere exposure can have everlasting effects on one's psychic senses. In my opinion, I believe the conscious and subconscious are at play here. I knowingly desire to improve my investigation skills, which include psychical uses; at the same time, I may be unintentionally cognizant of where my extrasensory strengths lie.

One of the misconceptions of psychic information is that it comes to us in a definitive, concrete fashion. This is not the case, as information imparted to us from the spirit realm typically comes in fragments. It is up to us to connect the individual puzzle pieces and make sense of what we are receiving.

Your intuition will guide you. When you have a sudden "Aha" moment, that's a good sign that you are accurately decoding the spiritual data coming through.

Clairvoyance

Psychic impressions can come in the form of pictures or visions. Clairvoyance is used when a person is able to see these pictures and/or visions that form in our third (psychic) eye. An example of using this gift is when individuals see a random ghost, spirit, or deceased loved one or pet. Now, a clairvoyant is more susceptible to physically seeing ethereal energies with his or her own eyes; however, it's seeing via the psychic eye that is most commonly associated with clairvoyance.

When I am investigating a certain location, I will often get glimpses of how a person looked while alive. I can see their physical attributes and types of clothing. Or I may see a certain type of setting, whether it be a house, the ocean or mountains, or a random building. Brief flashes of random objects associated with the spirits may come into my mind's eye.

Clairaudience

Psychic impressions can also come in the form of single words, phrases, or complete sentences. A clairaudient person may physically hear via his or her ears. Or he or she may receive words, phrases, or sentences in the form of psychic thoughts. It takes practice from the clairaudient individual to distinguish his or her own thoughts from extrasensory ones emanating from a spirit. Those who possess this gift can hear projected thoughts from deceased loved ones and pets, earthbound energies, spirit guides, or angels. When we pay conscious attention to what's coming through, we allow our soul to fully comprehend and make sense of the information delivered.

Even the living can project thoughts back and forth. This happens all the time with my mom and me. I will be thinking of her at a specific moment in my day, and two seconds later, I see that she's calling me. Another personal example is the telepathic connection my dear friend, Ali Schreiber, and I have. Many times during paranormal case studies, she will suggest exactly what I am thinking of, or vice versa. Or at the exact same time, we will propose the same phrased question to the energies. Many people on our "Spirits of the Adobe" tours at the Rancho Buena Vista Adobe have witnessed this. This psychic connection we have grows stronger with each project we take on.

Since ethereal beings are thought to not have vocal tones as they did when of body, the information they impart comes in the form of thoughts. In my own practice as a paranormal researcher, however, I have received various words or phrases that have distinct female and male intonations. In most circumstances, I would need to compare what I hear to the actual vocal tone of that individual when he or she was alive. This is hard to accomplish since what is imparted isn't always considered tangible. However, it can be attempted with the use of forensic voice analysis software.

Clairsentience

By far, this is one of my favorite psychic gifts to possess and one that is quite strong for me. Don't get me wrong; the other "clairs" have finely been tuned with my years of paranormal research and communicating with the spirit realm. But clairsentience came most naturally to me. When individuals are clairsentient, they are able to feel the sensations and emotions of others around them, the environment, and those in the spirit realm. This is a form of psychic detection that works around the clock, even when we're sleeping.

I believe clairsentience is one of the most common psychic abilities consistently utilized by many people. In a way, it's a survival mechanism to get us through the many challenges and obstacles of everyday life. To the untrained clairsentient, there may be difficulty in distinguishing one's own emotions and feelings from those of other living individuals or those in the spirit world. It can be problematic when this occurs, as one may take on unwanted feelings or moods as his or her own. Thus, it's vitally important to train yourself to discern whether the information imparted is your own or is coming from another source.

Clairalience

Scents have an uncanny way of evoking certain emotions and memories. This is a method spirits use to announce their presence or to impart a message. One of the least talked about methods of psychic intuition, clairalience is the ability to receive psychic impressions through smells. Many of the scents carry powerful, divine information. It takes knowledge on the part of the transmitter (spirit realm) and receiver (living individual) to make sense of the specific smell at any given moment.

Now, please don't confuse clairalience with typical everyday scents experienced by people from all walks of life. Encountering the pungent scent of body odor at the gym or potential halitosis from the person five feet in front of you is not an example of clairalience. Clairalience occurs when there's no physical, tangible reason for a particular smell to be sensed at that given moment in time. It's as if it emanates from a dimension beyond that of the mortal plane. Helen Lopinto loved to wear an older version of Estee Lauder perfume. It was quite strong and could be sensed from down the hall. Every now and then, I will get random whiffs of this exact perfume.

Clairgustance

By far, this is the least experienced psychic sense. It is the ability to taste something that isn't physically present. When this happens, a deceased loved one or friend may be communicating a memory regarding food or a certain event. On a past paranormal research project, one of my colleagues suddenly tasted tobacco in his mouth, even though he wasn't a consumer. We later learned that one of the resident spirits at the location was a prolific user of tobacco products. Perhaps this particular entity chose to interact with my friend in this manner as a way to announce his presence.

Claircognizance

A person who uses this modality has a keen knowledge of people, places, and events that he or she has no prior awareness of. This is similar to precognition, where an individual knows that a certain incident is going to happen prior to its actual occurrence. Individuals with this aptitude have consistent gut feelings, are exceptional at discerning honesty versus dishonesty, and can foretell future events. Nostradamus is one of the most famous seers, as he was able to predict future occurrences. When claircognizance happens, our logical minds want to understand the reasons why we have suddenly been bestowed with this information. In all actuality, there isn't a rational explanation for why this occurs. I have had claircognitive moments in my life, especially concerning geological conditions and natural disasters. Oddly, I am able to sense about 70% of the time when an earthquake is going to hit. Additionally, I have often had premonitions of wildfires and plane crashes. When this happens, it can be anxiety-provoking, but I have to remind myself to just go with the flow. At the moment of my premonitions, I have to remind myself that I am tapping into the all-knowing of the universe.

The Chakras: The Body's Energy Fields

Before delving into the following assignments, let's discuss the importance of the chakras and how they fit into this entire paradigm. I want to reiterate the notion that life is comprised of energy. Even inanimate objects such as rocks, gems, and crystals have some sort of energy running through them. A later chapter will discuss the importance of utilizing crystals when attempting spirit communication. Positioned near the spine from our base to our crown, the seven chakras are revolving energy units that help us with different aspects of our being. I admire author David Pond's analogy in his book, *Chakras for Beginners: A Guide to Balancing Your Chakra Energies*. He suggests that our spine is the elevator shaft and our chakras are "…the various floors from which we can experience life." These proverbial "floors" receive and transmit the widespread force that's within all of us. Each chakra embodies a specific universal frequency (Pond, 2003). Electromagnetic (EMF) energy fields are collectively dispersed. The chakras interact with the EMF spectrum and convert it to nurture our lives.

Each chakra is responsible for maintaining the health of a specific portion of our physical body. Additionally, all seven process and distribute energy coming into our auras, then transmute it into various emotional and physical sensations. They are responsible for balancing our physical, mental, and emotional energy, which provides for spiritual healing. The momentum moving through our chakras does not necessarily flow in a linear fashion. It can emanate from the earth and flow upward, or vice versa. It all depends on what specific chakra(s) need balancing. Properly aligned, they will be more capable of comprehending the energy around us, including forces coming from the afterlife. As you move through the different levels of chakras, you will gain a deeper perspective on your life's purpose and well-being. In conclusion, when our chakras are open and aligned, we permit our vital life force (*prana* in Sanskrit; *chi* in Chinese) to move freely throughout our physical body.

Chakra 1: Muladhara (root, base of tailbone)

Color: Red

Associated Psychic Gifts: Intuition, spatial awareness

The Muladhara opens downward toward the earth, which links us to it and our physical atmosphere. When properly balanced, it permits us to feel completely connected to our planet. It's responsible for maintaining health from just below the buttocks to just above the sexual organs. It helps regulate the spinal column, digestion, excretion, kidneys, adrenal glands, and sexual well-being. When the Muladhara is balanced, your survival instincts will be fully heightened. When this chakra is appropriately aligned, an individual feels great and has a sense of security, charisma, and confidence. He or she desires to give to others and is quite connected to friends and family.

Chakra 2: Swadhishthana (sacral, pelvic area)

Color: Orange

Associated Psychic Gifts: Clairsentience

This particular chakra maintains sexual energy, sexuality, sensuality, and intimacy. It helps regulate the pelvic organs, urinary tract/bladder, hips, legs, and feet. When it's properly balanced, our creative inspiration will be at its best, and an individual will feel an innocent sense of wonder. The Swadhishthana concentrates on a person's primal emotions, acceptance and/or rejection, and the sense of fitting into a group or being alone. Upon puberty, however, this magical sensation often vanishes due to obstructions in the second chakra. This happens because of society's prohibitive thoughts in relation to sexuality.

Chakra 3: Manipura (solar plexus)

Color: Yellow

Associated Psychic Gifts: Sensitivity to vibrations from various individuals and/or locations

Focusing on personality, the Manipura is situated in the empty area between the ribs, a few inches above the navel. This chakra maintains the appendix, blood, diaphragm, gall bladder, large and small intestines, liver, pancreas, and stomach. As the body's cooling and heating system, it helps regulate digestion, metabolism, and our nervous system. It also houses our creative potential and innate feelings. When this chakra is balanced, a person will be more capable of sensing vibrations from others. He or she will be able to control anger and have a sense of authority. The Manipura plays an integral role in peoples' linkage to the world around them. Some of the traits associated with a balancing of this chakra include an individual sense of love, respect, and worth. When this chakra is blocked, a person may experience fear, anger, anxiety, or possessiveness.

Chakra 4: Anahata (heart)

Color: Green or Pink

Associated Psychic Gifts: Empathy toward other people

The Anahata is aptly known as the entryway to the soul. It's positioned in the center of the chest at the spine's eighth cervical vertebra. It maintains the circulatory system, heart functions, lungs, and thymus gland (immune system). As one can glean, this chakra is associated with compassion, faith, and love. It assists with the different facets of love, including the process of acquiring, giving, losing, and receiving. When this chakra is balanced, a person feels an unconditional bond to humanity and a balance between experiencing anger, fear, joy, and pain. When unbalanced, a judgmental, egotistical attitude may be present. Or there may be a sense of insecurity and unworthiness or an absence of generosity toward the self and others.

Chakra 5: Vishuddhi (throat)
Color: Blue
Associated Psychic Gifts: Telepathy, clairaudience

Located in the body's throat region, the fifth chakra focuses on the otherworldly and the sources of hearing and sound. It manages the bronchial systems, ears, jaw, mouth, nose, teeth, thyroid and parathyroid glands, and vocal cords. As the communication center, the Vishuddhi governs the areas of dreaming, OBE experiences, self-expression via speech and writing, veracity, and belief in the self. When this chakra is balanced, both clairaudience and clairgustance are at their prime. Furthermore, an individual has a clearer perception of his or her ultimate purpose. When the Vishuddhi is unblocked, a person has a greater comprehension of clarity, self-identity, and the confidence to speak one's mind on various opinions and topics with integrity. When opened, this chakra allows a person to be conscious of psychological projection.

Chakra 6: Ajna (third eye)
Color: Indigo Blue or Purple
Associated Psychic Gifts: Clairvoyance

Located between the eyebrows, the Ajna governs the pituitary gland, or the body's control center, and endocrine glands. It manages the other six chakras in the body and is associated with clairvoyance and clairalience. This sixth chakra regulates all receiving and outbound thoughts and visions. When this chakra is balanced, a person is able to envision various aspects of his or her life. Ajna impacts concentration, dreams, imagination, intuition, and wisdom.

It also helps us differentiate between fantasy and reality. Via the third eye, one will become aligned with the yin and the yang of life and become further united with the soul's true purpose. When this chakra is in its healthiest state, people will be able to remember all of the years of their life, from infancy to the present. Additionally, there is a balancing of the six intuitive modalities, along with a better perception of paranormal events.

Chakra 7: Sahasrara (crown)
Color: Violet or White
Associated Psychic Gifts: Cosmic Awareness

Positioned at the top of the head, the Sahasrara maintains the upper brain and right eye. As the most powerful chakra, it's the center whereby a person can integrate the divine. Known as the spiritual epicenter, the Sahasrara is where a person can connect to spirit guides and angels, become one with the higher self, and fully unite with the universe. When this chakra is balanced, a person's energy fields become blended with his or her soul to achieve the concept known as soul love. This permits the rapid increase of spiritual growth. All of the six other chakras must be open and balanced in order to achieve this state of cosmic consciousness.

Exercises to Balance the Chakras

The Infusion of White Light

This is an exercise that I do quite often. Upon completion, I feel a sense of warmth and peace permeating my body. Here's what you need to do to practice this exercise:

1. Find a comfortable place, one that won't cause any distractions.

2. Sit on a chair, with your feet firmly pressing the floor. Close your eyes.

3. Concentrate on your breathing; slowly breathe in for eight seconds and slowly breathe out for eight seconds. Do this five times or until you feel grounded. Pay attention to the air entering and exiting your lungs. Imagine it as divine energy and picture it infusing your capillaries, veins, and arteries as it expands to your other organs.

4. Envision an opening at the top of your head (crown chakra). Then, similar to a waterfall, picture a stream of white, pure energy washing through your crown. Imagine it swirling in your head for a few seconds before moving down to the next chakra. As it enters, welcome the divine into your existence as it pushes out all of the clogged and unwanted energy. Take note of your physical, emotional, and spiritual sensations. Write them down if necessary.

5. Imagine the same stream of white, pure energy moving through the rest of the chakras, one at a time. As you do this, envision the clogged energy as a brown color. You will start to see the desired white color infiltrating your body as the brown moves out.

6. When you get to the root chakra, imagine the brown color completely leaving your body and dispersing back into the ground. Sit for a few seconds while envisioning a white, pure light of streaming energy swirling about in your body. Take notice that your chakras are now unclogged and balanced.

7. Say, "I welcome all that is divine and all that is pure into my life. I love myself unconditionally; I am one with the universe."

8. When you are ready, slowly open up your eyes.

9. You should feel a calm warmth and sense of peace upon finishing.

Over the Rainbow

This is a fun exercise. You can modify it to fit your imagination as long as you are applying the correct color and order of each chakra. John Edward has a similar exercise involving gemstones, which you can read about in his book, *Infinite Quest: Develop Your Psychic Intuition to Take Charge of Your Life.*

1. Close your eyes and take deep breaths, inhaling and exhaling slowly a few times.
2. When you feel you are centered, imagine yourself standing at the start of an arching rainbow with all of its seven colors. The seven colors of the rainbow match those of the seven chakras in order of how they descend down the human body.
3. Stand at the start of the red portion or first chakra. As you walk over this red line, envision the color red infusing the area of your first chakra. When it's fully imbued, say out loud, "I am now unclogging this chakra of all unwanted energy. I am now filling it with the vitality it craves for balancing." Then, imagine two separate scales moving about until they are balanced. Your first chakra is now equalized.

4-9. Repeat #3 for each of the remaining chakras.

10. You have now reached the gold or soul love/cosmic consciousness at the end of the rainbow.
11. Take a few deep breaths, inhaling and exhaling a few times. Slowly open your eyes and imagine your surroundings bathed with the colors of the seven chakras.

Exercises and Tips for Strengthening Your Psychic Potential

Please note that there are many different types of exercises one can do to hone his or her psychic senses. You may even create your own unique assignment or choose to adapt one that feels right for you. While these aren't pieces of training per se, becoming one with your creative side is a natural way to heighten intuition and psychic senses. Engage in and express yourself artistically, whether it be via photography, moviemaking, sculpting, drawing, painting, etc. Journaling and writing are other inherent ways to expand on these skills. Another simple yet effective way of harnessing your gifts is to simply ask for them. When you practice daily meditation, make sure to ask our creator or an ethereal guide to help you refine your innate aptitudes. The following are some exercises that have worked well for me and some of my colleagues.

Strengthening Psychic Senses as a Group

It's only natural for your psychic senses to strengthen when you surround yourself with like-minded individuals with similar extrasensory aptitudes. In fact, I once belonged to "The Psychic Gym," which was a meetup group here in San Diego, California. We met once or twice a week to collectively exercise our gifts. One of the ways that we accomplished this was to utilize as many of the "clairs" as possible for an item or photograph that belonged to a deceased person we knew. To avoid bias, we each wrote down our intuitive impressions regarding the following:

1. Discerning whether the spiritual energy attached to an item or photograph was earthbound or spirit
2. Notating the emotions and feelings surrounding that item or photograph

3. Writing down any words or phrases that came through from the spirit realm regarding that item or photograph

4. Concentrating on any specific events, memories, or circumstances surrounding that item or photograph

5. Writing down any scent(s) or taste(s) we felt were associated with that item or photograph

For the second part of the exercise, we each went around the room and shared the various psychic impressions that came through. Oftentimes, we found correlating perceptions. We also applied the above exercise to various historically haunted locations, private residences, and/or deceased individuals. If you decide to form a group to practice your extrasensory gifts, make sure you invite individuals who operate with honesty and humility. It's imperative that each member of the group is on the same page at all times. Of course, ego and judgment are not welcome.

Opening the Third Eye

When our third eye is opened, we become more aware of our unique intuitive landscape. Symbolically, when we open a door to something, we are permitting what it is we want to see, hear, or experience. Our third eye opens us to receiving the subtle whispers of wisdom imparted from the divine. Grounding is essential, as the information may seem strange and unusual to the logical mind. If we're stuck in a rip current while in the ocean, the best way to get out of it is to swim with it or parallel to the shore. In other words, just go with the flow and don't fight it. This also applies to the insight and messages received while our psychic eye is opened. There are several ways to apply this exercise. No one way is better than the other as long as you are going through the necessary steps needed to accomplish the task.

1. Quiet the mind. The setting in which you choose to do this varies between individuals. Some prefer to do this out in nature or in the solitude of their own home. Breathe in and out for eight seconds and ask the mind to take a rest. Be aware of the stillness and detach from your thoughts, especially those associated with ego. Close your eyes.

2. When you are ready, visualize the opening of your third eye. Imagine it as a movie projector; picture a pure, white light emanating from the third eye to a movie screen across the room. This movie screen encompasses the entire terrain of insight and wisdom your psychic eye allows you to see. As the metaphoric projector is turned on, be cognizant of your body's physical sensations and emotions. Pay attention to what your heart is telling you. Do this for about a minute or however long you deem necessary.

3. When you are ready, imagine your third eye closing as the light diminishes and curtains close over the movie screen. Take some deep breaths and slowly open your two eyes. Pay attention to any differences in your body or emotions after coming back to the present.

4. Repeat this exercise daily when you are most rested and energized. After some time, this training will become automatic and routine.

Obviously, the stability of our chakras has multi-faceted benefits. In addition to assisting us physically, emotionally, and mentally, their balancing can also help us connect with and understand our relationship with the spirit world and beyond. Furthermore, they permit the energy fields surrounding the living to further comprehend those encircling the ethereal domain. This helps forge a deeper and more profound rapport between the living and the afterlife. Remember that intention is everything.

Meditation is Integral to the Connection
Between the Living and the Afterlife

Meditation equates to quieting the mind and allowing the body to temporarily place preoccupation and material stresses on the shelf. It allows the body, mind, and spirit to coalesce in an undisturbed stillness. During meditation, the soul regroups and rejuvenates, ultimately thinning the veil between our world and the afterlife. In order to open the door to our unconscious, we have to quiet any thoughts and vibrations that don't serve us for our highest good.

Become aware of your breathing as you inhale for a few seconds and exhale for a few seconds. Do this repeatedly until you reach a relaxed state. Pay attention to your heart rate. Tell unwanted thoughts to leave, as they serve no purpose. Imagine your feet being rooted to the ground as you open up your head chakra, allowing purifying energy to enter. This pure force will move down your chakras as it cleanses your body and mind. Once you imagine a healing light encompassing your body, you then set the intention for whom you want to communicate with. This can be done by imagining that individual and/or asking your spirit guide to act as a liaison.

Learning how to meditate can take some time, as different meditative practices require various skills. Concentration meditation is one of the most popular techniques that involves focusing on a specific object, such as a lit candle, or repeating a specific set of words. When you start to lose focus, you redirect your mind back to that chosen concentration item. Speaking of unwanted thoughts, with mindfulness meditation, you acknowledge your feelings without letting them take over. This process allows you to see the patterns of your thoughts and how they can positively or negatively affect your life.

The purpose of meditation is to disassociate ourselves from the physical so we can discover our pure selves. There are great health benefits to incorporating meditative practice into your daily life. It can lower heart rate and blood pressure, improve blood circulation, reduce anxiety and stress, and improve overall well-being. Meditation is especially helpful for spirit communication attempts, as it places you in a relaxed, grounded state. Once you're in an introspective place, you can call upon your spirit guides to assist you in interacting with those of the ethereal realm. Being engrossed in silence can enable you to contact your departed loved ones and those who are close to you. The more time you devote to authentically receiving assistance with messages from the astral plane, the more you will be able to distinguish between true messages and any hopes or wishes you consciously make up.

Interacting with the spirit realm is typically accomplished via clairvoyance, clairsentience, and clairaudience. Some people are literally able to see a celestial entity, whereas others can visualize them in their mind's eye. As you commence your meditation, picture a pure, white light encompassing you that ricochets any unwanted energy that won't serve you in becoming your highest self. Imagine unwanted energy dissipating into the ethers. Once you have done so, use your imagination to invite a deceased loved one to communicate with you. Pay attention to your emotions and surroundings; by doing so, you can begin to feel his or her presence.

> "The first peace, which is the most important, is that which comes within the souls of people when they realize their relationship, their oneness with the universe and all its powers, and when they realize at the center of the universe dwells the Great Spirit, and that its center is really everywhere, it is within each of us."
>
> BLACK ELK

CHAPTER 4

Examining the Profound Connectedness Between the Living World and the Afterlife

E very single living entity experiences the profound effects of love and connectedness. Love, in its purest form, is something that ignites within the depths of our souls and something that physical death cannot destroy. Like an eternal flame, it is an essential component of the building blocks of life, establishing who we are meant to be as individuals. It is what fuels us in uniting with our true selves. The bonding connections we have with our family, friends, pets, and those we adore can be physically broken when death comes knocking at our door, but they can never be diminished entirely. After all, we are discovering through both collaborative study and experience that the very energetic essence of those gone but not forgotten remains with us and in our shared memories. How this phenomenon happens continues to remain elusive; perhaps, the mortal realm is not yet permitted to unlock the doors to understanding this and thus knowing the secrets of the cosmos. However, that doesn't prevent us from attempting to comprehend it. Whatever the case, there is a beautiful connectedness between the afterlife and mortality which deserves much-needed exploration.

For many people, the concept of death can be quite anxiety-provoking. Indeed, this is a controversial subject, whether due to a fear of dying or a lack of understanding of what occurs as we humans pass from the mortal bonds of earth. However, there is solace in knowing that we can acquire a better understanding of the dying process in various ways. Numerous inspirational stories from those who've endured near-death experiences (NDEs) or directly encountered the loss of a beloved friend or family member exist to grant us opportunities to not only reexamine how we culturally perceive death but also to reform any negative perspectives about it. In doing so, our individual viewpoints about this contentious subject can expand to reach a healthier, more positive dimension.

The Cosmic Psychic Reservoir Hypothesis may hold some answers to the survival of the soul after physical death. First coined by Professor William James, this conjecture holds that all things that have occurred since the beginning of time are deposited in the cosmos, whereby a channeler can access the information. This theory also proposes that spirit communications are considered to be portions of this cosmic memory. This theory also supports why the energetic essence of our individual makeup and life memories never diminishes. It exists eternally, available for future generations to access (Fontana, 2005).

Afterlife descriptions can be quite similar across the board for visual, auditory, and/or tactile experiences. Is the interest in studying and/or communicating with the other side the result of society's focus on the afterlife, or is there some sort of inevitable cosmic shift acting as the liaison between the living and dearly departed? Perhaps it's the perfect blend of both to help infiltrate society with the much-needed love and peace our world is starving for. Something is happening in the cosmos that is creating this paralleled relationship between the living and the departed. We are desiring to communicate with and learn from the spirit world, while at the same time, the ethereal realm seems to be extremely eager to reach out to us. There could be many reasons as to why; I truly believe the spirit world has evolved to understand a greater consciousness. With this said, it seems as though the afterlife is reaching out to us as a way to educate and offer assistance.

We live in times of high stress, constant demands, and endless competition, all of which take a toll on us physically, emotionally, and spiritually. We live in an era with an unfortunate abundance of ego, judgment, and ridicule of others. Nowadays, more than ever, people are hurting each other. This causes a ripple of negativity to permeate our environment and dampen our souls, leaving the undesired effects of physical and psychological illness. Indeed, acts of aggression toward others, times of unprecedented stress, and focus on the material are key signs that our world is crying out for help. Perhaps these reasons and others are the impetus for why the ethereal world desires to reach out to us. While we can't control how others live their lives, we can be cognizant of how we live our own.

One of the ways to help lessen the burden of stress is to realize that our lives are always changing and evolving. Life yields repetitious waves of splendor and heartache, euphoria and sadness, success and failure, etc. It's important to analyze both the minuscule and salient moments in our lives and see how they've helped us grow stronger and fit in with our ultimate purpose. Figuring out our mortal objectives can occur early for some and late for others; once we come to terms with this, the possibilities are endless. It's important that we realize how we're all connected and a part of something greater. There's a greater good in each of our individual souls; imagine the greatness and healing that could take place if we all access it.

Since life is always changing and evolving, experiences are placed before us as a way to help us grow, mature, and become the person we're meant to be. Life in the physical is about discovering what our mortal purpose is. I am of the belief that each person we come across and each experience we have in life are meant to be for some reason or another. With each dawning sunrise, we are granted new opportunities to discover what our earthly purpose(s) are. There's no race to the finish line, as every single individual is on his or her own unique path. Even though each living entity is on his or her own blueprinted route, all of us collectively belong to something greater. We all make up the universal consciousness as we share striking similarities and energy structures, linking to our very molecular core of existence.

Since life is never constant, it's often a whirlwind of change and transformation. We learn and grow from our mistakes, successes, and the people who come into our lives. Life gives us the opportunity to mature emotionally and spiritually, just as our physical organs and organ systems do. There are many similarities for all of us, even though we are each on our own individual paths in life. We each share what it is to be human, to be uniquely gifted and flawed at the same time. At times, we all experience joy, fear, anger, pleasure, heartache, and disappointment as these emotions help to define what it is to be human. This is something the spirit realm understands; as such, it pops into our mortal being as a way to help us look inward and take ownership of our lives.

The spirit world and universe combine to present certain situations to help guide us on our personal life journey; they also have a special way of helping to increase our awareness of physical life and death. In a way, each of the stories showcased in this book suggest not only the existence of an afterlife but also how it's possible to communicate with those who've reached the ethereal realm and heed the messages and/or help they offer.

More and more individuals are becoming attuned to their higher selves and are realizing that reaching this vibration can be the driving impetus responsible for profound, life-changing unexplained encounters—many of these encounters centering on experiences with ethereal entities or spirited messages from beyond. Reaching our higher self; connecting our mind, body, and spirit; and becoming more aligned with our soul's true purpose is not as elusive as once thought. In my opinion, there are daily reminding occurrences, some small and some big, that reveal how it's not as difficult as seeking the gold at the end of an elusive rainbow. Synchronous events continue to happen to each of us with almost impeccable timing, constantly begging us to pay attention to and analyze them in order to reach our true purpose.

After I gave a presentation about the history and paranormal phenomena aboard the RMS *Queen Mary* at the Escondido Public Library, my Aunt Shirley came up to me and said, "Sweetheart, you are doing God's work." This sentiment comforted my soul, as it's always been a heartfelt passion of mine to study the spirit world and communicate with those who've reached those pearly gates. While we don't have definite answers as to how or why consciousness seems to have the ability to survive physical death, there is still so much more to understand—and unearth—regarding the subject. For me, being a paranormal researcher entails much more than conducting research projects at haunted abodes; what's truly important is offering a helping hand to those who are afflicted with paranormal phenomena or want to learn how to communicate with a deceased loved one or friend. Furthermore, it's about building a rapport and connection with those who've walked the land before us and continuing to unite with our deceased loved ones.

Perhaps this paralleled relationship between mortality and the incorporeal is one of the reasons why more individuals are open to communicating with the departed. Does the spirit world have advice and/or answers to our mortal problems? Whether it's through Akashic record access or the natural knowledge that occurs with becoming a spirit, is it possible that the ethereal realm holds the key(s) to solving many unwanted problems in the physical world? If so, this could be why there is such a drastic increase in encounters with deceased loved ones, friends, co-workers, beloved pets, etc. When we pass from the mortal bonds of earth, we gain access to knowing so much more about ourselves and others. I can see why the spirit world has so much valuable information, messages, and experiences to impart. If the ethereal realm is the ultimate therapist for the living, how can we go about recognizing and opening up to hearing its messages? As you will read in the upcoming pages, there are many ways that we mortals can open ourselves up to communicating with the spirit realm and hearing what advice it has to offer.

Of course, there will always be individuals who are staunch disbelievers in the paranormal. Remember, as believers, it's not our individual job to alter their convictions. All we can do is share our experiences with the spiritual and uncanny and hope that hearing so many unique stories will help to open a cynic's mind to otherworldly encounters. It is for this reason and others that I am such a proponent of people sharing their paranormal, supernatural, and spiritual experiences, as it not only can help those to better understand the unexplained but it also can be therapeutic to those who have encountered something similar. While collected supernatural evidence is important for field study, what's more imperative is how the mortal world can help the spirit world, and vice versa. We can help provide comfort to certain ethereal beings who want to share their stories. We can be there for those earthbound entities who express that they need help in moving on and evolving without restrictive boundaries.

Aunt Lydie Appears

Lon Strickler is a respected researcher and radio host. He is the founder of his renowned blog *Phantoms and Monsters: Pulse of the Paranormal.* He has interviewed people from all walks of life about various paranormal encounters. A personal yet profound supernatural event is what catapulted Lon into doing the research he does today. In his own words, he shares:

Paranormal activity has been a part of me all my life. I have always had some psychic sensitivity but lacked the knowledge to properly use it. But one important event forced me to further examine my spirituality and how I would regard life here and beyond.

In 1977, it was confirmed that my great Aunt Lydie was suffering from lung cancer. The prognosis was not good, and the doctors stated that she had very little time to live, despite the fact that her illness wasn't slowing her down. After a stint in the hospital, she returned home and continued her normal routine.

Lydie was my mother's aunt and my grandfather's sister, and she would always open her home and kitchen to the family. The fact is that she practically raised my mother since my grandparents both worked. She and my uncle owned a well-kept home in the south-central Pennsylvania countryside that was surrounded by cornfields and woodlands. When I was a boy, I would take long hikes along the dirt roads, as well as hunt for squirrels and deer in their woods. When I'd return to the house, my aunt would give me a big hug and have food on the table. I was very close to my Aunt Lydie.

I had been married to my first wife for about a year and was living outside of Baltimore, MD. My mother also lived in Maryland but about 15 miles from me. The family kept daily contact with Lydie, and we all continued to visit her to make sure the house was maintained even though we lived an hour away. Lydie seemed resilient and didn't let her illness get her down.

One late night, my wife and I were in bed asleep when 'something' woke me. I rolled on my back, opened my eyes, and noticed that the room seemed to be illuminated somehow. By that time, my wife had also awakened and was wondering aloud as to why the room had lightened.

We sat up and looked around the room in amazement. I was just about to get out of bed to check on my baby daughter, when suddenly, a white, billowy apparition started to materialize by the foot of the bed. The form was about five feet in height and continued to take a distinct form. Little by little, the specter developed into the likeness of my Aunt Lydie.

As I looked at the apparition's face, I could see the mouth and eyes moving. It looked directly at me as it seemed like it was trying to tell me something. Both arms started to raise as if it wanted to hug me…the same way my Aunt Lydie would do when I'd walk through her kitchen door. My wife was motionless, shocked, and scared out of her mind! She jumped out of bed and ran into my daughter's bedroom, slamming the door behind her. By this time, the apparition started to dissipate and was completely gone after a few seconds.

I sat on the bed utterly astonished. Honestly, this wasn't the first ghost or phantom I had seen, but it definitely was the most unforgettable. Then, it struck me: My Aunt Lydie was dead. I looked at the alarm clock, which read 2:33 a.m. Just then, the telephone on the nightstand started to ring. I picked up the receiver, and it was my mother calling.

'Lon…don't get upset. But, did you see Lydie?' I acknowledged to her that I had. She continued, 'Well, Mom (my grandmother) called me and said Lydie had come to say goodbye to her and Daddy (my grandfather).' Well, by this time, I was totally freaked out. The fact that we all lived in separate locations many miles apart and that the specter of my Aunt Lydie had visited us at the same time was mind-boggling…at least to this, then, 20-year-old.

In the morning, we were told that my aunt had been rushed to the hospital a little after 2:00 a.m. and had died in the emergency room at 2:27 a.m. after suffering a massive stroke. This incident really opened my eyes and encouraged me to take a serious look at paranormal fieldwork.

Since that time, I have experienced a plethora of strange and unexplained phenomena…and I still have an overwhelming desire to find the answers.

Aaron's First Paranormal Experience

Aaron Collins of NW Paranormal is a good friend of mine. We have collaborated on projects and are both regular contributors to the famed Oregon Ghost Conference, which was founded and directed by our colleague Rocky Smith of Northwest Ghost Tours. As with Lon, myself, and many others, Aaron shares a rather unusual experience that commenced his investigation into the unknown and his desire to communicate with the beyond. In his own words, he mentions:

My name is Aaron Collins. I am married to the love of my life and my best friend, Christina. Between the two of us, we have six children. Three of them live at home. I was born in Memphis, Tennessee, in the summer of 1969. For as long as I can remember, my younger sister and I shared a passion and curiosity for the paranormal.

My first 'paranormal experience' terrified and excited me all at once. I was 10 years old, and I was spending the night with my friend who lived two doors down from us. His home had the same interior layout as my house. I awoke in the middle of the night to use the restroom. The house was so dark that I had to feel my way to the bathroom. When I was done in the bathroom, I had my left hand on the light switch and the other on the doorknob. I opened the door, and just as I was about to turn the light off, a woman dressed in a black robe with long black hair and no face appeared! I mean, there was skin pulled over her skull, but there was no definition to her eyes or mouth. The only recognizable feature was the nose.

I was absolutely terrified! In that split second, I turned the light off and ran in the dark, bumping into the walls as I ran to my friend's room. Just as I entered my friend's room, I leaped in the air, landing in his bed in sheer terror! As I landed in the bed, his chihuahua, which had managed to make himself comfortable while I was in the bathroom, yelped as I landed on him! Needless to say, I had to go back to the bathroom. That was it! I had to know what I had seen. That was the beginning of my quest for the paranormal. Some had asked me over the years if it could possibly have been my friend's mom. No. She had short hair and a face. I know what I saw, as the image has been burned into my memory since 1979.

Maybe the spirits in Aaron and Lon's accounts somehow knew they were destined to research the paranormal and communicate with the afterlife. Both Lydie and the female entity Aaron saw helped pave the path for them to become investigators of the unknown. Each person that convenes with a member of the spirit realm substantiates more awareness of those gone but not forgotten.

Dawn's Visions

Dawn Gaudette and I have talked about the paranormal at great lengths. She's had profound visions throughout her life. She's seen people's children before they were born, including her own daughter, Catherine. One day, she saw a little girl in a blue dress with dark brown hair. This small child walked by her and said, "I am your daughter." After working with her on various case studies, I can certainly attest to Dawn's ability to sense the spirit world. She truly has innate gifts for connecting with the afterlife.

Dawn discusses the time when, at a young age, she saw "flying angels" in her bedroom. She remembers laying in a crib as she visually witnessed angelic cartoonish animals and characters. At three years old, Dawn saw an older male figure before her that she called a ghost. She wasn't afraid, as he was really nice. She recalled him staying with her and keeping her company. When Dawn was a teenager, her mom showed her family photos, and she recognized the man she saw at three years old in one of these photos. It displayed a younger version of her deceased grandfather. The spirit world is quite mysterious, as ethereal energies can appear to us either younger or older than how we knew them in life. The reasons for this are unknown.

As an adult, Dawn and her sister, Sharon, went to see a psychic medium who knew no prior information about their grandfather. During the meeting, the psychic told Dawn that her grandfather was near her because he had a strong connection to her, even though they'd never met. Dawn feels that he is one of her spirit guides who has even looked after her son, Kyle, after he transitioned to the stars. She shares how her grandfather was extremely strong in her mind after Kyle passed away.

When she was 23 years old, Dawn went out with a friend to listen to a band. At the time, she was pregnant and experiencing fatigue. She decided to go out to the car and rest. Her friend came out shortly after, and the two drove down Broadway and El Cajon, two streets in Eastern San Diego. Dawn proceeded to lean forward when, in her head, she urgently heard a male say, "Get up!" She got up and put her hands on the dashboard right as they got into a serious car accident. Dawn remembers this man carrying her out of the sunroof. She saw blood but miraculously avoided serious injury. She ended up going to the hospital, as she had a small abrasion on her head. Her physician told her that she was extremely lucky because she could have broken her neck.

"I was meant to have children; my life was not over," recalls Dawn regarding the accident.

When discussing the afterlife with me one day, Dawn shared that she absolutely believes that the spirit world reaches out to the living. With her experiences as a child, she knows that there's another dimension. She can feel it and believes it takes a willing openness on our part to connect with the ethereal domain.

The Role of Psychokinesis in Communication with the Afterlife

We all have seen movies where cabinet doors open and close with relentless ambition. Or we may see people and items of various sizes levitate of their own volition. Many people refer to the aforementioned as poltergeist activity. In fact, a poltergeist is a German word literally meaning "noisy ghost." While this may be the case with certain situations, the true essence of psychokinetic energy doesn't have anything to do with the dead at all, but rather it emanates from the living. This is where the term "psychokinesis" (PK) enters the discussion. In the book *On the Cosmic Relations*, American author Henry Holt first described this term in 1914. Psychokinetic events occur when a person's psychic abilities are able to influence the movement of a physical object on their own without the aid of any physical assistance. Over the years and after studies into this perceived psychic ability, there remains a lot of controversy regarding its scientific veracity, as it is variably said to violate some laws of physics, be the result of a person's professed ability to cause such events, or be entirely simulated using magic skills (Holt, 2010).

People throughout history have alleged that they have psychokinetic aptitudes. One such person was Angelique Cottin, known as the "Electric Girl" of France, who was considered a PK generator. Those close to her asserted that she was able to move furniture and scissors across a room; however, observations potentially revealed fraud. There were many others besides Angelique who claimed to have this power but were exposed as deceptive. Regardless, psychokinesis and its influence on spirit manifestation is a prevailing theory used and discussed among paranormal researchers. Even though PK is considered a pseudoscience, as there is really no way to prove its existence or effects, it still remains a viable explanation for potentially why and how ghosts and spirits gain energy to interact with the living.

The human body is comprised of mainly hydrogen, carbon, nitrogen, and oxygen. Many of the small particles that make up our cells have existed for millions of years. Scientists claim that our body mass emanates from the kinetic energy of protons and neutrons and the connecting nuclear energy that holds them together. Our bodies even remit radiation while possessing many of the particles unique to the universe. Electricity is ubiquitous, even in the human body. Our heartbeats are triggered by electrical impulses that pass down through the heart muscle's sinoatrial node.

Could the minute particles and electric energy our body is made of somehow allow us to utilize psychokinesis? Perhaps it could be the link that permits the living and departed to sense and communicate with one another. Since energy can never be created nor destroyed, it could explain why spiritual energies seem to retain, albeit in spirit form, the types of physical energy unique to the human body. Psychokinesis and projected thought forms go hand-in-hand, in my opinion. Since we're made of energized cells, it makes sense that our thoughts are, too. A mere thought can take on its own life form if enough power and intention are focused on it. If you critically think about it, this could be one of the contributors to why there's an influx of the living and spirit worlds interacting with one another. Perhaps this yearning of both parties to interconnect is creating its own energy field that's rippling out into the atmosphere, thus gaining strength with each dawning day. If this is the case, this energy field could make it easier for the living and departed to interrelate with one another.

Think about all of the renowned historical places throughout planet Earth that are being investigated on an ongoing basis by eager paranormal researchers. Day and night, environmental monitoring and gadgets are being utilized to communicate with the spirit world. This is consistently waking up the afterlife and providing the impetus for it to interact with those in the physical world. It's synonymous with a revolving door at a department store; as it keeps moving and operating in a circular fashion, so do the living and departed as they come in and out of each other's existence.

Bob Encounters His Grandmother's Spirit

Bob Fountain is an ordained metaphysical minister and the founder and director of Spectral Tech, a paranormal research team based out of Tennessee. As a young child, he could always feel when he was being watched by unseen entities. After finishing college, he commenced technical writing and later began writing on the paranormal as a way of documenting his team's paranormal investigations. In fact, we both share a commonality, in that we both write for *Paranormal Underground Magazine* and have appeared on *Paranormal Underground Radio*.

Being generally skeptical of the concept of life after death, Bob's initial intrigue in the supernatural dawned when he visited a spiritualist church with his girlfriend at the time. While there, one of the female psychics gave him a reading and prophetically relayed that he would write in the future. Additionally, the medium also commented that she felt Bob was able to visually see his spirit guide. He replied that he was not able to because he didn't possess a strong belief in the afterlife. The lady then asked that Bob point in the exact direction of where he was intuitively sensing something. After he gestured to his right, the woman then remarked, "You are pointing right at your spirit guide." It was then that she persisted by telling him about his latent abilities and how she could help him develop them. Due to uncertainty and disbelief, Bob decided to not take the nice lady up on her offer; however, in retrospect, he did share that the seed of interest in the ghostly realm was solidly planted at that point.

Five years later, Bob rented an apartment in the same area where he grew up. He shared with me how, as he sat in his dwelling, he would occasionally notice strange oddities, including his cat at the time reacting to unseen forces. Bob's feline companion often hissed at and watched something come from the kitchen area, move to the dining room and then to the living room, before vanishing near the front bedroom. At the time, Bob didn't perseverate too much on these uncanny occurrences.

However, his thoughts on the encounters changed when, one day, he decided to conduct a mini experiment while the cat was responding to this unseen force. As Bob got up and stood in the middle of the living room, he immediately felt a significant cold spot, even though the temperature reached the 80s outside. He strongly felt as though he was momentarily standing in the middle of an ice box. The freezing sensation lasted a fraction of a second. After inspecting this unusual occurrence, Bob realized that it followed the course of residual phenomena, a psychically imprinted time loop where anomalous activity continually repeats itself like a record player.

The odd phenomena continued and eventually culminated in a very odd experience. One night as Bob was sound asleep in bed, he awoke to the life-like noise of someone breathing adjacent to him. Of course, his logical mind kicked in as he tried to naturally explain what was occurring. At first, he thought he woke up from snoring. Just two nights later, he heard the breathing sound again. While he was awake, Bob attempted an experiment where he held his breath for a few seconds; the breathing sound continued. However, it completely stopped when he quickly turned the bedroom light on.

As if the recent high strangeness wasn't enough, something else occurred that really alerted him: A couple of days later, Bob had a glass of water sitting on a dresser. As he was almost ready to fall asleep, he heard the glass fall and shatter into several small pieces. He figured that since the floors are a little off-balance, the moisture pool underneath the glass caused it to slide off the dresser. But he noticed a perfect ring on top of the structure where the glass stood, ruling out that it slid off of its own volition. At this point, he knew something—or someone—was trying to get his attention.

Twenty years later after he moved away from the apartment, Bob felt his grandmother's spirit brushing his hair like she did when he was a small child. She was in a nursing home at the time. He felt the hair move away from his eyes, and then he woke up. He received a call about 8:00 a.m. from his mom saying that his grandmother died about 5:30 a.m.—the exact time of his profound dream. It was then that he started believing in survival after death—that spirits are somehow living, conscious entities that the mortal realm can't always see.

Bob said that once his grandmother brushed his hair, he knew that she was alive somewhere and wanted him to know it. What was important in his life completely changed, and he started to realize what was truly significant in life. In fact, the summer prior to his mother's death, she made Bob promise to not come to visit her if she became really sick. She was 84 years old, and Bob sensed that it was the last time he would see her in the physical world. He shared that he was able to sense when his grandmother, mother, and uncle were about to pass from the mortal realm; perhaps, this was part of the latent psychic ability the spiritualist alluded to many years ago.

It was at this time that Bob wanted to join a paranormal research group and examine what happens to the soul after it leaves the human body. He did a lot of reading on the concept and even had dinner with late researcher Hans Holzer. Bob started recollecting the odd events leading up to encountering his grandmother's spirit. For example, he talked about his daughter's fear of fire. She would scream and run away if she saw flames. When she started to speak and form sentences, she would say things like, "You're not my real mom and daddy; I died in a fire." One day when she was in a car as it drove past a house that burned, she let Bob know that it was similar to the house she died in. His wife at the time was very concerned about this. When his daughter was older, she realized that she was most likely sensing and tapping into one of her past lives. Psychic ability tends to pass from one generation to the next.

The Living Soul Hypothesis

The authors of the book *The Afterlife Experiments* (2002) elaborate on this concept by eloquently saying, "If the living soul hypothesis is true, and we develop our abilities to 'hear' what the dead have to say to us, perhaps human deceit might come to an end. It's possible that we could enter a new era of human caring that Linda and I call integrity love. We would be strongly encouraged, to put it mildly, to take responsibility for our actions, transforming the way we live our daily lives. And as more of us openly look to the deceased for everyday guidance, this potential could make life easier, safer, and more rewarding." This is exactly what I was alluding to in the earlier phases of this chapter.

The human soul comprises the true essence of a human being. Think of a human soul as being the physical body plus all the spiritual elements of that person, the pure fabric that makes up the incorporeal aspects of an individual. Unlike how our physical body is dependent on numerous organ functions, the soul is separate from it and can leave the body at any given time. One can argue that it houses our intangible parts, including our memories, psyche, intuition, etc. Even though no human being is exactly the same, our individual souls are all made up of the same energy units, which allow us to be interconnected via collective consciousness.

Even though each of us walking the earth is different, with unique physical attributes, personalities, and desires, the deep mold that defines our soul is comprised of the same celestial framework. Thus, every living entity contains this divine structure, which enables us to share and understand morals, ideals, attitudes, emotions, feelings, aspirations, and so on. We are all different, yet we are all the same. Maybe it's easier to imagine that one giant soul exists that branches out to each of us; in other words, we each share a portion that makes us the inimitable person we are, while at the same time consciously connected to others among the human race.

Émile Durkheim was a founding pioneer in the field of sociology, spending much of his life's work studying how society can form and function while maintaining stability and order. He developed the concept of collective consciousness as a way to explain how individuals are linked together via social grouping and societies. Today, we continue to draw upon Durkheim's work to learn more about the glue that binds us together and the schisms which divide us. This shared consciousness permits us to experience a sense of belonging and identity and allows us to share behaviors, beliefs, perspectives, and values. Our innately individual intuition and psychic abilities are comprised of the same mold, allowing us to also encounter mutual experiences with the spirit world. If we as individuals are able to tap into communal situations while alive, it makes sense to believe that we also share similar experiences during the dying process. In fact, this is exactly what near-death experiences could be trying to teach us: That we humans are bound together in life, death, and beyond.

Does a situation such as a near-death experience or out-of-body encounter permit us to access these hidden parts of ourselves? Think of the soul as that invisible portion that connects us to something greater than just our physical body. Some consider the soul to be a divine matrix, which connects individual intelligence to collective intelligence. In order for the mind, body, and soul to work in unison, their individual energy fields need to coalesce without unnecessary disruption. Unwanted emotions and physical illness can be the body's way of letting an individual know that there is a disconnect between the mind, body, and soul.

Do Near-Death Experiences Hold the Key to Understanding Life after Death?

Dreams and visions of an afterlife have been discussed and elaborated on across human history. As is the case with near-death experiences, the ethereal terrain of an afterlife is believed to exist just above the Earth's plane. However, the vibrations of the astral field are stronger, with its space infinite. Interestingly, the spirit world is described as having similar geological attributes to Earth, yet it is flexible and able to be altered by the imaginations of those dwelling in this realm. This could be why those experiencing brief NDEs or out-of-body experiences recall seeing exceptionally animated colors and striking features unlike those ever witnessed in the mortal realm. Those who've died but were brought back report ascending upward toward a bright light, eventually coming into contact with an all-knowing sense of love, intelligence, wisdom, compassion, and truth. Medieval and modern depictions of otherworldly phenomena include a sense of clarity, transparency, warmth, and beautiful energy. People describe waking up in a paradise replete with surroundings and environmental aspects common to that individual's culture. While in this state, individuals describe a sense of sheer beauty, with vibrant colors and higher beings. Could this be what heaven looks like for those who believe in it?

Take the case of a young boy who died for three minutes following a ruptured appendix. Prior to being resuscitated, he claims to have visited heaven, sat with Jesus, and communicated with a miscarried sister of whom he was not aware prior to his medical dilemma. This story may sound strikingly familiar, as it was the basis for a best-selling book called *Heaven is for Real* (Burpo, 2010). During an NDE, a Harvard-based physician came into contact with an all-loving God, and he now believes that He and the universe have unconditional love toward all living things. This surgeon's experience defies medical explanation; even though the medical team deemed his cortex to be completely shut down, the doctor asserts that he couldn't have experienced the divine state if it was.

The most original written account of an NDE was evident in the Tenth Book of Plato's *Republic*, which talks about the occurrence of a soldier named Er. Er was brought back to life while lying on his funeral pyre, just twelve days after dying in battle. The revived warrior described being taken to a mysterious area and coming into contact with two adjacent openings. Judges resided between their entrances: Moral individuals were sent to the right and ascended to heaven with tidbits of their actions affixed to them. Those who were deemed unethical went downward to the left. Content souls documented visions of magnificence, while those from below wallowed in pain. Plato's story goes on with Er coming back to life to recall his experience (Plato, 2019). Is it possible that Er's NDE experience was influenced by his cultural and religious beliefs, as is the case with others who encounter near-death experiences? A logical answer to this question would be "yes." In other words, symbolic imagery used to describe such experiences could be due to individual belief systems.

The aspects of near-death awareness have been studied for years by many psychological and medical scholars. Beginning in the last quarter of the twentieth century and moving on into the next, new research born out of those who temporarily died shed light on whether there is survival after death. An accomplished physician, Raymond Moody was the founding father of the study of near-death experiences. In 1975, shortly after he published his widely popular book *Life After Life*, people from both Western and non-Western religions and cultures disclosed similar NDE experiences. Moody collected around 150 NDE accounts from various individuals that helped shape the nature of these types of otherworldly encounters. The International Association for Near-Death Studies was developed to further ignite research study into this almost universal phenomenon. The concept of NDEs has been studied by disciplines such as neuroscience, psychology, sociology, and religion (Moody, 2015).

Near-death experiences have been reported by people from all walks of life and, as supernatural as they appear, seem to feel more tangible than our material reality. They most often occur when someone is near death, as in the case of cardiac arrest, drowning, asphyxiation, or coma. Many patients, not knowing at first that they died, do know that they've been resuscitated and have this newly formed sense of love and compassion. Many experiencers, even those with different cultural preferences, have documented being stopped by a deceased relative or spirit form and told to go back because it wasn't "their time." Their lives also flash before them in review, allowing them to instantaneously recognize and come to terms with mistakes they've made. Many people who have classic NDEs report that it's intensely difficult to become one with the physical body after being in the Light, as they now know true love and compassion. This truly says something about the celestial nature of the divine, a place we all come across once we physically succumb.

There are certain aspects of near-death experiences that separate them from dreams, one of which is the consistency in anecdotal reports. Across the board, people from all over the world describe episodes of either darkness, coming into the Light, or overwhelming feelings of joy, love, peace, etc. After such a profound experience, it's common for people to lose interest in material objects and money and to have a heightened love and compassion for others. These individuals may no longer have a fear of death while having a renewed appreciation for family, friends, and nature. Furthermore, those who experience an NDE may find that their psychic abilities dramatically increase. Many will embark on a spiritual, psychological healing journey. One pediatric study revealed that twelve children who survived cardiac arrest described typical events common during an NDE. After reconvening with these children fifteen years later, it was found that they were balanced, did well in academics, consumed a healthy diet, and had faith in their intuition. There have been reports of electrical malfunctions around those who've encountered an NDE. For example, wristwatches have been known to cease functioning for these groups of individuals while operating perfectly for others. Researchers have discovered a commonality among NDE experiencers that is independent of religion or culture, suggesting an intrinsic nature to how NDEs are encountered. It's how near-death researchers Bruce Greyson and Nancy Evans Bush explain that "Cross-cultural studies, as well as Western case collections [of NDEs], reveal a recognizable pattern irrespective of background belief systems or specific content of a set of experiences" (Bailey and Yates, 1996, 226).

Many scientific theories on the subject have been adopted in the wake of Moody's 1975 hit book *Life After Life*. Some prospect that NDEs are due to psychopathology, transformed blood gases, sleep problems, and changes in brain activity near death. No matter what the study is or who conducts it, near-death experiences remain enigmatically mystifying. Perhaps a true understanding of this uncanny phenomenon isn't entirely meant for the mortal realm to comprehend, but glimpses of it are a way to let us know that something divinely exquisite awaits us after we transition to the ethers. Furthermore, NDEs are interesting in that human consciousness continues even after the person dies. A series of thoughts still exist and a knowing of being awake to experience an altered state.

New York University's (NYU) Langone Medical Center has recently conducted a study regarding human consciousness and its survival of death.

Dr. Sam Parnia, the center's director of resuscitation research, discusses that physical death occurs when the heart stops beating and the lungs cease to spread viable oxygen throughout the body. This undoubtedly leads to a cessation of brain function, whereby people are then legally declared deceased. He shares that via advances in modern medicine, physicians and researchers can bring individuals back to life and intricately study what happens to them as they die. Dr. Parnia discloses that the cells in the human body, specifically those in the brain, are not suddenly obliterated upon death. Rather, they go through a process of decay, which can take hours, thus granting time to bring someone back to life even though that person has been deceased for many minutes to hours after his or her organs shut down. Of course, this continually raises the proverbial question of what happens to us when we die (CBS News, 2017, :24).

Being an intensive care unit physician who has first-hand experience with death and resuscitation, Dr. Parnia talks about how, over the last few decades, millions of people have reported being able to see and hear what's going on around them even though they have been declared deceased. This particular NYU study, the largest of its kind in the world, was conducted in fifteen United States and European medical centers. Dr. Parnia and his team studied more than 2,000 people who experienced death and were not expected to have any sort of consciousness or awareness. Intriguingly, up to 40% of those who came back to life had a perception of what was happening to them even though they went beyond the threshold of death. Furthermore, 10% had a deeply profound spiritual experience, whereas 2% had full awareness. Whether some had perception but later forgot due to medical treatment and medications continues to remain a mystery (CBS News, 2017, 1:23). What this inquiry and many others have unearthed is how those who endure a deep mystical encounter seemingly change for the better once they recover. They end up living the rest of their lives more altruistically and with total love and compassion.

This particular study and others conducted in the last few decades are defying the scientific model that suggests that no consciousness should exist once someone physically dies. Science has not yet unlocked the keys to completely understanding the framework of NDEs and consciousness after death; however, it is shedding light on what happens to us when we pass on. The question remains as to how long the mind and consciousness continue after physical death.

Science has yet to fully explain why huge percentages of people have these experiences before death. In addition to NDEs, many dying patients have deathbed visitations with deceased family, friends, or spiritual beings in the days and hours leading to their eventual departure. Perhaps we mortals are not permitted to know the specifics as to why these events happen. Maybe it's a combination of brain chemicals, or a lack thereof, and medications that can predispose certain dying persons to this phenomenon. Does it occur to reassure the dying that they will be taken care of once they pass? Does it occur to help illuminate the path of where they are going next? Perhaps these visions happen because those near physical death are closer to the spiritual realm themselves, thus enabling them to connect with the spirit world. Could seeing deceased family and friends be a psychological projection on the part of the dying as a way to make the process a little easier? Does this mysterious process occur as a way to help grieving family and friends come to terms with the dying process? There is a beautiful enigma that surrounds near-death encounters and how these experiences can open people's hearts to life after death.

Benje's NDE

The following account occurred when Benje suffered a stroke in 2010. As you will read, his experience closely matches the occurrences people have when enduring a near-death experience.

Benje was in his bathroom when he suddenly felt as though he was drunk and hungover. He recalled the room spinning as he lay down on the ground. In retrospect, he realizes that he shouldn't have done that, nor should he have closed his eyes. The odd feelings he was sensing seemed to last for quite a while. During this time, he saw himself in a warped tunnel where he could visualize a bright light at its end. As the light got closer, he could see moving human shadows. When Benje got right up to the light, he saw a close-up figure. It was then that he thought, "I have to walk my daughter down the aisle." After realizing that he still had things he had to do and accomplish, he started seeing the light get smaller as he motioned backward. When he woke up, he was still on the floor as paramedics medically attended to him. Later on, Benje mentioned his out-of-body experience to his physician. His doctor said that he has heard of individuals having similar encounters but didn't know enough about the NDE phenomenon to comment on it.

"I didn't actually see God, but after the things I have seen and heard, I realized that this has got to be real," relayed Benje.

Benje has fully recovered from his stroke. However, he did have an incident afterward when he was sitting at his table. He felt that same spinning sensation that wouldn't stop. Dawn, his then-girlfriend, was there with him as the paramedics gave him oral medication to take for his unrelenting nausea. He thought he was having another stroke. After reading about the many NDE occurrences people have had and the similarities among them, I have no doubt that Benje experienced this often-misunderstood event.

Could Einstein's Theory Shed Light on the Afterlife?

By understanding Albert Einstein's assertion that everything is energy and energy cannot be created nor destroyed, you can see how these theories apply to the survival of consciousness. The human soul contains this omnipresent energy. When researching the theories of survival after death, are we to assume that the soul is responsible for spiritual communication between the living and departed? Is it a person's individual soul that gives a voice to his or her ghost or spirit? Perhaps society's intrigue in the supernatural is the Creator's way of teaching us that we are all interconnected. By studying various concepts relating to the paranormal and supernatural, a person has the opportunity to examine his or her soul's purpose and, by doing so, align with the all-encompassing power of universal communication.

When someone passes away, we must realize that his or her body is the only vehicle to cease functioning. An individual's soul survives physical death and continues to evolve in future lives. Going on this premise, it's safe to relay that the concept of collective consciousness also survives corporeal demise and stays with that person's soul for eternity. Can this universal awareness and perception be the medium that permits communication between the living and spirit world?

Quantum Theories and Life After Death

According to many scientists who've studied the concepts of life after death, there is substantial evidence that the soul continues on a quantum level. Quantum physics claims that our lives continue on in a parallel universe regardless of what happens to us in our current plane of existence. The laws of quantum physics convey that life is not comprised of matter but of vibrations that break away from time and space.

Munich's Max Planck Institute for Physics proclaims that the physical universe we reside in is only our perception, and an infinite beyond exists once our bodies cease to function. Many experts now claim that there is no death of human consciousness—only death of the body, the shell that houses the true essence of a person (Martin, 2016). According to renowned researchers, quantum mechanics permits consciousness to live on after the brain dies.

Stuart Hameroff of the University of Arizona, along with British physicist Sir Roger Penrose, asserts that our consciousness is merely information deposited at a quantum level. The pair describes this process as "Orchestrated Objective Reduction" (Orch-OR), merely confirming data that protein-based microtubules (or a structural constituent of human cells) hold quantum information that is housed at a sub-atomic level. This material within the microtubules cannot be destroyed once someone is beyond the threshold of death; instead, it dispenses out to the universe (Hameroff and Penrose, 2013).

"If the patient is resuscitated, revived, this quantum information can go back into the microtubules and the patient says, 'I had a near-death experience,'" Dr. Hameroff goes on to say. He further mentions, "If they're not revived, and the patient dies, it's possible that this quantum information can exist outside the body, perhaps indefinitely, as a soul" (Martin, 2016). Based on its celebrated research, the Max Planck Institute considers that this world— that is, our present-day—comprises just the understandable material level; however, there is a much larger scale infinite reality that our world is embedded in. This allows our lives in this plane of reality to be surrounded by a spirit realm. Thus, an ethereal quantum field lives on despite the death of the human body.

Renowned scientist Robert Lanza's concept of biocentrism is another intriguing theory that builds upon the ideals of quantum physics. Theoretical evidence suggests that physical death is a concept that our consciousness makes up. Lanza asserts that death cannot exist, as there is no marginal way to define it. Biocentrism's main distinction is that life creates the universe, as opposed to the latter creating life. It claims that life and biology are the integral duo for being, reality, and the cosmos. Biocentrism also proposes the revitalizing idea that life is immortal. Lanza eloquently mentions that when our bodies physically die, our lives then become a "perennial flower that returns to bloom in the multiverse" (Lanza, 2010). We are taught from an early age that our bodies eventually die. We know they die since we are connected to our bodies while living in the Earth's realm. In essence, biocentrism supports the notion that when we die, our energy lives on and travels to another universe or dimension. It maintains that consciousness exists in the energy housed in our bodies and is released once death comes knocking at the door.

The Orange Balloon

William Brower was the first person I interviewed when I was in the initial stages of this book. William is also a noted author, having written several books. The following story, albeit quite profound, is from William in his own words:

Life, and at times the afterlife, has a sense of humor, case and point being my first paranormal experience 10 years ago. Although I've read many books about hauntings, my view was always skeptical. For many years, I was cynical about almost everything except for my friends.

Gary was my closest friend who, although was 12 years older than me, still had the charisma of a teenager. I met him in high school through a mutual friend, and within the span of minutes, we had a fast bond. He had made a career of himself by being a clown and magician.

Every month he would host very wild parties that lasted into the next morning, each one filled with dancing and magic shows; in the sense of life imitating art, he was the living embodiment of Gatsby from the literary classic by Fitzgerald. This routine continued even as I graduated and began to discover my own talents; like clockwork, there would be a voicemail on the first weekend of the month.

As I opened my own business as a public speaker, it was Gary who called me over to his apartment and gave me a crash course on how to operate and expand my business. His advice took me through a statewide lecture circuit that lasted seven years. When I returned to my hometown, it was no surprise to hear that Gary was still hosting his parties.

In 2003, there came a change in Gary; his girlfriend had left him in November, and he was badly shaken by the departure. Although he continued to throw his parties, it was only his physical shell acting like he was happy-go-lucky. He even had attempted to hang himself with the hopes that the guests would find him, but that had failed. In my free time, I'd go over and keep him company and listen to him pour his heart out.

By 2004, he seemed to have slowly composed himself and continued with his magic shows and acts. Things seemed fairly normal until he started researching websites on near-death experiences and various methods of suicide. I continued to spend more time with him in the hopes that the friendship would help correct the situation. One afternoon while waiting for my girlfriend to finish work, Gary asked me a peculiar question: 'What do you think happens when we die?' I was frustrated by the question, not just because of the subject but because I, too, had personal problems that were getting worse. My harsh cynical side answered, 'People hold a funeral then cast lots on your property to see what they get.'

'You don't believe that the soul survives?' he asked.

It would sadly escalate into our first argument while I adamantly denied the theory of life after death. We parted ways for a few weeks while I focused on my situation. Gary, at last, checked himself into a hospital. On April 15, things were finally getting balanced in my situation. I was looking through the classifieds for a regular job when the phone rang; it was my old friend checking in! We spoke for a little while, and then he changed the tone of the call. 'Are you going to be ok?' he asked. 'Yeah I think I'll pull through and start fresh,' I answered.

He hung up after I reassured him that my troubles were coming to an end, and I left to pick my girlfriend up. We came home later that night, and less than an hour later the phone rang; it was Gary's mom calling to say he had taken his life. A few days later, all of his friends gathered at an empty apartment, tasked with the challenge of clearing it out. Each of us shared funny memories about our lost friend, but many of us were overcome by the silence. At times some of us glanced at the door waiting for it to open and see him walk through, but that never happened. All of us attended the funeral and gave him the highest honor an entertainer could ask for: a standing ovation.

Later that night after the funeral, my girlfriend and I attended the reception but only stayed for about twenty minutes. There were old videos from the parties being shown, and it was just too much for us. We had taken the back stairs to our friend's apartment and had accidentally parked three buildings away from where the reception was, so it came as a surprise and an epiphany when I returned to the car and found an orange latex balloon tied around my antennae! I recognized it at once as being from the pouch that Gary carried on his gigs, which had been deposited at the city dump the day before. I placed the balloon in my box of memories, where it stays tied around his business card. That strange gift alone opened my eyes

to the great beyond and gave me a smile as well; leave it to a magician to
pull one last trick out of his hat!

This is an example of how the spirit realm uses symbolism and synchronicity to communicate with the living. Those in the afterlife use the two as a way to provide comfort and solace when needed. The fact that this all happened on April 15th is direct synchronicity, as William is an RMS *Titanic* aficionado. As many already know, the *Titanic* met the bottom of the ocean in the early morning hours on this exact date. Synchronous moments teach us to pay attention to the signs that are all around us.

As to why we see certain departed loved ones appearing in a form from an earlier time of their life, many ethereal souls may choose to take on a recognizable form, especially one related to the most memorable, prime parts of their life. Spiritual forms may appear a certain way to some and different to others depending on how people best remembered them. Evolving in the spirit world parallels that of the living world, albeit in a more divine manner. When we ascend to an afterlife, our souls will continue to grow, evolve, recharge, and prepare for the next life, wherever that will be. In our astral forms, we will be able to look back on and analyze certain aspects of our mortal lives.

"A coffin may have a body inside of it, but the spirit has long since departed."

ANTHONY T. HINCKS

CHAPTER 5

Common Misconceptions of the Spirit World

S ince the ethereal domain isn't concretely explained, it's obvious that misconceptions about it exist. It's necessary to examine these misunderstandings as a way to navigate through the spirit communication process. Various misconceptions about the spiritual world can directly influence how an individual identifies with the beings that dwell in that domain. Over time, society has become the culprit for initiating these mistaken beliefs. Of course, it's not done maliciously; however, the lasting effects can leave an unhealthy imprint on how we collectively perceive the afterlife.

With the rapid progression of technology, the distribution of social media, and Hollywood's fixation on creating shows or films about evil, we are seeing an influx of many false impressions regarding the ethereal kingdom. Courage is needed to supersede these misconceptions. Those who, throughout the ages, have had endearing encounters with the spirit world should come forward and share their experiences. The aftermath will trigger a consistent ripple effect with the intent of dispelling these often-destructive beliefs. Let's examine some of the most common fallacies associated with the afterlife.

Do Ghosts and/or Spirits Harm the Living?

Quite the contrary: Ghosts and/or spirits do not harm the living. Although many think that the two are interchangeable, we already know that there's a difference between ghosts and spirits. Those with gullible and naïve tendencies can be highly influenced by the numerous cinematic and televised creations about horror and malevolent beings. Do not turn to Hollywood for advice or education if you truly want to learn about the authentic reality of the spirit world. Perhaps a recapping lesson on distinguishing reality from fantasy may be in order if you are easily swayed. Unlike the way they are depicted in various media creations, ghosts and spirits don't morph into creepy forms. They don't maliciously come out of the woodwork in chilling ways to frighten the living.

In paranormal investigation and research, it's a common conviction that any marks left on a person's physical body are signs of malice. Again, society's media arts have engrained people with the notion that scratches and/or streaks of red marks are signs of demonic entities. Let's apply some logical thinking here: Is it possible that the human body biologically responds in this manner to the touch of spirit entities? If the theory is that spiritual energies are comprised of heat and some electrical or ionic forces, it would make sense that the human body will turn a reddish color upon their touch. When one is electrocuted, the skin will turn color and burn. The human skin will either turn red, burn, or blister depending on the amount of heat it comes into contact with. If you push down on your skin, you will see white spots where your fingers were applied. If you scratch yourself, you may see pink or red streaks develop. Let's not forget to mention that many of the reported accounts of alleged anomalous marks left on the body occurred during sleep. In this case, the vast majority of grazes are caused by the sleeper during his or her slumber. It's not a ghost, nor is it a demon.

There are common reasons as to why ethereal beings desire to commune with the corporeal world. Maybe they are in need of help or sense that the living needs assistance. In the living domain, people get along better with some individuals as opposed to others. This is usually due to the union between specific personalities. This same principle carries over to the deceased as one's general disposition remains despite physical death. With that said, some entities may feel a bond to a particular living person because that individual has a similar temperament or reminds them of a family member, friend, or co-worker they knew while of body.

It's an honor to have an experience with a member of the afterlife. It's not something to exploit or take lightly. When such an encounter occurs, don't let years of socially embedded falsehoods about the spirit world dictate how you should respond to and perceive the event. Our egos don't understand the reasons for spiritual happenings. Listen to your inner wisdom and heart, as they are the conduits for providing the deeper meaning behind the connection.

In the case of tragic deaths such as suicides, automobile accidents, or drug overdoses, it's sad but common for the ghost to repeat his or her last moments in life. Also known as crisis apparitions, people may observe ethereal specters at the location where they perished. These types of apparitional sightings can be residual or intelligent in nature, meaning that the earthbound is cognizant of his or her situation. Oftentimes, these energies appear confused and move around in detached ways. In the case of a death where physical harm was evident, a specter may materialize with burns, bruises, abrasions, broken bones, bloody surfaces, etc. While this may be emotionally difficult to witness, don't let it scare you. Those energies who are aware of their death and/or environment may be simply looking for help and assistance. Humility and empathy will lead the way and help us recognize this so we can do what we can to help these energies transition to spirit.

Also known as spirit rescue or spirit resolve, the process of helping earthbound entities transition to a peaceful state in the afterlife is one of the most wholehearted types of support we can offer. While we can't force all ghosts to evolve and move on "into the light," if you will, we can extend our help to those who are open to it. Along with other researchers, I have had the honor of participating in this truly humbling experience.

One of the most profound sessions occurred on an aircraft carrier in San Diego, California. On a bright, sunny day, the museum curator invited me and some others on a private tour of the lower decks when the unspeakable happened: In one of the areas near the sickbay, I strongly felt the emotional energy of one of the resident spirits. After some channeling and communication with this ethereal energy, we determined that he was aware of his demise and didn't want to be stuck aboard the vessel anymore. We then initiated a guiding process for him to become acquainted with the all-encompassing white light. At one point, I spoke out loud to this presence and told him that he was free of any pain and suffering and to gently go into the light. I then told him that loved ones will be waiting for him and he will experience eternal peace and love. What came next was an apparent male vocalization of "thank you" as captured on our audio recorders, followed by a collective feeling of stillness and tranquility. We knew in our hearts that at that moment he had broken through the boundaries of being confined and evolved into the welcoming arms of spirit.

The Influence of Thought Projections and Tulpas on the Spirit Realm

I realize that this topic may be controversial, as some people will disagree. Nonetheless, it's vitally important to discuss. In the paranormal research field, there seems to be a shift toward believing that malevolent energy constitutes the majority of spiritual beings. This can be seen in the many created television and film projects; in turn, they can influence and brainwash certain individuals. I strongly believe that tulpas and/or thought projections are to blame for the majority of alleged "demonic" cases. Opinions and views can be so strong that they manifest their own type of energy. As such, negative vibrations may commence at a location if someone projects his or her own internal "demons" and negative beliefs. One cannot blame the paranormal when this occurs.

Describing a form of thought projection, the term "tulpa" is a Tibetan word, meaning "emanation" or "manifestation." For example, the Shangri-La, or fictional earthly paradise full of mysticism and harmony as described in James Hilton's novel *Lost Horizon*, is a prime example of a situation where constant thought about an object has practically caused it to come to life (Hilton, 2012). In order to power the tulpa, a person has to spend much time on the thought he or she is forming in his or her mind. The more attentiveness to it, the more it will generate energy and life. The whole notion of malevolent forces and demonic beings can, in a sense, be one huge tulpa that has gained momentum throughout the years.

Like a ripple effect, the power of destructive thoughts can pervasively spread unwanted anger and hate into the world. Picture a beautifully still lake at dawn, just before the sun arises from its slumber. Then, imagine skidding a pebble across the tranquil water and witnessing the circular, wavy lines expand outward until they spread through the entire lake. The almost constant focus on evil, wicked spiritual energy is creating the same type of phenomenon where the ripple pulsations are diffusing throughout the world. The paranormal field is acquiring more of a spot in mainstream culture and society, and we are seeing this particular trend dispersing exponentially.

Now, I am not stipulating that some negative energies don't exist; I just don't believe or put much stock into the current belief that *most* spiritual energy is malevolent. There is just too much inherent good in the world for that. If the paranormal community starts to focus less on the concept of extremely negative beings, I do believe that the tulpa's power will lessen. As mentioned, it's being propelled not only by a person's beliefs but by mainstream media, such as supernatural-themed films and television shows. Unfortunately, these programs are strongly confusing people by showcasing how spiritual energy is most wicked and cruel. Furthermore, these widely distributed entertainment ensembles do little to advance the paranormal research discipline, thus, earning them the moniker of "paratainment." Although these creations are essentially made for the purpose of amusement, they confuse those who watch them. The after-effect can cause certain individuals to succumb to the belief that the supernatural realm should be feared. Once again, the tulpa is charged.

The tulpa is being propelled by a number of other factors. We are seeing an influx of demonologists whose main goal is to study these alleged malicious beings. My point here isn't to be judgmental, as I am merely highlighting an observation seen in the paranormal research field. The question that I have is: Do we really need all of these specific specialists, especially when the majority of alleged evil beings are mostly caused by our mind's concentrated thought projections? Again, my stated opinions are not to offend or criticize those studying the occult or demonic energy. It's merely to relay that we all should strive toward a core understanding of the origins of thought projections and tulpas. By doing so, we will start to realize that the true composition of the majority of these alleged negative beings is nothing more than a human-projected belief.

This problem is also causing teams to receive many paranormal research requests from those who believe they have a malevolent entity in their home or business. Perhaps, if society in general didn't highly focus on these tulpa-fixed energies and instill fear in people, then we would see fewer of these particular case requests. We would ultimately have more time to devote to those investigation requests with genuine paranormal phenomena. Ghost researchers around the world need to educate humanity about the consequences of this situation. The more powered this specific tulpa is, the more it will influence certain religions that already have a preconceived notion that ghosts and spirits are malevolent. While striving to avoid disrespecting someone's religion, it is also critically important to help prevent certain dogmas that are caused by something that isn't actually real.

We all have our own personal "demons" or baggage to contend with. It's vitally important that we recognize the signs of projecting our own issues onto the environment. As a defense mechanism, it is sometimes easier to project or displace our personal problems onto someone else. As a veteran paranormal researcher, I am noticing that people are also blaming some of their own individual issues on ghosts and spirits instead of dealing with them head-on. By doing so, some of these folks are making it seem that the specter in their house is responsible for their emotional or mental issues. Now, in rare cases, this can be the result of some type of spiritual possession, but then again, this is rare.

When an investigating team acquires a case request regarding this type of problem, it is a delicate process to weave through. Generally speaking, the San Diego Paranormal Research Society does not take on any cases where a preponderance of evidence suggests that personal, emotional, and/or mental issues are the hallmark problem. With these types of requests, we urge clients to seek medical help, as combining paranormal research with a legitimate physical or psychological problem could pose serious consequences for that individual or family unit. It is for this reason that I strongly support supernatural researchers further educating themselves in medicine, psychology, abnormal psychology, sociology, etc., as it will help them recognize when the dilemma is originated from factors other than ghostly phenomena.

There needs to be more studies devoted to the differences between negative entities versus actual malevolent beings. In my opinion, these are two words that should be separated, as they denote two separate meanings. Negative energies or lower-level entities comprise the spiritual makeup of once-living individuals who were innately mean, traumatized, or lived an unhappy life. In ghostly form, these particular earthbound units showcase themselves to mortal beings just as they would when they were of the body: gruff, mean, and/or territorial.

Now, true demonic entities are categorized to be non-human creatures with the intent of harming the living. There are telltale signs of the presence of these organisms, which directly affect the person(s) they're after. For example, those dealing with an authentic malevolent haunting may experience a plethora of unwanted situations: odd sulfur-aroma smells, changes in personality or health, a sense of impending doom, strong psychokinetic (PK) interference, odd animal behavior, and so on. As paranormal researchers, it is our duty to educate people about the differences between these two types of beings. In order to quiet the tulpa, we need to help prevent the undesired consequences that accompany the misconceptions surrounding these energies.

In modern-day society, we are at a crossroads in regard to paranormal research. Collectively, we can go down the path to forwarding and advancing the field for the betterment of humanity, or we can go down the other path that will eventually cripple its foundation. Learning more about tulpas and thought projections is significantly imperative to the survival of supernatural field research. It is for this reason that I highly believe that both terms should be included in the classification list of ghosts and hauntings.

All of society's injurious acts and aggressions toward people are creating a giant manifestation of negative energy. It's very easy to blame certain external problems on the paranormal; however, we need to take responsibility for our emotions, feelings, and circumstances and understand how they can adversely affect humanity. Chances are, people who claim to be affected by wicked forces are probably dealing with intrinsic and extrinsic stresses, negatively-charged emotions, and/or personal "demons" that they are projecting outward. The celestial world is a beautiful place; you will reap its many rewards once you have faith in its inherent goodness.

The Misconception of Paranormal Television

This is a testy subject to contend with, as I know several competent paranormal researchers who are on paranormal television series. What I am about to relay has nothing to do with their experience, knowledge, or skills as investigators of the unknown. It's to address the intent and structure of these shows and how they don't always align with the world of research outside of the televised domain. Most importantly, many of these entertainment venues depict the afterlife in an unnatural light. Some are rather inadvertently persuasive, suggesting that people should get involved with studying the spirit realm for superficial reasons: i.e., for recognition and a shot at fame. Suggestive in nature, these shows can prey on the vulnerable and negatively influence that particular audience.

Along with many viewers, most researchers of the unknown understand that television's purpose is to entertain. It's a greedy industry where high ratings equate to bigger paychecks and network bragging rights. In order to achieve high marks, a reality program needs to be structured in a specific manner. Scripts may be used and potential evidence may be captured days or weeks before the hour-long "live" segment you see on camera. Editing can make certain scenes look different than what actually occurred. Let's not forget to mention the producers that are just out of frame, potentially creating artificial data. Filming for one episode can last several days, with sixty hours minimized to sixty minutes. The usage of equipment isn't always accurate. An example of this is evidenced by the handy EMF detector, where a producer or someone off-camera turns on a cellular phone to initiate spikes in the gadget. What results is a higher focus on drama with missed opportunities to educate people.

Some of the newer paranormal reality television shows utilize expensive and often specially-made equipment. To the untrained individual, this can give off the impression that a certain elite caliber of gadgets is needed in order to acquire data about the afterlife. This is not the case, as you don't need bundles and bundles of fancy contraptions to communicate with the ethereal domain. In fact, you don't need any equipment to commune with the other side. Our bodies and their senses are the best spirit magnets out there.

In many ways, paranormal television treats the spirit world like a bunch of circus animals, placing it unwillingly before an audience. Add provocation to the list, and you have an abusive recipe for exploitation and disrespect of the spirit realm. Maybe this is one of the reasons why the afterlife is reaching out to us: to tell us to stop the madness. Authentic research and entertainment are like oil and water; they just don't mix. Hopefully in the near future, this medium can be better utilized to educate and inform humanity about ghostly phenomena.

Of course, there are many benefits to the wide distribution of supernatural-related television. People from all walks of life can get a glimpse into a specific location and its history. In addition to helping spread awareness, these shows can serve as motivation for people to get involved in paranormal research.

Those who are devoted to paranormal research need to be cognizant of ways to advance the field of supernatural exploration. We need to advocate for the spirit realm and not exploit it. It's not here for our entertainment or amusement. It's here to be cherished and revered.

"To walk the spiritual path is to continually step out into the unknown."

WALLACE HUEY

CHAPTER 6

Communicating with the Spirit Realm— Standard Techniques

I t doesn't take being a rocket scientist to know how to effectively talk with spirits. It does, however, entail exhibiting a healthy openness, along with patience and a willingness to talk. Anyone who is balanced emotionally, physically, and spiritually can attempt a spirit communication session. Ego doesn't deserve a seat in these interactions, as successful communication between the living and departed is done via pureness of heart and intention. Interconnecting with the celestial world can be a positively life-changing experience, allowing us to feel closer to those who aren't physically with us anymore.

It is crucial that your mind, body, and spirit are positively balanced and protected before you attempt spirit communication. If not, you open yourself up to lower-level energies, specifically those which don't serve you in your highest good. Many people, including myself, believe that amateur attempts and negative thinking while interacting with the ethereal world can invite unwanted energy. If you approach your work from your heart and soul and with respect and reverence, you will attract that back from the celestial realm.

In addition to having stability, one has to know what he or she is doing when deciding to contact the astral world. Work with those who exhibit professionalism, knowledge, and humility. Never conduct a spirit communication session when physically ill or going through a lot of stress. Just as you need to be in tip-top shape for a marathon, you need to be vigorously healthy when delving into the unknown.

Today, paranormal research is stepping outside the shadows of pseudoscience. One can argue that since supernatural phenomena aren't defined in black-and-white terms, it will be that much more difficult to approach them from a scientific standpoint. However, we can learn a lot by using the scientific method during paranormal research, as it will give us glimpses into how certain phenomena operate. Furthermore, researchers can learn more about the intricacies of supernatural occurrences through the development and testing of more theories. Around the globe, this needs to be accomplished collectively. By creating these models, we will hopefully discover how certain supernatural phenomena function. Through intelligent research, paranormal investigators will hopefully be able to narrow down the what, when, where, why, and how of preternatural phenomena and how it interacts with our environment.

The Scientific Method: Stepping Outside of the Shadows of Pseudoscience

Typically, the scientific method may commence with a single observation or by acknowledging a pattern to certain observations. For example, a paranormal researcher may discover through several tests that spirit voices occur within the first five minutes of an audio communication session. Or, via many examinations, one may find that certain types of cameras are prone to light anomalies. (In fact, this has been discovered with digital cameras regarding orbs.) This model is adopted in all the major facets of science, including biology, chemistry, geology, physics, and psychology. There is no reason why it can't be instituted in paranormal research and investigation.

When these observations are discovered and/or patterns are noticed among them, it's imperative to apply certain steps to problem-solve and comprehend the reasons for and functions behind these observations. The crucial way to accomplish this is via the scientific method, which has five specific phases:

1. Make an observation

2. Ask a question

3. Form a hypothesis or an explanation that can be tested

4. Make a prediction based on the hypothesis

5. Test the prediction

Of course, a competent researcher will utilize the results to comprise a new hypothesis or prediction. A hypothesis is a possible answer to a question, whereas a prediction is an expected outcome should the theory be correct. The results for each test will either support or oppose the original conjecture. This entire #1-5 sequence can continue over and over until there's a verifiable answer to the studied prediction. The outcome of one tested sequence will undoubtedly provide feedback and insight into the next.

Imagine if every single paranormal researcher across the globe applied the scientific method to case study experimentation. I surmise that we would have a much better understanding of certain methodologies and the behaviors of supernatural entities by now if this were the case. Sharing leads to collective understanding; as such, paranormal investigators or research teams that develop specific hypotheses should distribute their findings. Better yet, there should be a website or main hub devoted to all of the scientific method experimentation for all branches of supernatural research. This is how the field will gain credibility and step outside the restrictions of pseudoscience.

As for paranormal research teams, it is important that each member is adequately trained in the following spirit communication methodologies. This is when the saying "Everyone brings something to the table" can go a long way. Since no two people are identically alike, each investigator can bring a unique style and different perspective to research techniques. Spiritual residents may be drawn to certain personalities. By having various people involved in the investigative process, a group can increase its chances of communing with various energies.

Audio Communication Methods: Electronic Voice Phenomena (EVP) and Instrumental Trans Communication (ITC)

I don't claim that our personalities pass on to another existence or sphere. I don't claim anything because I don't know anything about the subject. For that matter, no human being knows. But, I do claim that it is possible to construct an apparatus that will be so delicate that if there are personalities in another existence or sphere who wish to get in touch with us in this existence or sphere, the apparatus will at least give them a better opportunity to express themselves than the tilting tables and raps and Ouija boards and mediums and the other crude methods now purported to be the only means of communication. (Thomas Edison, *Scientific American*, October 1920)

Audio communication with the spirit realm is one of the most prolific and preferred methods paranormal researchers utilize. Known as America's greatest inventor, Thomas Edison was one of the founding researchers of the electronic voice phenomenon. In addition to creating a motion picture camera, phonograph, and electric light bulb, Edison also experimented with electrics, sound recording, and power utilization. He invented the "ghost machine" or "telephone to the dead" that could launch the lines of communication between the living realm and the afterlife. Since no blueprints exist as to what he exactly built, some people believe he created a large microphone that could detect spirit vocalizations.

American photographer Attila von Szalay was one of the first individuals to attempt the recording of spirit voices. He commenced his experiments in 1941 using a 78-rpm record; however, it wasn't until 1956, via the reel-to-reel tape recorder, that his experimentation proved insightful. Along with Raymond Bayless, he implemented a variety of recording sessions with a custom-made device that included a microphone inside a sequestered cabinet that was linked to an external recording apparatus and speaker. Attila von Szalay alleged that many of the findings belonged to incorporeal entities. One of his intriguing captures included, "Merry Christmas and Happy New Year to you all." In 1959, both men's research was published by the *Journal of the American Society for Psychical Research*.

Other EVP study pioneers include Konstantin Raudive, who was a psychologist and parapsychological researcher. Believing strongly that consciousness continues after physical death, he explored the concept of electronic spirit voices, which led to the publishing of his 1971 book *Breakthrough*. Collaborating with Friedrich Jürgenson, he recorded around 100,000 audio tapes of alleged spirit vocalizations (Raudive, 1971). Sarah Estep was another leading forerunner in the EVP methodology. Having founded the American Association of Electronic Voice Phenomena, Estep maintained that she has captured hundreds of EVP messages from deceased friends, relatives, and other individuals.

An electronic voice phenomenon is a vocalization or sound that is not heard in real-time by the human ear. It's later heard during a review of the audio session. This also applies to an electronic noise phenomenon (ENP). While it may or may not be captured on a recording device, an audible voice phenomenon (AVP) is a vocalization that is heard in real-time by the naked ear. An audible noise phenomenon (ANP) is similar to an AVP but specifically contains sounds. Furthermore, there are classifications for EVP, which are specified below:

Class A: The "holy grail" of authentic spirit vocalizations. When this occurs, the majority will comprehend the vocalizations without question and without the need for an external speaker or headphones.

Class B: Just under the quality of the Class A variety, those that fall under this category may need an external speaker and/or headphones. Furthermore, there may be differing opinions as to what's being said via electronic devices.

Class C: Perhaps the most common type of electronic voice phenomena, Class C's need external speakers and/or headphones. The majority will be undecipherable as they are merely whispers and inaudible vocalizations.

Class R: This type is quite intriguing. Class R varieties occur when you reverse the audio segment that contains the anomalous vocalization. When the recording is played in reverse, a researcher can comprehend a vocalization that isn't understood in regular playback mode.

Coined by Ernst Senkowski in the 1970s, Instrumental Trans Communication (ITC) mainly refers to communication via any electronic medium, including televisions, tape recorders, fax machines, computers, etc. Those who employ the ITC methodology also examine, via the Droste effect, a television and video camera feedback loop. This effect, known in art as "Mise en abyme," produces a smaller version of an image within itself in a recursive manner. While such devices can lend too much subjectivity, it is important that the researcher maintains a critical and objective ear when listening to all recordings.

"The Spiricom" was perhaps the first Instrumental Trans Communication device, invented by William O'Neill in 1980. He was able to hold two-way communication sessions with the spirit world through the apparatus. O'Neill asserted that the gadget was constructed to exact specifications that he intuitively received from deceased scientist, George Mueller. Created in 2002 by EVP specialist Frank Sumption, the "Frank's Box," or "Ghost Box," is aimed at allowing real-time communication with the afterlife. As with O'Neill, Sumption also claimed to obtain design instructions directly from the spirit world. The "Frank's Box" combines a white noise generator and AM radio receiver specialized to sweep back and forth through the AM band, which selects nanosecond extracts of sound. Modernized versions of the "Ghost Box" also include AM and FM radio bands. In addition to its subjectivity, many researchers consider these ITC devices to be electronic Ouija Boards.

EVP and ITC experimentation can be a fun and exciting way to interact with the dearly departed. With both methodologies, however, there is a high probability for both pareidolia (interpreting random sounds or pictures) or apophenia (perceiving certain patterns in arbitrary information). Thus, it takes some restraint and cognizance on the part of the researcher. Other potential problems to pay attention to include artifacts, which are caused when a researcher edits the audio in post-production. During this stage, a portion of the audio may be edited to help ascertain what's being said. Examples of this include re-sampling, frequency isolation, noise reduction or noise enhancement, sound boosting, stretching the audio, and so on. While these methods may prove beneficial in some cases, they can distort portions of the audio, causing them to sound entirely different from the raw recording. Furthermore, it's important to pay attention to the possibility of capturing errors or abnormalities generated in the process of acquiring audio signals.

Utilizing magnetic tape recorders (analog tape recorders) is the preferred method for recording spirit communication audio, according to many paranormal researchers. It is theorized that incorporeal energies can somehow emulsify their energy onto the magnetic tape, as they are thought to contain some form of magnetic energy. If you use this type of recorder, keep in mind that it's possible to re-record over an existing recording, thus creating false positives in the new file. Even if you erase a prior recording, thus freeing up the tape, it's entirely probable that fragments of the previous one remain on the new file. Again, this can create false positives in the new recording. In my opinion, this is why I recommend using a brand new, blank tape for each communication session.

Intriguingly, meteors can cause foreign vocalizations to be carried through radio waves. All radio transmissions above 30 MHz can cause the radio signal to be reflected by a meteor. When traveling through the upper atmosphere, these asteroids generate a trail of ionized electrons and particles. They replicate radio wave diffusion, which raises the possibility that an extraneous voice may interfere with radio receivers. These specific waves can last from 0.05 seconds all the way up to one second.

As with any other chosen methodology, it's vital to be respectful and reverent to the energies and the location(s) they inhabit. Following "The Golden Rule" at all times will pave the way for a unified rapport between those of flesh and those of spirit. Since some celestial beings may not know they are passed on, we always shy away from questions regarding their death. As we are here to lend a helping hand should it be needed, we let the spirits know that we are there for them and to let us know if they need any help.

Protocol for Audio Spirit Communication Sessions

We have had great EVP and ITC results by starting out with a statement of intent as opposed to just hitting "record" and commencing questions. This helps to set the overall tone of the session. It lets the energies know your good intentions and tells them what you hope to accomplish. Make sure to state the location you're in, the area within that location, as well as the date and time of recording. Have each investigator state his or her name in the recording. This helps with voice recognition as well. The following opening statement is just an example. While it doesn't have to be verbatim, it can go something like this:

> It's Nicole and Ali here and we are going to attempt a spirit communication session. We are in the majordomo room of the Rancho Buena Vista Adobe. It's March 21, 2020, at 9:35 p.m. We want to let you all know that we come with respect; we come as friends. We would love to talk with you and learn a little bit about you and the amazing history of this beautiful place. With that said, please know that sometimes it's hard for us to hear you with our ears, but we will do our best. So, if you are speaking to us and we're not responding, please know that we are not ignoring you. We have various electronic gadgets that can capture your voices and sounds. We promise to review those in the event we can't hear you. We look forward to communicating with you.

Prior to initiating the audio communication session, it's vital to understand the specific audio equipment you're using. Although it can be boring, it's imperative to read through the user manual for all the gadgets you decide to use. Since some vocalizations can be captured on certain recording devices and not on others, it's recommended to incorporate at least two to three recording apparatuses. You can sync each recorder so the start times are the same. Depending on the size of the recording space and/or the microphone type and strength, you may decide to implement an external omnidirectional microphone or experiment with binaural ones, such as the 3Dio models. Binaural varieties allow the listener to naturally feel as though he or she is in the space that's being recorded.

If you have a DVR system set up for infrared day or night surveillance, it may be beneficial to place a recorder in the spot each DVR IR camera is viewing, especially if it lacks audio recording capabilities. Or you can position one audio recorder in the center of the room and one in each corner of the room. When reviewing the results, it will be easier to ascertain in what part of the location the spirit vocalizations occur.

It's important that the audio session mimic that of a conversation rather than an interrogative interview. Remember to go with the flow. You can have a preset list of questions to ask, but know that they may not go in the order that you have them written down. Be creative. Have a variety of yes/no and open-ended questions, as well as comparative ones. For example, "Do you prefer vanilla or chocolate?"

As for Instrumental Trans Communication, there are various gadgets on the market. I do want to emphasize once again that this methodology is extremely subjective. The same goes for electronic voice phenomena sessions. There is a great chance for pareidolia or matrixing the audio into words and/or phrases that aren't really there. This is why my team chooses to use these gadgets sparingly and in conjunction with other methods. When using spirit boxes, such as the PSB-7 and PSB-11 varieties, as well as others, we pay attention to these crucial aspects:

1. Does everyone agree to the words and/or phrases that emanate through the device?
2. Do the responses coming through the device correlate to the location's history and/or the questions being asked?
3. Are the words and/or phrases clear and easy to understand?
4. Do certain male and female vocalizations consistently come through, even on separate days? When this happens, it's beneficial to forensically analyze the audio to see if there's a match.

In addition to standard EVP sessions, the San Diego Paranormal Research Society does employ the use of ITC and similar ghost boxes during its investigation projects and makes sure to follow these protocols. We have been able to document compelling ITC at the Rancho Buena Vista Adobe, which is a historic locale we've researched for almost twelve years. As mentioned, since radio fragments and/or static sounds can be matrixed into alleged voices, it's imperative to look for certain clues that reduce the chance of this possibility. When reviewing ITC audio via software such as Adobe Audition, Pro Tools, or Audacity, we look for responses that are clear, profound, and relevant. You can more confidently rule out the possibility of a stray radio station fragment if a captured word or phrase is readily heard and deciphered by everyone who listens while at the same time seems to be historically accurate or correlates to the questions being asked.

Here are a few of our most compelling audio vocalizations:

Still Am ITC Response

While hosting one of our fundraising tours in 2015 at the Rancho Buena Vista Adobe, I felt intuitively compelled to ask one of the resident spirits if he was friends with the Native Americans. The question I asked was, "Juan, are you friends with the Indians?" Now, I purposely didn't use the words "Native Americans" because, in his era, they would have used the word "Indian." Strikingly, we captured an absolutely clear, historically relevant male response of "Still am," which seems to correspond to the history of this particular spirit, being that he was most likely indigenous to the land. This and other compelling audio can be heard on the San Diego Paranormal Research Society website.

All About the Horses ITC Response

Again, while hosting one of our "Spirits of the Adobe" tours at the Rancho Buena Vista Adobe, we asked about the horses, specifically how many animals Cave Couts Jr. had on the property. After posing this inquiry, we received a clear response of "Two." We then proceeded to ask about the horses' colors, at which time Ali Schreiber may have heard the word "Appy," potentially referring to "Appaloosa." This prompted her to ask, "Do you have any Appaloosa horses?" Again, another male vocalization emanated through the device, saying "Three." Both questions about the animals are historically relevant to the property; Cave Couts Jr. went as far as to keep one of his prized stallions inside the adobe at night due to horse bandits.

William Heath-Davis House AVP Response

In 2013, we had quite an interesting case study at the Davis-Horton House. At one point, I heard the disembodied voice of a young girl. Lillian, the spirit of William Heath Davis's daughter, is known to frequent the historic location in the Gaslamp Quarter district of downtown San Diego, California. After hearing the young child, one of our guest investigators asked her to join us in the parlor. All of a sudden, I heard the youthful spirit communicate once again. Since this was heard in real-time, it was classified as an AVP. Upon review, it's obvious that she said, "I am trying to talk to you; my name is Lillian." Shortly after this, the door to the upstairs children's room opened up of its own volition. All investigators were seated at the time, and there were no drafts or open windows. This experience was featured on an episode of the television show, *My Ghost Story: Caught on Camera*.

RMS *Queen Mary* EVP Response

After investigating the *Queen Mary* many times, I have walked away from the legendary ship with many personal experiences and compelling evidence. One of my favorite EVP captures occurred in the aft engine room. On July 10, 1966, one of the ship's firemen and bilge cleaners was found unresponsive while wedged in the 13th water-tight door on the starboard shaft alley side.

This individual was only 18 years old and hailed from Yorkshire. He's also known as one of the liner's most popular ethereal residents. Out of respect for his surviving family, I will address him as J.P. and not his full name. One day, a former ship crew member asked, "J.P., are you back here?" Upon review of his audio, he heard a direct response of "Yes" to his question. This is considered a Class A EVP response. After sharing it with me, I immediately recognized the vocalization as belonging to J.P., since I have heard him audibly as well as via EVP.

A Dad's Message

I had an interesting phone discussion with Scott Oates, who has been an investigative member of Spectral Tech since 2014 along with his wife, Lisa. Even though he has always welcomed skepticism, Scott mentioned that he was never really a true believer in the paranormal and the afterlife. However, his convictions changed exactly one year after the death of his beloved father.

It was Scott's wife who encouraged the team to conduct an investigative project at the liquor store they owned. During the event, while Bob Fountain was setting up the laser grid device, Scott witnessed the shape of a person run in front of the grid, go along the back wall, and disappear. After finishing the data review for this particular case, Scott discovered an EVP on one of his recorders asking, "Can you hear me?" It was then that Scott informed Bob that the vocalization was his departed father's voice. To be extra sure, Scott's wife listened to the audio piece; her husband did not tell her who he thought it was until after she finished. She, too, recognized the vocalization as that of her father-in-law. Their grandson also positively identified the spirit voice after reviewing the audio clip.

Scott's dad passed away on August 11, 2013. Even though they were not that close while Scott was growing up, father and son grew closer in the senior's later years. After Scott's dad retired, he offered his son the liquor store he owned. The rest become history when Spectral Tech's founder Bob Fountain came into the business one day. He and Scott started talking about ghosts and hauntings. Since Lisa is a clairvoyant, she has witnessed the ethereal energy of a red-haired man manifest near where the vodka liquor bottles were stored. Interestingly, the previous owner of the depot, prior to Scott's dad, had red hair and enjoyed vodka.

After conversing about ghosts and spirits for a while, Bob mentioned to Scott that his team could conduct an official paranormal investigation of the liquor store. This ground-breaking research project occurred on April 19, 2014. Intriguingly, Scott's dad was also born on April 19th. The business closed its doors at 11:00 p.m. when the Spectral Tech team arrived and started setting up various gadgets and equipment designed for paranormal investigation. Additionally, one of the team members interviewed Scott and Lisa about their otherworldly encounters on the premises.

During the setup process, Scott walked around utilizing a KII meter, which measures EMF levels. He witnessed the device spiking to a different color at one point. He examined all possibilities as to why the gadget notified him of an EMF change; however, he could not replicate the experience. Meanwhile, Spectral Tech staff set up a laser grid, which is used to illuminate an environment for better visualization of ghostly shadow figures; if a figure manifests in front of a grid light, the altered beams can be better detected than what's visible to the naked eye. These laser devices come with various grid options in different colors, such as green, red, blue, and purple. When the setup was completed, the device was aimed at the store's utility area. Scott was sitting adjacent to a female Spectral Tech team member when a shadow figure was witnessed moving back and forth and then disappearing right before their eyes.

Utilizing a flashlight is another popular experiment employed during paranormal research; investigators can ask questions of the spirits and ask them to either turn the device "on" or "off." It's not always a reliable technique; however, it's more accurate when it corroborates other data or mysterious personal encounters. During this investigation, research personnel stationed the flashlight on the floor in the off position and commenced an EVP session. Scott proceeded to ask, "If anyone is here, can you turn it (the flashlight) on?" To everyone's immediate surprise, a bright light shined through the gadget as it turned on seemingly of its own volition. Following this strange occurrence, Lisa inquired, "If that's you, Grand-dude, can you now turn the light off?" As you have possibly gleaned, the tool then turned off.

With a warm feeling in his heart, Scott said out loud, "Happy Birthday, Dad." It was at this very moment that Scott became a firm believer in the paranormal and the afterlife. He and his wife joined Spectral Tech soon after and have thoroughly enjoyed learning about what goes into a paranormal research project.

A few days later, Bob presented Scott with some interesting audio data from the investigation. He told Scott that they captured an interesting EVP of a male voice during the session conducted along with the flashlight technique. Right after the flashlight turned off of its own volition, an electronic vocalization was heard asking the aforementioned "Can you hear me?"

Another uncanny occurrence happened in the liquor store a few days after the investigation. Apparently, a bottle of bourbon was found sitting on the floor; it was not there when the team closed the business after the investigation was finished. Let me mention here that Scott's dad loved bourbon. Soon after, Scott was bumped in the back of his head by another liquor bottle that moved toward the front of the shelf by itself. Despite it being wedged tightly on the shelving unit, it then fell to the floor without shattering into a million pieces. Scott's skeptical brother witnessed this event, looked at him, and asked, "What in the hell is going on in here?" Another encounter occurred one day when Scott's daughter was working in the store. The TV turned off by itself. Lisa was there also and said, "If that's you (Scott's dad), can you turn it back on?" As you have guessed, the device turned back on. Tears engulfed Lisa's eyes.

Scott told me that he feels his dad's spirit from time to time. He went on to share that the experience he had with his departed father during the premiere investigation of the liquor store has opened up his intuitive senses so he can experience other paranormal events at various locations, such as the haunted house he investigated in Mississippi. Evidently, the spirit of a young girl drowned at this Mississippi farmhouse. During a research project, Lisa positioned a toy tea kettle by the wall. After the team stepped outside for a brief moment to fetch more equipment, they came back inside and noticed the tea kettle substantially moved out from the wall. They also heard disembodied footsteps upstairs.

"Once you open yourself up to realizing that something is out there, you have more experiences," Scott relayed. It's true, as everyone has the ability to sense and communicate with otherworldly energies. It's similar to practicing a sport such as soccer or baseball; the more you practice and expose yourself to the spiritual realm, the more your psychic senses open up.

Spirit Photography

Spirit photography is one of the oldest methods used to capture evidence of ghosts and/or spirits. The goal is quite simple: to capture on camera what we may not necessarily see with our naked eye. In fact, this method dates back to around 1861. Bostonian William Mumler was credited with producing the first authorized spirit photograph. One day while developing some self-portraits in his own photography studio, he noticed an image of a young woman standing next to him on one of his developed plates. After close scrutiny of the picture, Mumler identified the specter as his cousin who passed away twelve years earlier. Interestingly, he also experienced a weird sensation in his right arm while posing for his photograph. This is an example of how a documented piece of data is backed up by a personal encounter.

Undoubtedly, Mumler's ghostly picture helped fuel the Spiritualist movement. His work was further inspected by foremost photographers and Spiritualists. After that, the figures of deceased individuals began to appear in some of his other photographs. As a result, his work was met with a lot of controversies; he was even exposed when individuals recognized that some of his supposed spirits were still alive and well. Without a doubt, Mumler's work commenced a ripple effect where others also disclosed their ability to make the deceased appear in photographs.

Especially during the Spiritualist movement, the practice of spirit photography was met with a ton of controversy, as the majority of alleged ghostly photographs were proven to be fraudulent. It soon became a deceitful way for people to make tons of money. It was easily discovered how these fraudulent photographers caused manifested entities to appear in pictures. This is somewhat ironic, since spirit photography is one of the only paranormal investigative approaches that uses scientific standards and procedures. As a well-known paranormal researcher Troy Taylor says, "…the amount of energy that goes into making such a photo can be measured by the way it appears in the image…" Furthermore, it's quite easy for researchers to devise ways to replicate a certain picture and document various explanations for how certain incorporeal photographs are made.

Obviously, early-day cameras were not nearly as technical as the varieties we see today. Indeed, one can argue that the more advanced a camera becomes, the easier it will be to discern why a photo does or doesn't contain valid evidence of the supernatural. For example, regarding the highly controversial topic of orbs, researchers have figured out why the majority of these white, circular shapes are not considered paranormal in origin. Of course, orbs seen with the naked eye are found to be more intriguing. However, when captured on digital cameras, orbs are typically explained away as either moisture, dust, bugs, or lens flares. There are many reasons for this, including fast shutter speeds, pixilation, the compact optical design of the camera, and/or the close distance between the lens and flash. The San Diego Paranormal Research Society was asked to investigate why a client was seeing moving orbs on her security surveillance cameras. It didn't take Ali Schreiber and me long at all to ascertain the reasons why. We determined that the cameras' infrared lighting was illuminating dust specs and/or the occasional insect. We even demonstrated this to the client, and she was totally relieved that it wasn't anything paranormal.

Although it's easier in modern times to differentiate an authentic versus a phony photograph, there are still ways the people of today can fake spirit snapshots. Individuals can alter pictures via Photoshop, Gimp, or any other photo editing software. However, the method most irritating to paranormal researchers is when they receive a manipulated ghost photograph made with an Android or iPhone ghost app. These apps contain stock images of many varieties of animals or people. In my paranormal research courses, I recommend people study these apps so they can easily spot a bogus picture.

There is no "one size fits all" for how ethereal energies can manifest on photographic devices. There are many theories that can possibly explain why. Photography may provide the raw foundation for a ghostly entity to manipulate in order to manifest. For example, creating light can be utilized to make the impression of a physical shape. It's theorized that the spiritual domain and other energies comprise portions of the electromagnetic spectrum, which aren't visible to the naked human eye. Cameras can thus capture what our vision doesn't. All researchers should rule out any potential natural explanations for what's captured on film or digital records. Another piece of advice is to know the settings of your camera(s) and to always take a series of three photographs of the same location for comparative purposes. One or two photos may show something strange, whereas the third doesn't. Study where visual phenomena occur in a specific location and set up infrared and/or full spectrum static cameras or surveillance systems in those areas.

The Relationship Between the Afterlife and the Environment

There are various environmental monitoring gadgets utilized in paranormal research. With this, please remember that there is no such thing as a "ghost detector." Over many years of supernatural exploration, researchers have developed plausible hypotheses regarding how the environment responds to spiritual phenomena. By putting these assumptions to the test, we are analyzing how our surroundings respond to certain paranormal stimuli. When certain environmental monitoring devices behave erratically, it doesn't mean that a ghost or spirit is necessarily present. However, it does point to some atmospheric disturbances that may or may not have a paranormal origin. Collectively, we need to examine our environmental monitoring results to see if there are unique patterns in the way electronic mechanisms are behaving during case studies. By studying these patterns, further information may be gleaned as to the relationship between paranormal occurrences and the environment. It's only then that we will begin to understand how and why ethereal entities manipulate a location. While this book isn't a "how-to" in regards to devices and gadgets, I will say that it's imperative that the researcher understand how the equipment functions and what purpose it serves in examining our surroundings.

Electromagnetic Field (EMF)

Researchers have measured strong magnetic fields as well as ones with atypical fluctuations. Some of these readings may be due to electrical equipment or geological formations or stem from the Earth's magnetic fields. It is widely believed among ghost researchers that paranormal entities can cause differences in the electromagnetic field or that the EMF field can directly cause paranormal activity. Even radiation can potentially fluctuate during a paranormal occurrence. It is for this reason that Geiger counters are used to monitor it during a case study. A "fear cage," or an area with a huge concentration of EMF, can interact with our human brains by producing various physical and mental sensations. Some medical researchers have uncovered that certain electrical stimuli can cause people to hallucinate or even experience ghostly encounters. When this happens, an individual can experience headaches, anxiety, nausea, dizziness, and/or other neurological symptoms. In fact, one of the theories for why people encounter supernatural phenomena at night has to do with how solar winds interplay with the Earth's magnetosphere, the globe's magnetic field which extends out on the side facing away from the sun.

There are a variety of different EMF meters on the market. Let's be clear that these gadgets are designed to measure electromagnetic pollution, not ghostly inhabitants. Most models can measure magnetic, electric, or a combination of the two fields. If you don't know what your device is measuring, look at the units. Electric fields are measured in volts per meter (V/m), whereas magnetic ones are measured in milligauss (mG) or nanotesla (nT). It's difficult to use EMF readings from meters as scientific measurements of ghosts and spirits. Different meters may produce varying frequencies. This can pose a lot of problems when you compare one device's reading to another. To help get around this, dataloggers are widely used to measure EMF readings during an entire case study.

There really isn't verifiable scientific data linking EMF fluctuations to the paranormal. Of course, there is circumstantial data of spikes in EMF at alleged haunted locations. Is it possible for an EMF meter to even measure a spirit entity fluctuating in the EM field? In my opinion, we won't truly know this until we can determine that ghosts and spirits are linked to actual hauntings and the experiences people have associated with these hauntings. When incorporating EMF meters during case studies, it's vital to take baseline readings. Be aware, however, that the electromagnetic field is constantly fluctuating, so it's impossible to get a true baseline reading. To get around this, the Association for the Scientific Study of Anomalous Phenomena has a recommendation. The group suggests a "positional baseline," where you use two identical meters. One that is positioned in the "hot spot" area and one in a control area with no documentation of ghostly phenomena. Using this method, you can see if there are higher EMF readings in the "hot spot" location as opposed to the control. This is best accomplished with the use of a datalogger that feeds the results straight into a computer or laptop. In conclusion, there needs to be more concrete scientific studies into the potential connection between EMF and paranormal activity.

Ionic Energy

According to the Association for the Scientific Study of Anomalous Phenomena, any surface charged with static electricity will invite ions. When a ghost or spirit is trying to come through, it may disrupt the air's ion count, either creating an increase or decrease in the number of present ions. For this reason, researchers use a device known as the air ion counter. However, it's important to be very careful when using such a device, as altered readings may have nothing to do with ghosts. For example, winds and breezes blowing across the gadget can produce varying results. Certain electrical equipment can alter results as well. Just a little amount of static electricity can set off negative ion detectors.

Although there are differing opinions as to why it happens, a widely accepted theory proposes that ghostly inhabitants are linked with an abundance of negative ions. Negative ions are typically associated with similar amounts of positive ions; thus, if there are a lot of negative ones, there will also be quite a bit of positive ones, too. The majority of ions are fashioned from cosmic rays and radioactivity. They can attach to certain objects and create a charge. As with negative varieties and EMF, it is theorized that ghostly energy can also cause changes in the static electric field; however, there is very little supporting scientific data on this.

Temperature

It has long been theorized that spiritual inhabitants can draw heat out of the environment when attempting to manifest energy. When this happens, those in the corporeal realm can feel a rather identifiable cold spot. These cold spots are isolated to one area and can disappear as fast as they occur. These icy areas are produced separately from any freezing drafts, air-conditioning vents, or open windows. Spiritual residents traveling from a different dimension into ours can cause an altered air pressure, which may also affect the ambient temperature. Some researchers have detected noticeable hot spots as well; however, these have not been documented nearly as often as the cold varieties. Many EMF-detecting devices, such as the Mel models, measure electromagnetic readings and ambient temperature simultaneously. If you document a random spike in EMF at the same time as a temperature drop, you are left with two pieces of the puzzle that could point to paranormal phenomena. It is imperative to get baseline temperature readings in each room of the location you're investigating. Remember, though, that temperature, like EMF, is constantly fluctuating. Combining various thermometers with thermal imaging cameras can study how heat behaves in an alleged haunted site. Thermal imaging cameras are great for observing the surface temperature of various items and seeing if a noticeable heat signature is created.

Infrasound

Ghostly energies can utilize our environment for communication purposes through infrasound, or sound with a frequency under 20 Hertz. As with high levels of EMF, some people may experience odd sensations when exposed to infrasound, even feeling as though an entity is present. Other symptoms can range from nausea, dizziness, blurred vision, and fear. Infrasound can be produced via violent weather, seasonal winds, and earthquakes.

In 1980, engineer Vic Tandy found out that it could also be the cause of perceived paranormal activity. He even discussed his experiences while working in a laboratory that was known to be spooky. Apparently, people disclosed that they were anxious and unnerved inside the facility. Tandy discovered there was a fan that emitted noise at a 19Hz frequency; after he turned it off, all strange sensations ceased. He repeated infrasound experiments at many locations known for having haunting occurrences. Ghostly sightings that occur inside buildings may or may not have anything to do with infrasound, but it's something to explore further in case studies. Thus, it's worthwhile to invest in an infrasound measuring device.

Paranormal Vigils

In my opinion, a vigil is an important and necessary component of the entire case study process. Typically implemented at the beginning or end of each research project, it allows individuals to become acquainted with their environment. Additionally, it grants the research team an opportunity to experience the documented phenomena from other observers and to further discern if those occurrences have a natural or paranormal explanation. During the case study, it may be necessary to hold vigils for specific purposes or to try and find answers to particular questions.

During this phase, it's vital to pay attention to all of your senses and how they respond to certain environmental stimuli. Intuitively inclined people can utilize this time to get a sense of the spirits residing in a particular location. Vigils can be broken down into smaller sessions, whereby paranormal investigative team members watch and wait for anomalous phenomena to occur. They can be done during the day or night; however, the latter time is preferred. Remember, it takes around 20 minutes for our eyes to adjust to night vision.

Note-taking is a must during paranormal vigils. Subjective observations should be shared amongst the group only after the completion of the vigil. This is done to avoid bias and the power of suggestion. It may be beneficial for a few team members to go in blindly, meaning they haven't been told what other observers have witnessed. For objective viewpoints, it's okay to disclose opinions, as it may lead to quicker problem-solving in more specific circumstances.

You can have fascinating experiences utilizing these methodologies. Please remember to uphold respect, reverence, and humility when communicating with the spirit realm. Ego doesn't deserve a seat at the table. A healthy sense of skepticism balanced with an openness to discovery will further provide for a conduit between the living realm and the afterlife. The next chapter elaborates on other alternative ways, including divination, that can be used to contact the spirit realm.

"Remember the entrance door to the sanctuary is inside you."

RUMI

CHAPTER 7

Communicating with the Spirit Realm: Alternative and Divination Techniques

It's essential to experiment with other methods of spirit communication, especially considering the afterlife is not defined in black-and-white terms. Over many years, people have had great success contacting the other side while utilizing the techniques mentioned in this section. To put it into perspective, I'd like to offer a simple analogy: In the corporeal world, we know that people with certain personality types are drawn to specific careers and areas of study. Some are right-brained and travel down the artistic route; those inclined to left-brain thinking cater more to analytical and methodical approaches. Now that we have established this scenario, let's apply it to the spirit world. Depending on their unique energetic makeup, some ethereal entities may be drawn to standard, scientific ways of communing with the living domain, whereas others may choose unconventional, metaphysical practices. It is for this reason that we should implement various styles when attempting to contact the other side.

The Power of Crystals and Gemstones

In a crystal, we have clear evidence of the existence of a formative life principle, and though we cannot understand the life of a crystal, it is nonetheless a living being. (Nikola Tesla, 1900)

For many years, people have been interested in stones and crystals. In fact, the use of talismans and amulets dates back to ancient times. The Sumerians used crystals in magic formulas, whereas the ancient Egyptians used varieties in their jewelry mainly for protection and health. Talismans and crystal amulets were used to improve health or provide protection in Roman culture. Those in Greece incorporated the use of these sentient rocks in many different ways, such as rubbing hematite on soldiers' bodies before war as a way to make them unconquerable. In India, crystals have been revered for healing emotional and metaphysical imbalances. In fact, the Hindu Kalpa tree (wish-granting tree) is comprised out of crystals and precious gemstones. The ancient text Hindu Vedas refers to many different stones and their healing aptitudes. Since the very beginning, jade has been valued among the Chinese, with uses dating before 3000 BC. Native Americans and other indigenous cultures hold the consecration of many stones. With the advent of New Age culture, the utilization of crystals and gemstones for healing resurfaced in modern society in the 1980s.

For thousands of years, precious and semi-precious rocks have been applied for mental, physical, and spiritual well-being. Crystals and gemstones have been utilized to cure illnesses, prevent disease and injury, grant mental balance and stability, and promote spiritual growth. They can also be used to clear any mental, spiritual, and emotional blockages; restore homeostasis; assist in daily meditation or grief; align people with their higher selves, intuition, and creativity; and so on.

It was Nikola Tesla, a brilliant inventor, electrical and mechanical engineer, and physicist, who proclaimed that all universal things are forms of energy with their own frequency and vibration. He later proved how certain energy structures can change the vibrational character of other forms of energy. This is the main reason why so many people assert their faith in the positive influence of crystals and other gemstones in healing capacities.

Crystals and gemstones are sentient beings. As such, minerals, crystals, and rocks make up the physical matter of the entire universe. They can be incorporated into our lives to help to create balance and harmony. We've obviously learned a lot from our ancestors because in modern-day society people still rely on the healing qualities of these ancient rocks. Positioning crystals near an energy imbalance can permit healing processes to take place and become more successful.

All living objects are made up of energy; again, according to Einstein's brilliance, it has been unearthed that energy can neither be created nor destroyed. It simply exists and, along with vibration, is the main common denominator that brings human beings and these ancient, uniquely conscious stones together. All energized entities vibrate; however, the vibration is usually not measurable by the five human senses. Nonetheless, science has discovered that vibration does exist, with each object possessing its own exceptional vibratory framework. In the case of human beings, this equates to our chakras, the energized junctions running throughout our bodies (meridians), and auras, the energy fields neighboring the physical body that permit us to perceive our own vitality and that of others.

There are many varieties of crystals and stones you can use to connect with the afterlife. Below are some of my favorites:

Amethyst: This stone is known for its grounding and protective capabilities, as it increases higher consciousness, peace, and clarity. This is a great stone to use when meditating, as it can quiet the mind and increase perception. It can also facilitate out-of-body encounters, vivid dreams, and psychic aptitudes.

Celestite: This stone can open one up to higher realms by enforcing your link to angelic beings. It's especially useful to help you relax and clear away unwanted thoughts, worries, or stresses. Celestite can calmly move you into a dream-like state and help you process and comprehend incoming information.

Selenite: Selenite is also good for spirit communication and can assist you in dream recollection.

Clear Quartz: This is by far one of the most healing stones. Quartz amplifies, changes, communicates, and directs energy. Connecting to our crown chakra, it helps increase energy to the highest level while enriching psychic abilities and aligning you with your spiritual purpose.

Labradorite: This stone has unique abilities, such as raising conscious awareness and spiritual development while arranging the physical and etheric bodies. Labradorite can connect and ground spiritual energies while also increasing intuition and psychic abilities. It has the ability to ricochet any unwanted energy away from the auras.

Moonstone: As one can deduce, this stone connects to the moon's energy fields. Typically, it is worn to increase psychic gifts and clairvoyant development. It opens our minds to coincidence and synchronicity.

Turquoise: Used for centuries as a protective stone, it protects the communication systems of our bodies. It can be very effective as a healing stone, as it deflects negativity while helping to balance the physical and spiritual arenas. By placing it on the Third Eye, you can help foster intuition and meditation.

Apophyllite: Strengthening intuition and mental clarity, this sentient being is beneficial when interacting with the spirit realm. It can help connect you with the ethereal world, fine-tune meditative states, and assist you in recalling afterlife messages in dreams.

Many people believe that crystals and gemstones, due to their sentient energies and affinity for natural intuition, pick the human energies they are destined to go home with. This is quite uncanny and mystical, but I agree with the others who put faith in this notion. It's also beneficial to spend some individual time with your new crystal as this further strengthens the bonding relationship you have with it. Simon Lilly's book, *Crystals & Crystal Healing: Harnessing the Unique Power of Crystals and Gemstones for Health and Inner Harmony, With Over 200 Beautiful Photographs* (1998) outlines the steps of this process:

1. Visually inspect your crystal from a variety of different angles. Then, for a minute or two, hold it in your hand with your eyes closed. Notate any impressions or thoughts that come up.
2. Position the crystal near your solar plexus and visualize the breath passing over the end of the stone as you exhale. Then, imagine your breath coming through the crystal and into your abdominal area as you inhale. Continue this cycle with phases of relaxation.
3. Sit quietly with eyes closed. Then, open your eyes and look at the crystal. After a few minutes, close them again and pick up the crystal, paying attention to any differing feelings.
4. Hold the crystal with your left hand, place it down, and pick it up with your right hand. Do this several times.
5. Position the crystal on the center of your chakras, with the most sensitive being the solar plexus, heart, and brow.
6. While lying down, position the crystal adjacent to your body, notating how it feels as you move the crystal near different parts of your body.

Divining (Dowsing) Rods

Divining rod practice goes back to ancient times. Grecian historical documents refer to the art of divining, which was implemented back in 400 BC on the island of Crete. In the book, *The Divining Hand* (2000) by author Christopher Bird, the art of dowsing made its appearance in 1650 via an essay written by famed English Philosopher John Locke. Adopting the phrase "dowsing rod" from the defunct English dialect of Cornwall, Locke suggested that minerals and/or water could be found by using such a device. According to Lloyd Youngblood in his article "Dowsing: Ancient History," a group of French explorers in 1949 unearthed a large arrangement of caverns known as the Tassili Caves that depicted impressive pre-historic paintings dating back 8000 years. This is quite fitting since their mission's purpose was to search for lost civilizations in North Africa. As they closely examined the murals, they found an art gallery that showcased spacecraft and extraterrestrial beings. One of the most interesting paintings illustrated a dowser holding a forked branch while seeking water (Youngblood, 2016).

In addition to being a spirit communication device, divining rods are metaphysical tools to locate underground water sources, buried metals, oil, gemstones, gravesites, etc. In fact, many areas of the globe utilized dowsing rods. There are thousands of books on the subject, which can be found in many libraries. As evidenced in their drawings, Egyptian people were also known to practice the art of dowsing. Other designs reveal the archaic Chinese Emperor Yu holding an apparatus similar to that of a dowsing rod. There are references in the Bible that indicate the use of divining mechanisms, whether to find water or to decide which city should be attacked.

As for contacting the afterlife, there is no scientific proof of its efficacy and as such is considered a type of alchemy. In regards to supernatural research, it can be an effective adjunct tool to other gadgets such as audio recorders and ghost boxes. The blending of standard techniques, as discussed in the last chapter, with atypical methods can connect more pieces to the supernatural puzzle. For example, let's say we capture an EVP at the same time our divining rods cross to indicate the same answer. That's two pieces of corroborating evidence. I prefer to use divining rods during EVP and ITC sessions.

Y or L-shaped rods are the types most commonly used for spirit communication. Longer rods are more sensitive. You can purchase them online; in fact, Ali and I bought ours on Amazon. We prefer to use copper varieties, as it is the second-highest electrically conductive metal. This could explain why dowsing rods made of this metal seem to have more interesting results than their brass or wire competitors.

Just as we do prior to conducting an EVP and/or ITC session, we include an introduction to our divining rod session, which sets the tone and instructs the spirits on what we're doing. Unless you are completely grounded and have trust in the spirits you are working with, it's best to not tell the energies that they can use your energy. Once we're set and ready to go, we start asking yes/no and/or comparative questions and designate whether the rods should cross or extend outward when answering. For example, we can tell the energies to cross the rods for "yes" answers and separate them for "no" answers. Utilizing this method can be exhausting for some people; for that reason, it's important to feel rested and energized prior to using this tool.

One widely accepted notion throughout the scientific community is that the movement of rods is thought to be an unconscious muscular response. Hand movements are amplified by the ideomotor response, or the subconscious mind's ability to influence the physical body without consciously thinking about taking action to do so. Those subscribing to metaphysical practices assert that the spirit realm speaks through the living medium, causing the rods to move. Although people may have their unique styles in using divining rods, the following is the procedure I use:

1. Stand tall with feet spread about a foot apart.

2. Once you are firmly holding onto the rods, make sure they're parallel to the floor about six inches apart. This is called the neutral position.

3. Make sure that your thumbs aren't pressing down on the portions of the rods that move.

4. Designate how you want the rods to move, i.e., cross for "yes" and outward for "no," or vice versa.

5. Let the energies know your intention.

6. During the session, if the rods do cross and are touching each other, it's okay to refresh and go back to the starting position.

7. Make sure to not rush the questions, as it's important to grant the energies time to answer.

8. Let the spirits know when you are about to end the session and kindly thank them for their participation.

It does take some practice to get used to the dowsing rod process. Rod movement after a proposed question feels a lot like getting a tug on the line when you go fishing. Not all spiritual energies will enjoy communicating in this manner, but for the ones that do, you will find it to be a very engaging process.

Pendulums

Experimenting with pendulums goes back to the 1600s, when Galileo first examined a cathedral's swinging lamp. Christiaan Huygens, a Dutch scientist and inventor, constructed the first pendulum clock in 1656. Over the years, many individuals have used these gadgets to communicate with the spirit realm and/or to tap into their higher selves.

A pendulum for this type of communication is a small, weighted object on the end of a 5- to 10-inch piece of chain, string, or twine. Although you can practically use any item as a pendulum, it's widely popular to utilize crystals, such as rose quartz or obsidian. This type of divination has been incorporated for thousands of years for healing or dowsing purposes, to prophesize the future, and to assist in seeking the appropriate answers to a specific dilemma. People can use the pendulum to ask questions about life in general, whether they revolve around health, career, family, emotions, day-to-day trials and tribulations, and so on.

Incorporating pendulums for spirit communication is similar to using dowsing rods. You don't have to be a psychic medium to employ divination tools. You can use your pendulum by having it hang on a stand or holding it in your hand. However, if you have shaky hands, it may be best not to hold the device. Then, direct the spirits to move the item back and forth, side-to-side, clockwise, or counterclockwise when answering questions. By tapping into human energy fields, these tools reflect and mirror our personalities, which makes them unique when discovering more about one's self or the ethereal domain. In addition to aiding sessions with the afterlife, a pendulum can help you acquire information from your subconscious mind and genetic makeup. As with dowsing rods, a person's subconscious moves the pendulum during spirit communication sessions. By practicing this technique, you will build a strong rapport with your pendulum. The best results come from a state of transparency and a lack of ego.

There are so many varieties available; choosing pendulums with crystals that vibrate to your unique energy fields and/or those you are drawn to is probably your best choice. If you are near a metaphysical store that has these items for purchase, make sure to hold the ones that resonate with you. It's hard to explain in words, but you will feel a connectedness with the one that's meant to go home with you. Or you can choose to buy them via online retailers, such as Amazon or eBay.

Before you commence a session with the ethereal world, make sure you meditate and take a few deep breaths. This helps set the intention of the session. Make sure to designate the movement of your pendulum. This can be forward, backward, side-to-side, clockwise, or counterclockwise. When asking "yes" and "no" questions, you can appoint the pendulum to move clockwise for "yes" answers, counterclockwise for "no," and sideways for "I don't know" answers. As with dowsing rod meetings, make sure to not rush your questions, as it allows time for the spirits to respond. Some individuals prefer positioning the pendulum a couple of inches above the open palm of their other hand, as this creates a free flow of energy. As with divining rod sittings, when you finish the session, make sure to thank the energies for their participation.

After you use your pendulum, it's important to clear it of any residual energy. This way, the energy of its former use won't compete with or dilute that of its future use. There are many ways to cleanse and/or empower the crystals on your pendulum. One method is to bury it in the soil for 24 hours and let the earth's elements do the trick. Or you can run it under cold or hot water, have it bathe in the moonlight overnight, or light sage around it. Research what's safe for certain gemstones, as certain liquids can damage certain varieties. In addition to these aforementioned techniques, it's vital to focus on healing and purifying thoughts to help get rid of negative and imbalanced energy before conducting a session.

The website *Ask Your Pendulum* discusses other ways to energize your pendulums. It recommends using a smudge stick containing cedar or dried white sage and/or other herbs of your preferred incense. The next step is to blow out a lighted candle flame and move the item or crystal a minimum of four times through the smoke. It also endorses placing your pendulum in a pouch or container with citrine for 24 hours, especially since citrine is a self-purifying stone. You can also put your pendulum on a chunk of selenite for a day or position the pendulum on a cleansed set or basket of crystals and leave it there for many hours. Dry brown rice can be of help; you can immerse your metaphysical item under its surface. As with moonlight, sunlight can also be sanitizing. To use this tactic, you put your pendulum in direct sunlight (preferably morning or late sun) for up to four hours. This isn't the best method for all crystals, as some, such as fluorite and amethyst, may lose their vibrant colors.

Automatic Writing (Channeled Writing)

Considered a type of mediumship, automatic writing allows information from the spirit realms to be channeled via the living through writing or drawing. Controversial to some, this process of communicating with spirit allows your unconscious mind to facilitate your writing, permitting your spirit guides to use you as a conduit for their writing. More or less, you are permitting a higher power to either create or facilitate the words you write. In this practice, you are essentially quieting your conscious mind as you meditate with intention and purpose. Automatic writing can occur in both a trance/hypnotized state and when someone is awake. During this activity, an individual holds a pencil or pen on a sheet of paper, letting the spiritual energy and/or subconscious mind take over and inscribe books, letters, and short messages.

In the 16th century, occultists John Dee and Edward Kelley claimed that Enochian angels spoke to them via this process regarding their type of language. This vernacular is a key component of Enochian magic, which is a ceremonial process based on the conjuring and decreeing of spirits. Automatic writing became especially popular during the Spiritualist movement. Sir Arthur Conan Doyle's wife actually talked with spirits using this specific technique. In his book *New Revelations,* he discussed that automatic writing occurs via the writer's subconscious or through ethereal energies communicating through the living agent (Doyle, 2009). Upon transition to the 20th century, however, automatic writing shifted away from communing with the spirit realm towards communicating with those of various etheric worlds.

If you desire to try this technique, buy a special journal and keep it by your side. Concentrate on the spirit you choose to communicate with and let him or her know your intentions in doing so. Even though this form of contact is debated among researchers, if you know what you're doing and your mind, body, and spirit are balanced, you can be amazed at the inspiration you receive. Those who engage in automatic writing are typically in a state of altered consciousness, one that expedites the diffusion of information from other realms. It's similar to being hypnotized or in a dream.

There's much debate regarding the origin of the acquired data. Some people assert that the writing generated comes from an individual's mind or repressed memories. Every channeler is different because of his or her unique perceptions. Some may gain insight from the physical, whereas others may be tuned more into the non-physical. As incorporeal energies vary in their understanding of the living realm, they, too, will offer different types of discernment.

Séances

During the Spiritualist movement, séances to communicate with the spirit realm were popularized by the Fox sisters. From the 1840s to the 1920s, many psychic mediums appeared, willing to facilitate these sittings. In the mid-1800s, séances were typically held in a circular format, with participants known as sitters surrounding a round table. The purpose of these meetings was to create a continuous energy field to entice spirits. According to the directions of the operating psychic medium, sitters may have held hands or placed them in a flattened position on the table in front of them. Some mediums chose to sit in a select cabinet, while others joined attendees in the circle. Typically, these sittings were opened with prayers and/or hymns and contained a balance of male and female attendees. The purpose of the early séances was to entice the spirits to manifest in the physical world.

Various early tools were utilized during séances to aid in hearing the spirits. Spirit trumpets were considered a type of speak tube to amplify an entity's whispers or vocalizations. Spirit slates were two chalkboards bound together like a book. The psychic medium could open the slates to potentially expose an ethereal message. The tables used hardly weighed anything so they could rotate or levitate when spirits came through; however, this was easy for hoaxers to manipulate. As you know, some psychic mediums chose to sit inside select cabinets tied with rope so they couldn't fake anything during the séance. These cabinets were pioneered by the Davenport Brothers during the 1850s. One drawback of the cabinets was how the facilitator could use the privacy to engineer sights and sounds, pretending that they originated from the spirit realm. Other tools such as pendulums, tarot cards, and Ouija boards were also employed.

Séances are typically done in a room with low lighting with a psychic medium who channels the ethereal subject and delivers its messages. The act of mediumship involves the specialist (psychic medium) endeavoring to receive messages from the departed and/or from other energies that come through. Some practitioners choose to remain fully conscious, whereas others go into a partial or full trance. Mediums in the latter case typically do not remember the information imparted from the spirit. Occasionally, Ouija boards or talking boards are utilized during the session, where one or more of the applicants place fingers on the board's planchette while the medium asks questions of the spirits. Many assert that those trained in acting, drama, and/or vocal impersonation can easily fake the channeling of spiritual energy.

Séances should be as controlled as possible, and the medium conducting the session should know what he or she is doing, or else undesirable spiritual energy may bleed through. Séances have raised a lot of skepticism over the years. Many alleged psychic mediums exploited the dead by fraudulently conducting these sessions, especially during the Spiritualist movement. Some early séance guidelines were established. One recommendation was to not hold more than two or three per week with a two-hour maximum time limit.

Assuming that the ethereal energy coming through is authentic, it can take a variety of forms. An earthbound entity or evolved spirit can utilize any one or more of our five human senses, including the proverbial 6th sense. Attendees may smell a familiar scent that was common to a particular specter or even feel one's disembodied touch on a hand or shoulder. Witnesses may hear a phantom vocalization or potentially see an apparition or some form of a light anomaly. Lit candles may suddenly go out, or a gentle breeze may be felt. The séance room may suddenly feel cooler. Modern-day séances blend older methods with newer ones.

Talking (Ouija) Boards

It was in February 1891 when advertisements started boasting about a magical gadget that could answer questions about the past, present, and future with exact precision. The Ouija or talking device erupted from the fascination with Spiritualism and the belief that the corporeal world could contact the deceased. Baltimore, Maryland, resident Charles Kennard arranged a group of four other investors in 1890 to start the Kennard Novelty Company. The main purpose of this business venture was to exclusively design and market the original talking apparatus. At first, the board was without a name. It was Helen Peters, the sister-in-law of one of the investors, who assisted the group in developing a proper name by sitting around a table and proposing to the board what it should be called. "Ouija" came through; after asking what it meant, the board replied, "Good luck." After a successful demonstration of the board, a patent was bestowed, acknowledging its accuracy. Soon afterward, the mysterious Ouija board became a lucrative money-maker.

Marketed as a mystical visionary and family entertainment device, the Ouija board soon became a mainstay in homes across America. Its appeal reached people of all ages, backgrounds, and education. Along with a planchette to hover over the device, the smooth board contains alphabet letters arranged in two semi-circles above the numbers 0-9, with "yes" and "no" featured in the top corners and "goodbye" at the bottom. While placing fingertips on top of the planchette, two or three individuals can propose a question and watch in anticipation as it moves over letters, seemingly spelling out a word of its own volition.

The question remains as to its authenticity in reaching the spirit world. Some researchers, including myself, assert that the mind's psychokinetic abilities are responsible for spelling words as the planchette moves about the device. The words generated match what the human agent is thinking. Several years ago, I participated in a session at a known haunted location in California. I consciously thought of a specific word throughout the entire meeting but didn't tell anyone what I was thinking. After a few minutes, I wasn't the least bit surprised when the planchette ended up spelling the exact word my sentient mind was concentrating on. Of course, in order to prove that there's a psychokinetic component, several studies and experiments are needed.

Utilizing the Ouija board or any other type of black magic apparatus raises a lot of controversies because many, including myself and the San Diego Paranormal Research Society, feel it's potentially dangerous. Here is my opinion on why: The tool used, in this case, the Ouija board, isn't the problem or the reason why the practice is deemed unsafe. It is the negative cultural connotations associated with the board that can be hazardous. I feel that the associated negativity almost emulsifies on the board, so there's already a cloud of adversity present before one even begins to use it. Furthermore, it is quite possible that mediums and/or those utilizing the instrument may subconsciously move the planchette. Additionally, many individuals who aren't trained in paranormal research and the importance of mind/body/spirit balancing attempt using the Ouija board, potentially opening themselves up to lower-level energies. The board is a common tool used by curious teenagers or, sadly, those involved with religious cults; most likely, these two types of parties don't necessarily know what they are doing and aren't consciously aware of the dangers that could result from abusing this tool.

Scrying

Considered an ancient esoteric technique, the purpose of scrying is to expose the unknown through our intuitive second sight, allowing us to see things that can't typically be observed via our five senses. The term implies staring into a shiny surface for divination purposes. It can help people to connect with their unconscious and discover the meaning and purpose of one's life. The art of scrying was first brought up in the ancient Persian manuscript *Shahnameh* in the 10th century. Various cultures have implemented this archaic form of oculomancy; in modern times, it has progressed into a pagan tradition.

Scrying is usually conducted in a low-light environment alongside a reflective surface, whether it be a mirror, water, or crystal globe. A person can use the reflective medium to see what messages, symbols, or visions may appear. Staring at this surface can last anywhere from a few minutes to an hour. Keep a journal nearby and make sure to write down any sudden thoughts, images, and sensations that come up. It's common to not always recognize the messages that emanate from other realms. When this happens, try not to make sense of it immediately; make sure to sit with it for a few days until the answer comes. If you can't derive an explanation, perhaps it's meant for a family member or friend.

Regardless of the method used to communicate with the spirit realm, it is imperative to be humble, kind, and respectful. Don't just rely on one or two methods; experiment with various techniques. If you knew an ethereal resident when he or she was of body, you will be more inclined to know what communicative style he or she preferred. Or, through long-standing case studies of a particular location, you will learn the methods that work for the ghosts and spirits at that certain site. Remember to treat all entities how you want to be treated, regardless of their background.

There are many ways the spirit world can communicate with the living realm. Many of these methods have been utilized by the ethereal realm since the dawning of man. Anyone can talk with the dead, especially when he or she exhibits a healthy openness to it. As mentioned, it is imperative that your physical body, mind, and emotions are in a healthy, balanced state regardless of what method you utilize to communicate with spirits. The mind, body, and spirit are interconnected and can never be separated. The three of them act in unison, guiding each other to homeostasis. Remember, no matter what tool or method you use to contact the departed, always be cognizant to never, under any circumstances, abuse and exploit the spirits you are interacting with or the techniques you use to contact them. The spiritual realm should not be treated as though it's a dog and pony show; as such, consider it an honor when those residing in the afterlife connect with you in the living world. Any contact should be preserved as a hallowed, sacred experience. Remember the two "R's" at all times: respect and reverence of those who've passed from the surly bonds of earth. Only then will you reap the amazing benefits of interconnecting with the afterlife.

"The best teachers are those who show you where to look, but don't tell you what to see."

ALEXANDRA K. TRENFOR

CHAPTER 8

Fostering the Connection: The Power of Spirit Guides

Spirit Guide Awareness

T he concept of spirit guides gained popularity during the Spiritualist movement when churches integrated mediumship into their services. It's hard to define exactly what spirit guides are, as there aren't any clearly delineated characteristics to them. Anyone can connect with his or her ethereal assistants, whether you are an advanced medium or someone learning the basics of utilizing intuition. We all have that little instinctive voice inside that guides us in our daily lives. Perhaps spirit guides are a combination of the internal wisdom each of us possesses with the ethereal chaperones assigned to us from the very beginning of our lives in the physical realm. Spirit guides, after all, are here to help, protect, assist, and motivate the living realm to reach its highest potential. Those who work with these astral helpers have a special relationship with them, whether due to emotional or past life connections, spiritual obligations, or any set of attributes responsible for bonding two parties together.

I personally believe that all people and animals have ethereal guides that can be a consistent source of knowledge and inspiration. We may need different types of spirit guides depending on where we are at any point in time. For this reason, there are various cosmic chaperones that come in and out of our lives throughout our mortal framework. Noted author James Van Praagh hits it on the head of the nail when he says that by working with the living realm, these spiritual assistants are undergoing their own interdimensional training. It's a shared relationship, in that they help facilitate our learning and maturity while we aid them in improving their skill set(s).

Spirit guides come into our lives for the purpose(s) of aligning us with our life's destiny and helping all to achieve that higher state of being. They are comprised of incorporeal energies that expand their own awareness and gifts by learning from and helping other beings. Some of these ethereal guardians have lived on Earth as teachers, counselors, medical practitioners, leaders, etc., while others have never experienced a mortal shell. The close relationship between a spirit guide and a mortal soul is completely mutual. In a way, our ethereal assistants are evolving just like us, albeit in different ways. They are not perfect beings that we should strive to live up to, as that's a common misconception of who they are and what their purpose is. Some guides are with us for the duration of our entire mortal lives, whereas others come and go. The ones that connect with you match your genetic vibration.

We all have spirit guides that help us stay on the course of whom we're meant to be as people. Some individuals are naturally able to get in contact with their guides whereas others need education on how to do so. Before we delve into the various ways to contact your spiritual assistants, let's discuss what these beings are and what their purpose(s) may be.

Spirit guides are around us all the time to give us direct information on how to better live our lives and move into higher consciousness. They have a keen awareness of our needs and interests; however, it's up to us to listen to and apply their teachings and guidance. They visit us in various forms, including deceased family members, friends, and colleagues who aim to watch over us. Appearing in ways that allow us to easily distinguish them, our guides can help us with the most mundane decisions, whether it's regarding what to have for dinner or where to go on vacation. They can also be a guide for our moral compass, steering us toward becoming the person we're meant to be and uniting us as one with the universe.

Types of Spirit Guides

James Van Praagh is world-renowned for his agility in communicating with the other side. As someone who has a deep understanding of spirit guides, he has developed a classification for the different types of ethereal assistants, which are as follows:

Ascended Masters or Angels

Acting as a chaperone throughout our many embodiments is the master guide that educates us on spiritual evolution and growth. These types of spirit guides vibrate at a very high vibrational frequency, allowing us to perceive them as pure light. It is believed that these beings can travel throughout our dimensions and beyond as they connect to those on similar paths as their own. While typically working with collective groups of souls, these types of guides may be attracted to those in educational professions or those who practice energy work, for example. With access to Akashic records, their primary focus is helping humanity achieve a higher state of being.

Angels are ethereal energies that were created or evolved to be without any physical body. Even though we are all considered immortal, angels haven't gone through birth and death as humans do. There is a multitude of angels, each set possessing its own abilities, knowledge, and wisdom. Many theological references describe angels as messengers; still, other holy passages discuss angelic guardians that serve various roles.

The Gatekeeper

The gatekeeper or protector guide's main responsibility is to keep us away from any detrimental energies that could pose a threat or cause injury. This guide helps to expand our souls by teaching us compassion, humility, unconditional love, forgiveness, creativity, and so on. They come into our lives to assist us with what we need or want in life. For example, people who want to learn how to play the piano will attract an ethereal guide who can inspire them with expertise in that area. Involved in our total health processes, this healing guide or spirit doctor will aid us in optimum well-being by making sure our energy fields are appropriately aligned.

Ancestral Guides

Ancestral guides have a kinship with us and belong to our genetic lineage. Spirit guides in this category can include deceased ancestors and relatives who are part of larger soul groups that incarnate together to assist certain people and teach new life lessons. Many people classify these types as guardian angels since they knew and loved us while in the physical plane.

Teacher Guides

Teacher guides connect with us for a purpose and may symbolically represent someone else, depending on the lessons they choose to impart. These spirit assistants teach you and guide you along your path while helping you to problem-solve based on your needs. Those individuals that we bonded with in life will continue to guide us in spirit. As relationship guides, they help us to make pure choices and guide us in choosing personal connections that we can benefit and learn from. They may come to us via dreams or meditations and stay close to us as long as we need them. This group consists of guides from past lives, other spirits, or someone in your soul lineage who passed before you.

Animal Guides

Animal guides are widely discussed. A spirit animal is a teacher or messenger that has a close bond to a specific individual and typically mirrors some of the same attributes that a person sees in himself or herself. Many of our beloved animals who have passed on to spirit may choose to connect with us for a specific purpose, such as helping us through the grieving process.

Depending on what culture or religion you are predisposed to, it is highly believed that we each have animal totems or symbolic depictions of our animal guides. In this case, a specific animal may choose to connect with us to provide guidance, wisdom, teachings, life lessons, protection, etc. Totem animals or animal influencers belong to a group we are extremely bonded with. You may have one or many of these spirit guides throughout your life, depending on the specifics of your life's path. Acting as your main spiritual guardian, it is thought that the animal on the highest part of the totem is one that guides you in the emotional, mental, physical, and spiritual phases of your life. As with other spirit guides, animal ethereal assistants connect with us in a multitude of ways.

Understand that our spirit guides are comprised of protectors, gatekeepers, message barriers, healers, teachers, etc. At any given time, we could have one or a combination of these guides watching over us as they impart the knowledge and life lessons we need. All you need to do is genuinely ask for their help and look for the many signs of their presence, all of which can manifest in so many unique ways. You may connect with your guides via dreams, meditation, prayer, or the five senses.

There are many spiritual guides willing to step forward to help us in various aspects of our unique mortal journeys and beyond. For example, we may have those who instinctively know how we should access and utilize our creative abilities, or we may have those who help us with interpersonal relationships and communication. In a way, every person that steps into our lives—whether for a short period or long—acts as a mirror for us. However, it's up to us to recognize what we're seeing in that mirror and comprehend and retain the inherent message. We all have educational spirit assistants whose purpose is to assist us with understanding logic, laws, ethics, and morals.

Some people are able to visualize the physical attributes of their guides; however, it's not mandated that you do so in order to connect with them. As mentioned, they typically do appear in recognizable forms. However, imagination is the gateway to connecting with your guide(s). You don't have to visualize all the minute details; in fact, you can imagine these pure beings however you want, as long as it opens the doorway to genuine connection.

In a way, think of your spirit guides as personifications of yourself completely in tune with your higher character and connection to universal consciousness. It's thought that the guides who are chosen to help us are those who are a part of the same soul tapestry, as they can truly understand our genetic makeup and purpose(s). Our spiritual assistants are here to help our soul reach its highest dimension; once it does, our soul can start to acquire knowledge of our past and future lives and gain access to the laws of the universe.

Our mortal selves are limited in knowledge. However, our spiritual guides can help us dissect aspects of our lives that may seem utterly confusing and give us the keys to better comprehend our daily trials and tribulations so we can move to that higher self-state of being. Even though our guides communicate with us in various ways, they do so via pure intent. Thus, in order for us to hear their messages and guidance, we need to put our egos on the shelf and access our guides through our hearts. There's a working relationship between ourselves and our guides; we help them and they help us, creating beautiful evolutional growth for both parties.

Perception is Key: Spirit Guide Contact

Spirit guide contact can be easy for some and difficult for others, depending on how one perceives the contact process. Getting in touch with your guides will be easier once you are aware of and can readily sense their presence. Our ethereal assistants have a keen understanding of our mortal vibrations, aiding them in helping us with certain life processes and goals. It's imperative to have conscious awareness of your guides, as many of their teachings are subtle and easy to miss.

It is crucial to put forth genuine intent when connecting with your spirit guide. Reserve a special place in your home, one where distractions are absent. Allow yourself to attain a meditative state aided by relaxation and focus on deep breathing. As you breathe in, allow positivity and pureness to enter your body while exhaling all negativity and unwanted emotions. Allow your imagination to explore beyond what the physical body is limited to as you gain access to new experiences and subconscious memories.

Once your energy is attuned to that of your guide, you will be mindful and cognizant of its presence. Be aware of your guide's presence and the sensations and feelings you acquire as a result of the connection. Awareness of your surroundings is crucial as you pay close attention to the situations and aspects of your day. Look for subtle clues or repeated patterns, as they can be direct messages from your ethereal assistants.

Once you realize that your guide is with you, ask the being to convey the messages you are meant to hear. Also, ask how these messages will be imparted to you. Again, this process is to be accomplished with unconditional love and not with ego or judgment. Pay attention to your heart's feelings and vibrations; utilize your senses. Your guide may respond to you in a way that's easier for you to comprehend. For example, if you are clairaudient, your guide may choose this method when communicating with you. Whatever technique is most viable, it is imperative that you pay attention to what each of your senses is picking up and attuning to. Observe sounds, smells, touches, and visions while staying true to your unique energy field.

This process takes practice; once you master this, you will benefit from the inspiration and teachings of all your guides. Make sure to tell your spirit assistants on a daily basis that you want to connect with them. Talk to them as you would a relative, friend, or co-worker by putting forth conscious effort in doing so. Ask them to show you that they're around. Remember that they are here for your highest good.

What's intriguing about us mortals in modern times is how we collectively want to learn more about our spirit guides as we desire to evolve into our higher selves. This, in a way, is the first sign that our guides may be reaching out to us, especially when it's the heart that wants to learn about them, as opposed to our analytical brain. It goes back to that parallel relationship between the living and the afterlife where both parties are reaching out to one another, thus creating this cosmic vibrational connection between the living and departed.

Our guides are here to help steer us on the paths we are destined to follow. We shouldn't judge the experiences we have, whether positive or negative. There is a reason for all of our life's experiences; they occur as a way to foster soul growth and maturity. If someone all of a sudden develops an innate interest in something, or if that interest has been perpetuated since childhood, it could be a sign that your spirit guide is communicating with you. Your guide may be speaking to you if you keep receiving or coming into contact with little hints here and there regarding something you should do, such as a career path or relocation to a new area. In the paragraphs to come, you will read about my own experience with this and how my ethereal assistants have maneuvered me toward paranormal research and studying the unknown since my childhood years. So, if you are experiencing a soulful type of excitement and interest in something, don't ignore it, as it may be destiny speaking to you.

Our spirit guides are very creative when communicating with us. Many times, they won't be direct and will instead interact with us by showing us certain puzzle pieces that we are meant to connect. These clues may involve any or all of the five senses, but they will be placed strategically as a way to connect us with the message our guide is trying to impart. We all have types of epiphanies and "aha" moments in our lives, which can be direct signs from our guides.

A personal example involves the RMS *Titanic* and how, throughout my life, books or photos about the iconic ship appeared before me, whether I was at work or leisurely enjoying my weekends off. To this day, I still randomly come into contact with items relating to the *Titanic*. I fell in love with the RMS *Queen Mary* many years ago and have been studying the glorious vessel's history and paranormal phenomena for many years. In addition, I have written three books about the *Queen Mary*, which are sold in her gift stores as well as via online retailers. Both ships have often been compared to one another, with *Titanic* exhibits available on the *Queen Mary* at certain times. In retrospect, I do believe my spirit guides were luring me to the *Queen Mary* and maritime studies by ingeniously placing all those *Titanic* clues before my eyes. Even in my infancy, I often drew pictures of ships, especially those with smokestacks. Coincidence? I don't think so at all.

Speaking of the lost liner, I have since found out that two of my relatives tragically perished when the *Titanic* met the bottom of the ocean on April 15, 1912. Indeed, it's very intriguing as to how our spirit guides give us signs and clues that we are meant to pay attention to. It's as if my guides instinctively knew before I did, that I would develop a passion and desire to study ships and maritime history.

Spirit Guide Messages via Dreams

Many of our daily distractions are put on the shelf when we sleep, allowing us to be more perceptive to our subconscious and thus open to spiritual guidance. Our spirit guides understand this and many times will choose to communicate with us via dreams. We can have one singular dream about our guide or several themed ones relating to the message that's being imparted to us while we slumber. Our ethereal assistants can metaphorically speak to us during our sleep, but it's up to us via our perception to decipher the inherent messages. Our vivid, often lucid dreams that strike the very core of our existence are all signs of spirit-guide communication and assistance.

Speaking of my love for ships, I often dream of ocean liners and the seas. Whether this is a past life coming to the forefront or just a subtle reminder that I am on the right path, these dreams signify a themed message that I should pay attention to. Interestingly, I have lucidly dreamed about being in a lifeboat and watching a large ship sink into the ocean. Many past life regressionists feel that I was perhaps aboard the RMS *Titanic* in a past life, ultimately surviving the catastrophe, especially since my accounts are so vivid. Maybe my relatives who didn't survive the tragedy, desire to communicate with me via dreams.

Spirit Guide Messages via Synchronicity

Perhaps the most famous spirit guide contact is done via synchronicity, or the simultaneous series of events which are extensively related without having a recognizable underlying connection. The concept was first examined by Carl Jung, an analytical psychologist. He described the events of synchronicity to be "meaningful coincidences" if they happen with no fundamental relationship while at the same time holding some sort of significance. Jung asserted that events may be intertwined by causality and meaning. Those occurrences that are linked by meaning don't necessarily mandate an explanation in terms of causality.

Jung also utilized this concept when discussing the existence of supernatural phenomena. He emphasized that this notion directly paralleled concepts such as the relativity theory and quantum mechanics. Jung further believed that synchronicity serves the role of helping people shift from egocentric thinking toward higher consciousness or wholeness.

Synchronicity occurs at precise moments when we need to hear the messages being imparted to us. It can also help allay one's sadness during the grieving process, especially when someone hears a song that reminds them of the person he or she lost. As is the case with many people, I often see the numerical sequence of "444," which is interesting since my maternal grandmother and my beloved cat Max passed away at 4:44 a.m. and 4:44 p.m., respectively. Perhaps seeing those three numbers in unison from time to time is their way of letting me know they're at peace, or their way of popping in to say "Hello." My maternal grandfather used to love the song "Unchained Melody" by the Righteous Brothers. Sadly, he succumbed to Alzheimer's disease in 1993 when I was just a budding teenager. As previously mentioned, ever since his passing, I frequently hear his beloved tune on the radio or on Pandora. It certainly brings a smile to my face and warmth to my heart.

I have been speaking about various supernatural topics at conferences, events, and libraries for many years. In early 2015, I was researching paranormal-themed events around the United States. For some reason unbeknownst to me, I kept running into "Oregon Ghost Conference" on the World Wide Web. This went on for several days until I finally paid attention to it and contacted Rocky Smith of Northwest Ghost Tours. I sent him a brief e-mail introducing myself and the presentation topics I usually offer, one of which is my popular talk on the RMS *Queen Mary's* rich history and paranormal phenomena. The same day, I received an emphatic reply from Rocky. Without coincidence, he wrote how he loves the *Queen Mary* and has been looking for a speaker to present about the ship at his conference.

Thus, I traveled to Oregon City in the spring of 2015 to attend the Oregon Ghost Conference. Since that time, I have been a regular contributor and speaker at this notable event, which is considered the largest paranormal convention in the Pacific Northwest. Rocky also asked me if I could volunteer my time as the conference's California coordinator, to which I gladly obliged. Most importantly, I have developed close friendships with many people in the Oregon and Washington areas as a result. There are some tremendously talented and devoted ghost and spirit researchers in this region of the United States.

Another example of how the stars aligned at just the right time is when I was introduced to Gary Mantz and Suzanne Mitchell, the popular hosts of *Mantz and Mitchell*, one of Seattle's well-respected alternative talk radio programs airing on KKNW 1150 AM. My cousin Ryan's wife Julia is a publicist in San Diego. One day, she contacted me asking if I would be interested in appearing on the *Mantz and Mitchell* radio show. At the time, I had not heard of Gary or Suzanne and learned from Julia that they were seeking a paranormal researcher from San Diego to appear in their program. It was a match made in heaven as Gary, Suzanne, and I have become close friends since my first appearance on their radio show. There is a mutual admiration and respect between us; as such, I asked Gary and Suzanne to write the foreword to my book, *Spirits of Rancho Buena Vista Adobe*, which elaborates on the history and spiritual landscape of the iconic Vista, California landmark. This was most likely the work of one of my guides who knew before I did, that they would be the perfect match for this book.

One day, I contacted Gary and Suzanne and asked them if they would write the piece. They happily obliged and asked me to share some of the histories of the adobe with them. After a few weeks, I opened my e-mail to read their foreword, a piece of work so eloquently written. It honored those that walked the land before us and brought me to tears, albeit in a positive way. Intriguingly, both Gary and Suzanne shared that they, too, shed tears when writing their words. There was a paralleled sense of emotion and sentiment that the three of us shared regarding the Rancho Buena Vista Adobe; it's these feelings that the cosmos understood before we did, hence why their written words were the best choice for the book. None of this was a coincidence. It was meant to be on all levels.

These examples with Rocky, Gary, and Suzanne showcase perfectly how we are meant to cross paths with certain people. Furthermore, these illustrations depict the mutual benefits of meeting various individuals who come into our lives. Each of us can endure brightened horizons by engaging with people from all walks of life and with those who share common interests. We all have living guides in addition to spirit assistants. There's a purpose as to why people come into our lives for a short duration or for eternity, each of them offering guidance and inspiration and allowing us to observe aspects of ourselves that aren't always easily recognizable.

You must put forth heartfelt dedication when deciding to connect with your guide. Focus and intention are the keys to uniting with them. Think of your intent as a force of energy that vibrates to your guide. He or she will be able to tap into your vibrational energy, and an immediate connection will be established. You can create this rapport via meditation or some other form of conscious thought, but do it with confidence and conviction. It's not about sitting on your couch twiddling your thumbs, hoping your guides will come forth. They need to know that you are putting forth the effort to reach them.

One of the important rules to remember when contacting your spirit guides is to not allow the mind to interfere with the process. Our minds are always formulating specific plans and processes for how we carry out our daily duties. However, with spirit guide connection, you don't need to understand the specifics of how you make that connection, as those specifics may lie outside the boundaries of what our human brain can comprehend. Just let it be and trust that it will all fall into place.

Ways to Get in Touch with Your Spirit Guide(s)

This is where the saying "Intention is everything" comes into play. Let's make it clear that your ethereal guide can come to you at any moment in your life. However, there are things that can be done to set the tone when one desires to intentionally connect with his or her spiritual assistants. Becoming acquainted with a spirit guide(s) is one of the most profound humanitarian gifts bestowed on the living. There is really no right or wrong way to accomplish this, but openness of heart and pure love will innately influence the process.

1. Get in the mood: Make sure to clear your space of any unessential items. Take some time to meditate and ground one's mind and soul. You may choose to light a candle, put on some soft music, or dim the lights. Talismans or sacred items may help facilitate the process. Ask for protection and guidance as you go through this process.
2. Create the path to intention: Prior to this, draft some specific questions you want to be answered and be honest about the help you may need and with whom you want to connect. The more open and clear you are about what you want to accomplish, the

better chances you have of being acquainted with the appropriate guide(s).

3. Patience over ego: As mentioned throughout this book, pure communication with the spiritual realm is done via heart and soul, not via ego. Don't get me wrong: all humans possess an ego, which can come in handy for certain survival situations. However, the ego does not deserve a seat at the table of authentic spirit communication and/or help from the ethereal domain. Please love yourself and be patient with yourself, as the messages emanating from your guide to you will not necessarily come overnight. Also, many of these spiritual messages will be subtle and creative in the way they are delivered. This is a reminder to allow your heart, not your analytical brain, to be the receiver of them.

4. Be calm and serene: Train yourself to deep breathe. With each breath, set your intention(s) and allow your mind/body/spirit to coalesce. Inhale all that is welcome for your highest good. Put all daily trials and tribulations on the shelf. Focus on the exact moment.

5. It's okay to make noise: There's a lot of truth in the theory that many of the primal sounds we make align with the vibrations of the universe. One of the most common chants you can make to help facilitate this journey is to say "om" seven times to align with the divine.

6. The welcoming shift: After a while, you will start to notice a shift in your energy. You may even feel yourself among an infinite expanse of space. The scenery may take on different forms. You may feel yourself enter a beautiful vast pasture with vibrant colors, or you may see yourself in a welcoming cosmic space. Upon

arrival, your energetic frequencies will unite with your ethereal assistants. Invite your guides and give them express permission to dance with you.

7. Ask for signs: It's okay to ask your spirit guides to give you an affirmatory sign regarding the messages and/or help you're seeking. Now, rest assured that your ethereal assistants will not impart these in clear, concise ways. I am one who occasionally enjoys listening to music while I write. As I was writing this section, the song *The Sign* by Ace of Base came on. Talk about a synchronistic moment in time! Let me remind you of some of the lyrics to this popular musical melody:

I saw the sign and it opened up my eyes, I saw the sign
Life is demanding without understanding
I saw the sign and it opened up my eyes, I saw the sign
No one's gonna drag you up to get into the light where you belong
But where do you belong?

Of course, people will have different ideas as to the exact meaning of this song. That's not really my point. My intention here is to highlight how it randomly came up in my YouTube music as I was writing about the importance of asking spirit guides for direct signs. This is absolutely an example of the delicate, almost imperceptible ways our spirit guides deliver their messages and divine wisdom. So, it's imperative that we pay keen attention to the abstract manner in which they communicate.

Kathie Guetzko's Story

I have known Kathie Guetzko's son, Adam Shroyer, for many years. Many years ago, he and I used to be members of a now-defunct paranormal research team in San Diego, California. As time has elapsed, Adam and I have kept in touch. When I shared my ideas about this book with him in the latter months of 2018, he suggested that I contact Kathie, as she has experienced a plethora of paranormal and spiritual encounters in her life. Our lengthy yet intriguing phone conversation took place on a cold, brisk day in Boise, Idaho, when I was visiting family.

As a paranormal researcher, I have learned that not everyone is willing to disclose the peculiar and unusual events they've experienced with the dearly departed; however, Kathie emphatically told me that she is perfectly at ease revealing the odd encounters she has come across over the years. Furthermore, the second-generation American also imparted her assumption that everyone experiences a supernatural event at some point in time, especially since her various family members have also walked the path of encountering paranormal events.

On one occasion, Kathie's daughter, Sharrie, came to visit her with her son, Christopher, who is now a young adult. When the boy was around seven years of age, he sat at the top of Sharrie's stairs shaking his head. When his mom asked him what he was doing, he responded, "I am talking to the ghost." Shocked, she said, "What?" Christopher then nonchalantly said, "He just went downstairs, Mom." Kathie remembers her daughter impulsively grabbing her son and quickly fleeing the home. To this day, Kathie isn't quite sure as to whom he was communicating with or whether it was a family spirit guide you will read about in upcoming paragraphs. She feels it may have been the ethereal energy of a Native American, since there are an abundance of tribes in the area of Minnesota where she resides.

In fact, Kathie shared with me that she believes she previously belonged to the Ojibwe (also known as Ojibwa, Chippewa, or Saulteaux) tribes, an Anishinaabe group of indigenous people in North America. She has even read several books by a Minnesota-based author who covers the historical tapestry of many areas in the Northern Minnesota region. When she was younger, Kathie often dreamed of the Wendigo, a mythical man-eating monster or human-possessing spirit residing in the northern forests of the Atlantic Coast and Great Lakes area of the United States and Canada. Historically speaking, the native children feared this particular boogeyman, so Kathie wonders whether she was tapping into a past life during her dreams.

Another mysterious occurrence happened one night when Kathie's teenage granddaughter, Emalie, was visiting. While having a conversation in the living room, the two of them heard a sound; both looked and saw that one of the dining room's tall candles tipped over of its own volition and fell out of its base. As any logical person would do, Kathie went over to the dining room and put the candle back into place. A few moments later, it fell out yet again, and Kathie placed it back into its holder. When she sat back down on the couch, they both saw the candle lift up out of the base and hit the floor. Instinctively, Emalie said out loud, "Great-grandpa, is that you?" "Do you think it's one of them?" Kathie inquisitively inquired. Strangely, the conversation the women had been having was about the afterlife and whether the spirit of Emalie's great-grandfather was around!

Whether due to certain biological or physiological factors, some individuals are more prone to experiencing and communicating with the spiritual realm. With this notion in mind, some people are just born with an innate sensitivity to the supernatural. This appears to be the case with Kathie and her family. Kathie always had a strong connection with her father, who's been deceased for many years, and it was this bond that allowed her to know the second her father had passed—prior to getting confirmation from his medical team. He underwent what was supposed to be a routine surgical procedure without complications but tragically succumbed hours later.

As another example of her family's intuitive inclination, her mother and father always seemed to possess this telepathic knowledge of when their assistance was needed. With an uncanny ability to know when their daughter needed them, Kathie's parents would often visit her home unannounced during the time when she was a single mother of Adam and Sharrie.

Like my younger self, Adam would endure strep throat and/or ear infections quite often as a young child. While fighting these challenging infections, he would typically acquire a high fever and hallucinate as a result. Kathie shared that he would abruptly wake up crying and yell, "Chinese eyes, Chinese eyes." The family didn't know any people of Asian descent, nor did any of them have any Asian friends. Kathie always pondered why Adam experienced this phenomenon and wondered if it was a result of the stories he read as a child.

It wasn't until ten years later that she may have solved the riddle of Adam's sighting of the man with Chinese eyes. One day, she traveled to Minneapolis to see visiting husband and wife psychic mediums who traveled around the country and appeared on television. The wife was apparently a spiritual medium, with her husband there as a guide. Kathie shared her skepticism of this woman's apparent ability to channel spirits and conduct intuitive psychic readings. Some of the television hosts were quite disbelieving of the couple and were often rude to them. Despite being dubious, Kathie thought it would be interesting to go see this husband-and-wife team in person. She met them in a session with a group of ten individuals whom she had never before met.

To preface the following, the husband-and-wife duo did not know anything about any of the spectators as they went around the room asking, "Does anyone have any questions?" The other attendees inquired about some of their odd encounters. Then the female psychic medium evidently channeled a man named Dr. Durrand (spelling unknown) and pointed in Kathie's direction and said, "Do you have any specific inquiries?" Kathie asked why she sometimes feels as though the bottom of her bed moves as if someone sits down on it. The first time this incident occurred, she thought it was Molly, her beloved feline companion; however, at the time, Molly was securely asleep near her head.

While the woman was channeling this Dr. Durrand, he seemingly came through, telling Kathie, "Yes, don't you know? That's your protective spirit. His name is Chang Ling; he is an ancient spirit guide. In times of stress, sorrow, trials, and/or tribulations, he will always be there. He will protect you as long as he is with you and as long as you keep him in your thoughts." It was at this moment that Kathie had a major epiphany and said to herself, "This must be the man Adam visualized during his high fevers as a young child." Just like that, the pieces of the long unresolved puzzle came together like clouds forming on a rainy day. Was this entire experience coincidental, or was there something more to it altogether? Chang Ling stayed with the family for many years.

Another intriguing event occurred that same day as Kathie sat unsuspecting yet skeptical in the audience. Right after Dr. Durrand mentioned Chang Ling, he also asked Kathie if she remembered him as her spirit guide. Credulously, she looked upon him with confusion as she uttered her answer of "no." The hair on the back of her neck stood up as he articulated, "Oh, Katrinka, don't you remember when you sat on my lap as a child, and I would sing this song to you in Russian?" As the channeled Dr. Durrand motioned to sing the tune in question, the hair on her entire body stood erect. Kathie's family is from Finland, and since her country of origin and Russia border each other, she felt that this Dr. Durrand was a distant relative or someone from a past life who came through the psychic medium. Again, was this another sheer coincidence or some form of spiritual communication?

While continuing along the theme of spirit guides, Kathie also shared with me another interesting experience when Adam was in the Navy. One weekend, Adam traveled via his motorcycle to Phoenix, Arizona, to visit with his dad and paternal grandfather. He could only stay a couple of days since his ship was departing from San Diego at the end of the weekend. En route back to California, Adam encountered a torrential blizzard while motorcycling through the Eastern Mountain range of San Diego. Highway patrol ended up closing that part of the freeway, which caused immense anxiety for him as he feared missing his ship's departure. He told the police, "Please, you don't understand; I am in the Navy and I need to go through, or else I will miss my ship leaving port." Reluctantly, law enforcement personnel permitted his passage through the mountains, which received an astonishing four to six inches of relentless snow that particular evening.

Adam remembers driving with his feet treading the ground to keep him steady on the road due to poor visibility. When exhaustion finally set in, he turned off the next exit, crossed over the freeway, and came down to a "T." He had two choices: either turn right or turn left. He decided to go with the former, but his bike jammed as he attempted to turn it. He tried again to turn right but to no avail. Thus, he was coerced to turn left, and surprisingly, his motorcycle cooperated beautifully. As he reached the bottom of the hill, his weary eyes set foot on a hotel. It was almost as if someone was guiding him to this safe destination for the night. When Adam walked inside the premises, he told hotel staff that he tried to first make a right turn. They told him that if he had, he would have come across a bunch of gravel. To this day, Adam feels that it was the spirit of his beloved grandfather who guided him to safety.

When I asked how all of these experiences have impacted her view of the afterlife and spirit world, Kathie relayed, "I would say, for the most part, it has had a positive impact on me; whatever doubts I had are gone now. I believe that there is another realm for us, somewhere else to look forward to once we pass away from this life. I have absolutely no doubt that we go on to a better place. I feel sad for people who can't experience the positive things that can come out of spiritual encounters. With positive, there's negative, but there are some beautiful experiences we can have."

Pete Orbea's Story

Pete Orbea resides in the beautifully quaint town of Port Gamble, Washington, and is a part of my network of Pacific Northwest friends and colleagues. I was extremely fortunate to visit this idyllic area in 2017 while attending the Port Gamble Ghost Conference, an annual event Pete organizes for those intrigued by the supernatural realm. The following story is one of those that will leave a resonating effect on your heart and soul, as it showcases the authenticity of spirit guides and the effects of synchronicity on our lives.

While I was talking on the phone with Pete, he discussed his very first paranormal encounter that occurred during his childhood years. Originally hailing from Boise, Idaho, he, along with his grandparents, used to travel to Sedona, Arizona, during the summer months. While traveling through Navajo country on one of these particular trips, both Pete and his grandfather saw two Native American spirit warrior apparitions adorned in traditional garb appear before them in the middle of the road. Their car continued forward and ended up driving right through these twin spirits who ended up disappearing before their eyes. Pete's grandfather slowed the car to an almost stop so they could inspect the area to see where these two ethereal figures went. Obviously, they vanished and were nowhere to be seen. Pete strongly believes that one of those spirits belonged to his group of spirit guides that he would come to later recognize at his debut visit to the Oregon Ghost Conference in 2013.

With an open mind and a healthy dose of skepticism, Pete mentioned that he grew up having intriguing paranormal experiences involving disembodied vocalizations, odd sounds, and a general belief in life after death. In fact, his mom told him that during his infancy years, he would describe this tall man who stood in his room with him. Of course, in later years as Pete discovered more about his psychic senses and interest in the supernatural, he came to believe that this specific ethereal being was that of his great-grandfather. Pete further relayed the close bond he had with his grandfather, his great-grandfather's son. Regardless of these occurrences, Pete desired to gather hard proof of the supernatural via scientific data collection, especially when he commenced his career organizing the Port Gamble ghost walks and the Port Gamble Ghost Conference.

Let's fast-forward to Pete's adult years, during his very first hosted Port Gamble Ghost Conference. Still holding onto his skeptical side, Pete encountered his first psychic glimpse of the ethereal during a psychic's presentation at this conference. Pete described this figure that appeared behind the presenter who, at the time, was conducting intuitive readings for the audience. At first, Pete was hesitant regarding the authenticity of his experience; however, he came to realize its truthfulness when a fellow researcher illustrated exactly what he saw. Of course, this provided the validation Pete needed.

It was just six months later when Pete attended the Oregon Ghost Conference for the very first time. He still held onto his skeptical side while visiting this popular Northwest paranormal convention. He disclosed that he had odd, anxious feelings while attending this conference but didn't know why. It was here that Seth, one of our fellow friends and colleagues, first approached Pete and asked to sit next to him at the meet-and-greet dinner.

The following day, Pete decided to get a psychic reading from Seth, a well-known psychic medium from the Pacific Northwest. They went to the building's atrium as Pete's stomach was actively churning due to nerves. Seth imparted, "I am going to have you do your own reading," as he instinctively knew Pete's innate intuitive gifts. He then said to Pete, "You don't know what you have, do you?" referring to the latter's medium abilities. Completely dumbfounded, Pete responded with an emphatic "no" but did relay to Seth that he had been feeling weird the last couple of days. Seth proceeded to write some of his own intuitive impressions down on a notepad, without Pete reading over his shoulder, as a way for the two to corroborate results.

Seth then told Pete, "You have eight guides with you. There is one in particular, and I want you to tell me what you see." Pete then described a Native American man with long hair wearing traditional clothing and a loin cloth. Seth then inquired, "What do you see?" With an open mindset, Pete went with it and said that he visualized an appaloosa horse. It was at that moment when Seth revealed what he wrote down on his notepad. It turns out that Seth had written down everything that Pete was psychically picking up.

Pete was shocked and felt a heaviness all over. Seth then conveyed, "Your guide wants you to learn his name, but he's not telling me because he wants you to learn it on your own." With an almost enigmatic precision, a crow flew up and landed right in front of Pete's face. It stared at him for the rest of the session.

As Pete continued to process his feelings from this enticing psychic reading with Seth, the latter picked up on the former's connection with animals. Pete grew up assisting in pet hospitals. As a child, his job was to comfort the animals who were sick or injured. Seth told Pete that he would be conducting psychic readings within a year. Reminding him of the inherent gifts he possessed, Seth let him borrow the *You Are Psychic* book, which Pete held onto until the following year's Oregon Ghost Conference.

After this rather emotional psychic reading, Pete's mind and body felt a multitude of swirling emotions. Then something rather intriguing occurred:

The name "Chocktaw" popped into Pete's head. He wondered whether this was the name of the spirit guide that Seth wanted him to learn on his own. With almost unifying synchronicity, Seth approached Pete, holding a clay sculpture in his hand that he had appropriately named "Breakthrough." Seth then said to Pete, "I don't know why I made this one, but it's for you." This piece of art depicted a Native American reaching out his hand and had been sculpted many years before the two met each other. Pete told me that this particular artwork bore an uncanny similarity to his own intuitive visualizations of his Native American spirit guide.

The sculpture Seth made for Pete. Courtesy of Pete Orbea

Ever since that 2013 convention, Pete's psychic senses started coming together for him. One night as he attended a paranormal investigation with some friends in Oregon City, he felt strange vibrations in certain areas. In one spot, Pete picked up how a homeless man passed away near the train tracks. He later learned that he was correct, as that was exactly what happened some time ago.

Perhaps the unifying aspect that tied all of this in for Pete occurred after the Oregon Ghost Conference. He never met his biological father and knew very little about him. Holding on to the two photos of his dad that his mom gave him, Pete looked for his dad sporadically throughout his life. For some odd reason, Pete felt completely compelled to look for his father one more time, as if something was urging him to do so. He conducted a search via Facebook and discovered who he thought was his sister, as she exhibited the same smile and teeth. Pete then looked through her friends list and found his dad, appearing to look the same as the photos, just with more gray hair.

Pete contacted his sister first and set up a phone call. While on the line with her, she said that she resided around the block from their father and was driving over there at that moment. As his sister pulled into the property, one of Pete's brothers named Jeff was outside. Shockingly, Pete was unaware that he had brothers. He talked with Jeff and let him know that he was searching for his dad.

Furthermore, Pete wanted to know where he came from and what his origins were. Right away, his brother said, "Well, let me tell you; you're Chocktaw Indian." As he about fell out of his chair, Pete conversed with his dad, telling him about the experience at the Oregon Ghost Conference and how he was experiencing paranormal events. His dad informed him that he, too, retained an interest in the supernatural. It was at that moment when Pete told his father about all the recent spiritual experiences and how they connected with each other. His father happily imparted, "Well, I know where you get your psychic gifts from. My grandmother and the five generations before her were known as seers down in Louisiana."

All of the above culminating experiences were absolute awakenings for Pete. Seth was absolutely correct in his vision, as Pete was conducting his own psychic readings within that next year. In the months following that life-changing reading with Seth, Pete began conducting readings with friends with the sole purpose of experiencing deceased family members. Of course, this provided consistent validation for all involved.

The ultimate positive outcome for Pete was how all the above-mentioned life events led to him finding his dad and discovering that he had half-brothers who welcomed him with open arms. Additionally, his life changed as a result and altered how he viewed the paranormal, religion, and faith. All of this was meant to happen for Pete at that specific point in his life, alluding to the power of synchronicity and its effect on our lives. His whole experience is proof that spirit guides exist and that there are those on the other side who are here to help and learn along with the mortal realm. As Pete puts it, "The reading with Seth changed my life. It was a royal flush."

Auriel Grace's Story

I have known Auriel Grace for several years. In addition to being a natural medium and published author, she has hosted her popular *A Gang of Girls* radio show for quite some time. I am so elated that she agreed to be interviewed for this book, as the following story is quite beautiful. As with many paranormal researchers, Auriel has endured many encounters with the spiritual realm; however, her experience at Bandelier National Forest in New Mexico some thirty years ago is one that truly resonates with her.

While in Bandelier, Auriel and her husband were given a special tour of the park's ruins, as it was during the off-season and people were permitted to visit secluded areas not usually open to the public. Since her husband was part of a film crew, the production company permitted them to engage in some really neat activities. The crew worked five, twelve, or eighteen-hour days, with weekends off to rest and rejuvenate. It was on these weekends that Auriel and her husband visited Taos Pueblos and traveled to Santa Fe to enjoy museums and shopping.

Describing the time and location of her spine-tingling spiritual encounter, Auriel shared how the area was particularly stunning, as you could visually spot turquoise, gemstones, and portions of pottery on the ground. Prior to visiting the ancient ruins, the tour first traveled to some circular adobe buildings. The group walked through them as the tour guide discussed how the natives resided in the cisterns. They then walked up a trail and saw a series of caves that the native populations utilized for different reasons. One particular cave was placed adjacent to a cliff; once everyone was safely inside, the tour guide gave a presentation as the sun pierced through. Auriel stood still in total amazement as she looked at the earth-toned and black-stained petroglyphs that were used for cooking and ceremonies many years prior.

Auriel felt as though she walked into a different time and place once she entered the cave. As she stood in the site's center and looked at all the drawings on the walls, she was suddenly surrounded by ancestor spirits. A shaman stood in front of her shaking his turtle rattle as he talked in his native language. She clearly saw his facial wrinkles, turtle shell lines, and jacket beads with front and side fringes. He danced around Auriel in circles. This shaman spirit's hair was braided and included feathers. His moccasins were unlike those in modern times; they had laces wrapped around the outside. He had white paint going all the way down the middle of his nose and two lines underneath his eyes. The ethereal figures of indigenous women and men adorned in traditional clothing appeared in a circle around Auriel. They had black paint on their faces as well as under their eyes and noses.

While the rest of the spiritual energies were chanting, the shaman approached Auriel and said, "You can see me now," as he touched the top of her head with his turtle rattle. The sun or what appeared to be sunlight then came through the hole at the top of the cave, infusing the space with gold light. The shaman then said, "This is your path; this is what you came here for. You came here to see." He then danced around Auriel while shaking his rattle, once again touching the top of her head. She was able to directly depict his aura as well as the colors of the cave. She told me that the colors were different from the ones we see every day.

As if in a time slip, Auriel felt as though she were inside the cave for hours. As the sunlight diminished, eliminating the light inside the space, all the ancestor spirits around her completely disappeared. The entire energy inside the cave shifted, and Auriel could once again hear her husband talking to her. She turned around and asked him, "Where am I?" She had completely lost sense of where she was. He then said, "Are you going to come? There's a really cool cave up here and I know you are going to like it." Even though it felt like her profound experience lasted for hours, Auriel's spiritual encounter occurred over a very short time.

Auriel has shared that, ever since her life-changing experience inside that cave, Native American individuals seem to find her. At the time of her encounter, she was still very young, trying to figure out who she was. The experience clarified her path and answered many of her pervading questions.

Auriel shared that, prior to her encounter with the shaman spirit, she was in the process of asking the universe for help and guidance. In retrospect, she believes that this uncanny event was the exact help she was searching for. It took the entire duration of her visit to fully process the meaning of her encounter.

After Auriel shared with him her exceptional experience, her cousin said, "We have to figure out how we use our intuition." Auriel disclosed how she traveled to metaphysical fairs during her younger years as a way to learn more about her innate intuitive gifts. Many of the participating individuals asked her why she wasn't conducting her own psychic readings when they sensed her abilities. Auriel was quite skeptical of psychic mediums, as she had always been quite practical; however, her seemingly divine meeting with the shaman in Bandelier solidified her natural intuitive talents. With heartfelt gratitude, she considers this event to be the biggest gift she has ever received.

"It hit it home for me," Auriel proudly relays.

Auriel has a distinctive way of practicing her mediumship. She connects to other peoples' spirit guides while attaining information through them. Her life-changing experience reminds us to look at events in our lives and see how they can bond with future situations. It's important to examine synchronous occurrences to see if there are inherent messages, because, after all, we are all interconnected.

> "Grief never ends. But it changes. It's a passage, not a place to stay. Grief is not a sign of weakness nor a lack of faith. It is the price of love."
>
> AUTHOR UNKNOWN

Fostering the Connection: How Moving Through Grief and Loss Can Help You Further Connect with the Spirit Realm

Universal Experiences: The Five Stages of Grief and Loss

When a person expresses grief, he or she is enduring a profound sense of sorrow, along with other emotions associated with a particular event or situation. It is common to experience anguish and bereavement from the death or separation of a beloved family member or friend. However, grief can show its face due to a variety of situational transitions and psychological demises. What's quite intriguing is how each individual progresses through the natural stages of grief. Some will welcome these five relentless stages with grace, whereas others will rigorously ignore and snub any unwanted emotion associated with heartache.

The works of Elisabeth Kübler-Ross have changed the way society views the end of life. Having worked with the terminally ill, AIDS patients, and the elderly population, Kübler-Ross is considered the foremost authority on the concepts of death and dying. It's comforting to know that messages from the afterlife can provide a sense of peace and healing to those who are grieving. These messages go to show that the core essence or soul of a person lives on and thrives after physical death knocks at the door. Kübler-Ross once said that when she "transitioned and graduated," people should celebrate, as she would be "dancing in the galaxies among the stars."

The grieving process is universal; no matter what your religion, culture, or demographic is, every single person has experienced the anguish of losing a loved one. With that said, working in the paranormal research field has allowed me to further understand the dying process and how life continues after physical death. There are five key stages to grief, with no exact order as to how one experiences them; however, it's typical to encounter them in sequence. The phases are reactions to feelings and, as such, can last minutes to hours or even longer as we move in and out of them. They help us come to terms with what we are feeling after someone close to us passes away. It is vitally important that a person doesn't repress or hold in the feelings that accompany grief; it's healthy to know that grief can trigger many different emotions. During a time of loss, it's essential that people take good care of themselves physically, emotionally, and spiritually.

Denial

Often misunderstood, denial allows us to experience shock and numbness; in this stage, we don't want to believe that we've lost a loved one. People are riddled with confusion and disbelief, which causes a wave of numbness to strike. During this phase, it's normal for people to imagine that they are dreaming, that the death they've just found out about isn't real. Questions such as, "Is this true?", "Did this person really die?", "Are they really dead?" are perseverated on during this phase. Anxiety is prevalent, which causes a vulnerable sense of things being out of one's control. This can undoubtedly stir up similar repressed childhood emotions that can further inhibit the healing process.

Denial permits people to unconsciously deal with their pain; suddenly, their lives seem quite overwhelming while they ponder how, if, or why they should go on. This stage is a natural way of letting us experience only as much as we can manage; as it eventually diminishes, one comes to terms with the actual loss. Once this occurs, people will commence an inward search for understanding as they deal with loss.

A bright sunny day in the spring of 2016 was overshadowed by an obscure yet unbelievable reality when I found out that my co-worker jumped to his death from the Coronado Bridge in San Diego, California. Out of respect for him and his surviving family, I will not disclose his name. After hearing the news, I remember driving to work in a completely numb state, pondering whether this was nothing but a nasty nightmare. Once I arrived on site, I parked my car and met up with fellow colleagues for a debriefing. There, we all sat in chairs thinking how implausible this news was. Fortunately, time has helped heal the sadness.

Anger

The anger stage can manifest in a variety of ways and occurs when you realize that you are safe enough to know you will get through your grief. More sensations suddenly hit, such as hurt, loneliness, and panic. You may find that you become angry at yourself for not being able to prevent the loss. You may feel enraged at friends, co-workers, family members, doctors, and even the All Mighty. You may question why someone was taken from you when that person was the quintessential "good" person in life who went out of his or her way for humanity. You may ask yourself, "How can this type of person be taken from us?" Allow yourself to feel the anguish; cry or scream if you need to. Engage in healthy activities that can help you externalize your anger. The truth is, those who've been intrinsically and extrinsically rewarded for good deeds and/or superior health will eventually pass on.

Anger is necessary and part of the healing process; as such, it will cease once you allow yourself to feel it. Harness it, as it can give you a sense of balance as you go through the void created by loss. For this reason, it's best not to tell people who are experiencing this stage of grief to move through it too fast. Allow them to move through anger at their own pace. Pain is the layer underneath the anger, and it's okay to feel it. If someone you know criticizes the way you are feeling, realize that it is his or her problem and that he or she will experience the pain associated with loss someday.

After my co-worker's suicidal leap from the Coronado Bridge, I was angry at myself, thinking that I could have done something to prevent the tragedy. My mom knew this person as well and even worked with him more than I did. She, too, wondered why she didn't see the prevailing signs of his suicidal ideation. In fact, she shared with me that, the day prior, this individual brought in donuts for all the staff and seemed happy. As a nurse who's trained in identifying depressive signs, she was flabbergasted at herself for not being able to detect that something was wrong.

Bargaining

Prior to a loved one's death, people will say that they will do anything to prevent that person from dying; after that individual's demise, bargaining may seem similar to a truce. The "What if…?" or "If only…" questions surface first. Then, it typically shifts from past to future thinking. Instead of, "What if I could have prevented her illness?" the line of thinking will shift to, "Will I see her again once I reach the stars?" In this stage, people want to turn back the clock to thwart the situations that led to that person's death. During this phase, you will do anything to not feel the pain of loss; this phase can be a temporary absolution from that pain. Bargaining helps us transition from one state of loss to the other; it gives us the time that we need to adjust to the void. No matter how a person moves through this stage, one will eventually come to terms with the fact that his or her loved one is truly gone.

Bargaining transitions grievers into the present where they feel emptiness and depression. You may find yourself withdrawing from life as you walk around in a dazed state. Those that don't understand this feeling or its classic symptoms may tell a person that he or she needs to snap out of it. On the contrary, dealing with situational depression after the loss of a loved one is a very natural response. It can help us rebuild ourselves after experiencing devastating loss; in many ways, experiencing what I call the "dark night of the soul" allows us to rise again like a Phoenix ascending from fire. Classic depression warrants medical and/or psychological treatment; however, that which arises from grief helps keep our bodies and nervous systems protected. As with the other emotions that are part of grief's tapestry, allow yourself to experience this emotion and be confident that it will leave once it's served its purpose.

A couple of months after my colleague's death, I drove across the Coronado Bridge. Maybe this was my way of trying to feel closer to him or to see if I could intuitively unearth why he took his own life. As I inched closer to the ominous bridge on Interstate 5, I suddenly felt a swirl of emotions as my heart rate increased dramatically. Once I arrived, I cried almost uncontrollably, begging for the clock to turn back. I felt a hollowness and gloominess while hoping that I one day would be able to see my beloved associate again.

Depression

People in this stage often experience a cascade of symptoms. Individuals may feel sad, confused, overwhelmed, and numb. Some may withdraw from others and endure feelings of despair and hopelessness. There are various ways to adequately move through this inevitable period of heartache. It's imperative to accept support from friends, family, and counselors. It's helpful to accept the flood of emotions that come through without self-judging them. Engage in activities and rituals that commemorate the loss of your loved one. Finally, let time take its course. I endured sadness for several weeks after my co-worker passed away. Talking about his passing with fellow colleagues really helped me stay on top of my grief.

Acceptance

Acceptance does not translate to someone feeling okay with what's happened. This stage is about accepting the reality of someone's loss and creating a new life without a loved one's presence. This phase is the final stage of healing as you learn to cope with and live in a new normal. A person may experience many recollections and remembrances as he or she starts to adjust. The anger diminishes, and we begin to accept that it was our loved one's time to pass on. It may sound contradictory, but enduring all the emotions associated with grief and loss allows us to be closer to our departed loved ones.

One day after some much-needed time, I acquiesced to the fact that my co-worker was gone but certainly not forgotten. I started to adjust to my new normal as I went to work every day knowing that I wouldn't see his smiling face. In fact, my mom and I sat down one evening and talked about all of the memories we had of working with this individual. She has even saved the last e-mail she received from him. Healing took place as she and I made a point to honor our departed associate by striving to do our best and carry on his legacy.

I think it's safe to say that you don't really get over someone's death; you just learn to cope with it and get through it. Experiencing a profound loss forces us to feel deep within our souls; by doing so, we grow stronger as individuals as we begin to invest in our lives in the ever-present absence of the person we lost. Loss takes us on a journey of examining the deep meaning of our existence, allowing us to come to terms with aspects of our own lives. Moving through the stages of grief, whether over months or years, permits us to form new relationships and/or make amends with others as we commemorate our departed loved one. Enduring the pain from losing someone close to us forces us to grow and evolve as we learn to live life all over again.

Bereavement Hallucinations: Visits and Messages from the Dearly Departed

Those who've transitioned to the ethers remain with us. Although not physically, the dearly departed are with us energetically, with the beat of their soul dancing right alongside ours. Every day. Every night. Those who have journeyed to the stars linger in our hearts, our minds, and in each of our senses. Mourning is an intense emotional state. As such, it's highly possible that the griever via a hallucinatory condition sees, feels, or hears the individual(s) who've passed on. When this happens, the mourner constantly senses the person he or she has lost. Typically, these illusions are comforting and make the living feel as though they haven't endured any loss.

According to Ronald Pies, M.D., in his article "Hallucinations of Loss, Visions of Grief," post-bereavement hallucinations could be considered a disordered grieving process called "complicated or pathological grief" (Pies, 2018). This has even been recommended as a new diagnostic classification in psychiatry's DSM-5 diagnostic guidebook. In addition to a single person experiencing these mourning mirages, groups of individuals have collectively experienced these hallucinations, typically following a very traumatic occurrence. For example, Singapore General Hospital reported many ghost sighting accounts from survivors and rescuers after the highly catastrophic 2004 Thailand tsunami that claimed the lives of over 200,000 individuals. In fact, some people were so terrified by these visual perceptions that they quit their jobs at the hospital.

What's interesting to consider is whether these hallucinations have any paranormal and/or spiritual origin. Are these illusions simply holograms of people no longer living in the physical world? Or does our immense sadness act as a capacitor, allowing the ethereal energy of the deceased to come to us? Do living individuals produce these hallucinations out of intense grief, or do the spirits of our dearly departed sense our sadness and, as a result, manifest to our senses? It may be a combination, and it is definitely a topic that warrants further research. Neuroscientists have examined the underlying brain compositions and operations that may shed a light on the reasons for these grief hallucinations. There is still a lot to be uncovered, however. Scientists and medical personnel are exploring a condition known as Charles Bonnet Syndrome (CBS), where an individual witnesses vivid visual hallucinations that are not linked to delusions or psychological problems. Typically afflicting older people, CBS could be caused by eye damage or destruction of the visual cortex.

Nowadays, there is more acceptance and discussion of spiritual happenings projecting themselves out into the general cosmos. With this changed atmosphere, spiritual beings may feel more comfortable and willing to commune with the living, especially after a premature and/or tragic death. Then again, we also need to realize the cultural implications, as these so-called grief mirages may have different implications and explanations across various cultures. Anthropologists have discussed how beliefs and death ritual ceremonies vary across the globe, but there isn't as much known about how differing ethnicities spiritually experience the deceased. As with many other facets of supernatural phenomena, there needs to be more exploration into the causes of and experiences with grief hallucinations.

These hallucinations are very real and quite heartbreaking. Vaughan Bell, author of the article "Ghost Stories: Visits from the Deceased," discusses a 2002 case report by German researchers who examined a mother's experiences after the tragic death of her daughter. While intensely grieving her daughter's untimely death from a heroin overdose, the mom regularly witnessed her child and occasionally heard her say "Mamma, Mamma!" and "It's so cold" (Bell, 2008).

One Swedish study examined the prevalence of hallucinations among elderly widows and widowers within the first twelve months after the spouse's demise. Half of the participants occasionally felt the presence of their beloved. Approximately one-third documented seeing, hearing, and conversing with the departed. We have to acknowledge how the yearning for the presence of someone we love is so heavily engrained in our everyday fabric. When that person is no longer present, our unconscious fervently desires to fill the void by bringing the deceased back into our present. In a way, bereavement hallucinations may be of help in coping with the newly found sense of loss. Furthermore, many people can find healing solace while encountering the presence of someone no longer with them.

Healing Your Loss While Honoring Your Loved One

When my father was ill and close to death, I remember being at his home, going outside at night, and sitting on his front porch. Knowing that he was going to be passing, I looked at the clear, night sky and the stars. Up until that moment, I had felt such pain and sorrow; all of a sudden, all of that lifted, and I felt a sense of peace within. Shortly after that, he passed. (Norma Strickland)

There are many coping mechanisms you can utilize to help move through the stages of grief. It has helped me greatly to set aside a few minutes each day to acknowledge my deceased loved ones and think about the wonderful memories I had with those individuals. Designate a special place in your home or office for a monument to that person's legacy. You can make an arrangement for photos, cards, poems, flowers, mementos, etc. Writing a letter or note to your departed loved one can be calming, as it's a way to communicate with that person as if he or she is still alive. Dedicate some time to partake in things that person enjoyed doing while of body. Chances are, that individual, now in spirit form, will take notice and communicate with you from the ethers. Live your life as your loved one would want you to; honor departed individuals by continuing their legacies, whether personal or professional.

Engage in activities and hobbies that you've always been interested in but have yet to partake in. Some of these may include pursuits that your deceased loved one enjoyed doing. Perhaps you can finish an activity that he or she started but never got to complete. You will undoubtedly feel closer to deceased individuals by participating in activities they enjoyed. Honor yourself and the deceased by helping someone in need or volunteering at a homeless shelter or animal hospital. A young high school student was tragically murdered in San Diego several years ago. She was a scholarly student and gifted athlete who specialized in long-distance running. As a way to honor her memory, the community started an annual fundraiser as a part of the foundation named after her.

Family get-togethers and celebrations of life are healing and comforting. This is a time for loved ones to commune and partake in the healing process together while acknowledging the departed person's unique life. Many families choose to visit with one another on the anniversary of their family member's birthday or passing. Each person can share a unique aspect of the individual they lost, which can be a reminder of shared memories and fun times. There is a collective comfort garnered with shared grief and mourning, a reminder that you are not alone in the pain of losing someone.

I was devastated after losing my dear friend and San Diego Paranormal Research Society consulting historian, Gabe Selak. Gabe worked for the San Diego History Center as a program manager; in 2011, he asked me to present about paranormal research at Balboa Park. We clicked immediately and worked together on other projects. A week or so after his passing, I went to the local store and purchased balloons. Along with my mom, we went to a specific spot in my neighborhood of Tierrasanta and let go of the balloons as a symbolic gesture to Gabe's departure to the stars. As the balloons took flight and ascended toward the bright blue sky, I visualized Gabe completely healthy and free. I cried, and it was an emotional release. In the short aftermath, I felt a strong sense of peace and solace.

Turning to nature is the ultimate way of moving through unwanted emotions and pain. Taking some much-needed time to go on a nature walk or hike and be one with the earth's elements can infuse peace. Meditate to the rising sun in the morning or the rising stars at night; this allows you to be one with the universe and access your collective consciousness. Getting your hands in the dirt and gardening can also be quite therapeutic.

While I was taking some nursing courses, one of my classmates got in a severe car accident one evening and died suddenly at the scene. Our cohort spent many days with this individual, and we collectively felt his loss. It was such a sudden and tragic passing of someone with such a bright future. To honor and remember him, the school dedicated a tree in his memory. One sunny afternoon, classmates gathered and shared in the planting of this tree and the placement of the dedication plaque. It was a way for us to all share in our grief while at the same time memorializing him. Although gone from the physical realm, this person is forever remembered and commemorated.

After my beloved cat, Max, passed away from heart disease, I went to my local Walmart's gardening section, picked out a succulent plant, and later planted it in a special section in my front yard. This plant symbolizes Max's life and contributions to our family. Art is another idea; either painting it yourself or having someone create a painting of your loved one can be a symbolic reminder that he or she is always with you. My Aunt Shirley painted a portrait of Max, which I see every night before going to bed and each morning upon waking up.

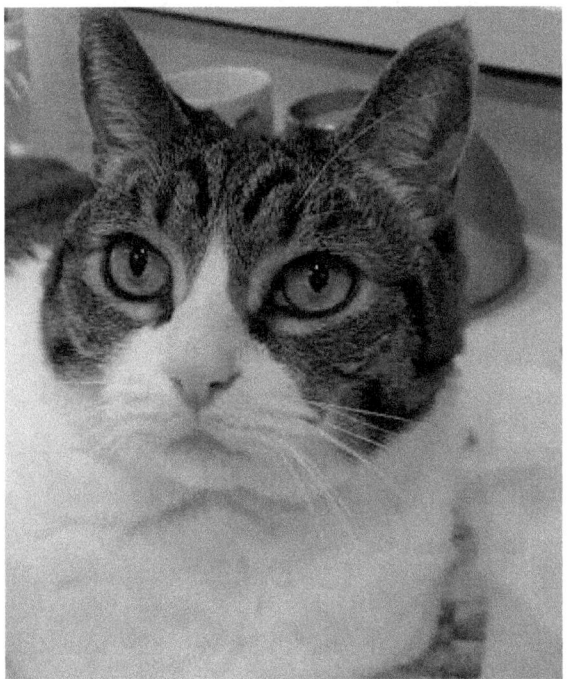

This photo of Max Strickland was captured just a few days before his transition.
Author's Private Collection

Norma also shares how she processed the grief of losing Max so suddenly. She says, "After four months, the intense pain comes and goes, but there is a sense of understanding that Max would not want us to be drawn into such depression. He wants us to remember our lives with him on Earth. He wants to walk and move freely through our daily lives without feeling bad about his transition. After all, we will all transition, and no one should be made to feel guilty for that."

I have had many animals in my lifetime, and I have loved each of them with all my heart. However, there was something utterly special with Max. He and I shared an unmatched bond. His untimely death struck the very core of my existence; undoubtedly, the grieving process was quite difficult. Then, one day, I felt Max's spirit enter my soul, if that makes any sense. Of course, I missed his physical presence, but I knew that he became a part of me. With that, I knew that Max would always be with me.

The time Norma spent as a hospice registered nurse helped her understand the dying process—not just for her, but also for the families that were losing loved ones. She remembers a time when one of her patients, a woman in her 30s, was in the active dying phase. Norma had become close to the patient's mother. At the time of this woman's last few breaths, Norma leaned in close to her and said, "Look for the light. Just look for the light." Hopefully, she found it.

"As people, we go around not thinking of death. Being a nurse, I had experiences in hospitals with dying patients. These experiences make you realize that this is something that we have to experience—and for the families, too. Hospice made me more aware of the loss and grief families go through," relayed Norma. Furthermore, she says, "Talk to the deceased, as I do believe we're going to derive most comfort from those passing…just letting them know how much you love them. Any unfinished business all becomes healed when you talk to them."

Some people turn their heads at the thought of seeing a therapist; however, psychological therapy can be extremely beneficial in allowing someone to accept and move through the stages of grief. Having someone there who can listen to you as you talk about your heartfelt pain is so crucial to the healing process. Professional psychologists and grief counselors are trained to help people access and come to terms with losing someone they cherished. They can help you learn to recognize the different stages of grief and not indulge in self-judgment. Furthermore, therapy can remind a person to take one day, or even one minute, at a time.

Grief is a biological, psychological, and spiritual journey that we all experience. One of the most important things you can do while enduring the pain of loss is to love yourself unconditionally. Be patient with yourself and never judge the emotions that come up. They are presenting themselves as needed to help you grow, evolve, and eventually heal. Especially important during grief is to get adequate sleep, eat healthy, exercise consistently, and always be in touch with your emotions.

Healing from the Loss of a Beloved Sister

The following story exists to show us that there can be beauty amidst the physical loss of someone dearly beloved. I have been graciously given express permission to share this account with you from JC Rositas and his mother. Hopefully, it can leave a mark on your heart and demonstrate how the dying process for some can be a comfortably welcomed experience.

JC is a thoughtful paranormal researcher who takes his work quite seriously. Even though the nexus of this account occurred over forty years ago, JC told me during our interview that his mother imparted this story to him only just a few years ago. "My mom revealed this to me because someone needs to know about it; who better than her son who happens to be a paranormal researcher?" he went on to say.

JC's parents wed at a young age in 1970. The family resided in a four-townhome complex in the state of Indiana. JC was born in October of 1973, the oldest of three siblings. His youngest sister encountered an untimely accident. Having sustained a traumatic brain injury, she had to be fed through a feeding tube and endured abnormal growth from that point forward. JC went on to share that his parents were always very strong and unconditionally devoted to their children. The loving parents they were, they did everything they could to foster happiness and comfort in all their children.

On the evening of Halloween in 1979, JC's mother took him and his brother trick-or-treating. JC's parents were separated at the time, so his dad came over to care for his younger sister. The older children had a full night of collecting delectable sweets in cute little costumes; his father excused himself and went home. After mandatory candy inspections, everyone slept in the living room that night as opposed to their individual bedrooms.

JC's mom was employed at a job that required her to rise very early in the morning. At daybreak on November 1, 1979, just two days after JC's sixth birthday, she noticed that her daughter (JC's sister) was stirring around unusually in her bed. After playing with her for a while, JC's mom started to notice paranormal-like oddities occurring in the house. Various doors throughout the townhome opened of their own volition. JC went on to share that when his mom went upstairs to close the doors, the basement doors simultaneously opened. This commenced a cat and mouse game of opening and closing doors that seemingly moved on their own accord. His mom could not logically figure out the cause of these happenings, especially since nothing like this had ever happened during the nearly seven years they'd lived in the home.

After finally getting the situation under control, JC's mother went back to check on his sister, who seemed quite unaffected by these eerie occurrences. Throughout it all, his sister retained her affectionate smile and playful demeanor. "Boy, this is sure scaring me, but it isn't scaring you at all, is it?" JC's mom posed to her daughter. As soon as JC's mom had spoken, JC's sister got the largest smile on her face, paused to look at her mom, and then passed away peacefully. She would have been two years old in January of 1980.

Being only six years old at the time of this tragedy, JC did not possess the understanding or awareness of what occurred then like he does now as an adult. When his sister passed, he was laying on the couch with his brother. He recalled seeing the paramedics arrive and then deliver the unspeakable words, "I am sorry; she is gone." His mom explained to her surviving children later on that their youngest sibling passed away.

Many years have transpired since JC's sister ventured to the stars. Now that he is an adult, JC looks back on this encounter and considers it a very positive experience. He feels that there are reasons for why events occur—reasons that are not meant to be understood but are meant to happen. In JC's mind and heart, he feels that it was merely his sister's time to venture to the heavens. He said that she was very comfortable and accepting of her passing, especially being so young at the time. Her young age permitted her to acknowledge her death without question or hesitation.

JC believes that his sister, not even quite two years old while simultaneously enduring health issues, had angels accompany her at the time of her physical death and help her transition to where she needed to go. "How else could this be explained? How is it that an innocent child who was going through so much pain and the horrors of her own health problems pass so peacefully?" he went on to ask. Indeed, JC believes that his dearly loved little sister ventured to a better place. She was called home.

JC realizes that, for whatever reason, things happen the way they do. Of course, he will never fully comprehend the workings behind what happened to his sister; however, he believes there are explanations for it, justifications we mortals are not permitted to comprehend. JC relayed that he has accepted his sister's death since she was called home at such an innocent age.

I had a sense of peace and comfort within my soul while hearing JC convey this heartwarming yet tragic story. It goes to show that we do go on to a better place when it's our time to pass from the surly bonds of earth.

Memories allow us to cherish the special moments, especially when our beloved is taken from us unexpectedly. JC vividly recalls times when he'd play with his sister and make her laugh. Indeed, her laugh and contagious smile live on in the heart and soul of her family for eternity.

A Profound Experience at Pomerado Hospital

The following experience occurred at Pomerado Hospital in San Diego, California, at a time when I volunteered at the facility. It's one of those memorable encounters that reminds us of the power of spirit and how we can still communicate with the living once we pass on to the ethereal realm. At the time, I had been volunteering for approximately three months and dealt with several patients of varying ages. However, my time spent with one in particular really stood out.

I met a nice elderly female patient on one of my day shifts at the hospital. I soon developed a rapport with her and spent time with her in her room. She talked about her beloved family and noteworthy times of her life. We soon struck up a strong friendship. This woman was hospitalized for about three days prior to her passing.

The night before her demise, I was volunteering on a night shift when I noticed how uncomfortable she was. What shocked me to my core was how her attending RN seemed oblivious to her suffering. So I did what I could to provide her some peace and contentment; however, it shattered my heart to hear her wails and witness her troubled breathing.

I drove home with sadness in my heart as I knew this woman was going through the active dying process. Needless to say, I didn't sleep too comfortably on this specific night. Since I had back-to-back volunteer shifts, I drove back to the hospital in the early morning. When I arrived, I noticed a crowd of medical personnel inside this woman's room. It turns out that she passed to the stars within minutes of my arrival at the facility. Since I was a volunteer, I was allowed in her room to witness two nurses checking for vital signs, which is the mandatory protocol for a patient who has just died. With no heart rate or breathing detected, the RNs officially declared her deceased.

What happened next was truly beautiful: Shortly after this woman's passing, the look on her face was that of total peace. Then, all of a sudden, the room started to get lighter as I felt a sense of warmth. I then saw her spirit appear before me. Just as my grandmother looked when I saw her ethereally, this woman looked to be about ten to fifteen years younger. She was adorned in bright, colorful clothing, maybe to represent a newly restored vitality that physical death could not possibly interfere with. She smiled at me, perhaps to thank me for helping provide comfort during her last moments in the physical. After a few seconds, she disappeared before my eyes, leaving a pure sense of love, peace, and serenity in her hospital room.

Of course, I couldn't share my experience with other volunteers or hospital staff for obvious reasons. However, I didn't need to, as my heart and soul were as full as they could be. As the previous night's drive home was filled with anxiety and sadness, this particular drive was undisturbed and complete with serenity.

This experience is just another one in the link of encounters that showcases the power of spirit and how the very energetic essence of an individual can transcend physical death. It strongly exhibits how we continue on with life albeit in another plane of existence. I absolutely believe there is life after mortal death, and this encounter showcases the connections spiritual energies have to those they knew while in the mortal realm.

A Healing Message in Numbers

I want to share an experience I had shortly after 9/11/01. In fact, this experience occurred just a couple of weeks after that gut-wrenching day. Completely overtaken with sorrow and grief, I decided to watch an *Inside Edition* segment concerning the last 911 calls from those stuck in the doomed towers, on the ground, and in the ill-destined flights. As if my heart wasn't already bleeding enough, it completely bled out, metaphorically speaking, after watching this particular television episode. After this segment ended, I sat there, almost in disbelief, as tears ran eagerly down my forlorn face.

To help calm my soul, I took a warm bubble bath and spent some much-needed time alone. I reflected. I thought. I cried. I grieved. Believing in universal consciousness and how we are all uniquely connected, I made the decision to talk openly to those who perished in this unforeseeable tragedy. I told them how much my heart ached. I told them how much they're loved and missed. I told them about the tears of our nation. That's when I proposed a question: I said, "I know this may be too much to ask but can you—or one of you—give me a spiritual message of sorts that you are okay and at eternal peace?" I didn't want to appear selfish or intrusive by posing my inquiry, but I let them know my intentions in asking. Knowing somehow via a divine message that these individuals peacefully transitioned to the stars after tragically walking through the valley of untimely, physical death would commence the healing process, not just for me but also for others across the world.

With candlelight flickering and warm water embracing my body, I then thought to myself, "How amazing would it be to get a message in the form of numbers?" After several more minutes of relaxation, I decided to dry off. I looked out my bathroom door at my alarm clock, which was facing me.

"That's it," I thought. "How awesome would it be to get my wish granted through a message on my alarm clock?" As I pondered how unlikely that would be, I said to myself, "Yeah, as if that would ever occur." Even so, my hope for this message prevailed.

The author on top of the Empire State Building in New York City. Author's Private Collection

Let's now fast-forward to the following evening. I watched a movie while stretched out on my couch since I was coming down with a cold. About halfway through, I decided it was time to turn in and go to sleep. I slept for maybe an hour before something mysteriously beautiful occurred: You see, it was as if a divine force awakened me and turned my body around to allow my eyes to meet the infamous alarm clock. What I saw next allowed light to slowly overcome darkness, a frown to morph into a smile. It was at this moment that I received the message I doubted only a day before. My eyes met the three bright red numbers of "911" on my alarm clock. They stayed bright and motionless as I stared at them in shock for what seemed like an eternity. A feeling of hope embraced my soul; a blanket of tranquility enveloped my body. It was at this exact moment that I knew all these individuals were in the hands of God and resting in eternal peace. They were no longer bound by the mortal emotions of fear and terror and instead united together among heavenly pastures.

Indeed, something spiritual happened that night. I could have awakened at any other time, but oddly, my eyes opened at the exact time my alarm clock flashed "911." Perhaps it was a synchronous experience since I don't personally believe in the concept of sheer coincidence. This one singular yet powerful encounter was a message from beyond. These individuals heard me, that much I know. When I think of the unspeakable atrocities of that unforgettable day in 2001, I am reminded of the pure power of spiritual communication and how it can further bond us all through the veils of time. We are all interconnected and intertwined, whether mortal or incorporeal. We are one.

When I relive the pain from this horrific travesty, I am reminded of this beautiful message. Of course, I want to share it with you, too, so you can think about it every year when wounds are opened. We miss them. We love them. They always live on in our hearts as we honor their memories and legacies. Of course, we will never forget.

A Symbolic Message After My Grandfather's Transition

After reading about my profound encounters with the spirit of my grandmother, you can obviously garner that the departure of my grandfather was equally difficult. Helen Lopinto's treasured husband, Andrew F. Lopinto, M.D., was an accomplished individual, achieving goals that many only dream of. In addition to owning his own thriving medical practice in San Diego, California, Andrew also mastered ice skating, playing the violin, and learning different languages. A much-loved family man, he was essentially revered by all who knew him. In retrospect, one can look back on my grandfather's life and consider it the epitome of sheer happiness and success, except for one impediment: the diagnosis of the all-invading Alzheimer's disease during his later years.

It all started on a January morning in the early '90s when Helen phoned my mom to let her know that my grandfather didn't know what day it was. With my grandmother anxious and fearful, my mom left work and drove over to her house. When she arrived, she instantly detected a significant change in Andrew, and that commenced two agonizing years of witnessing the life being sucked out of him. During that span, our immediate family saw my grandfather steadily decline, going from just memory loss to being bedridden and completely disabled. I was only 13 years old at the time, and it was difficult for me to understand this relentless disorder. However, I was sure of one aspect: Alzheimer's could never penetrate or destroy Andrew's soul and spirit. That much I knew.

My mom and I stayed with Helen during the last few days of my grandfather's mortal life. On a semi-warm morning on April 3, 1993, I abruptly awoke from a sound sleep, sat up in bed, and instinctively knew that Andrew had passed. As I heard the garage door opening, I reluctantly got out of bed and proceeded downstairs to the kitchen where my mom and Helen were sitting. The look on their faces confirmed that my instincts were correct, as my grandpa had departed the surly bonds of the earth just a couple of hours prior.

It was my decision to go inside Andrew's room and say goodbye; upon entering, his physical body appeared serenely peaceful, with Alzheimer's no longer in control. I even detected the slight smell of a rose, a scent that often presents itself when someone passes. I held my grandfather's hand and told him how much I loved him. I told him that he will always be with me in spirit and to let me know when he was ready to communicate with me from the ethereal realm.

The author with her grandparents, Andrew F. Lopinto, M.D., and Helen Lopinto
on the Huntington Beach Pier. Author's Private Collection

Andrew's military funeral services were held at Greenwood Memorial Park just a few days later. He was a medical officer and lieutenant on the USS *Ormsby* during World War II, so he had the entire honors, complete with the 21-gun salute and the emotional playing of "Taps." I sat in between my mom and Helen, often glancing their way as an endearing gesture. My grandmother's body shook with the sound of each rifle firing; however, I knew that she was determined to honor his rite of passage. After the services, family and friends gathered at a local Mexican restaurant, sharing fond memories and stories of their times with my grandfather. My mom, Helen, and I were emotionally and physically exhausted as we arrived back at her house in the evening, going to bed rather quickly as much-needed sleep was pertinent.

When the next morning dawned, I immediately noticed something out of place on the bedroom floor. As I inspected it more closely, I saw that a framed photo of Jesus on the cross had fallen off the wall, with the glass frame cracked in many pieces. Of course, it's logically possible that the picture had come loose during the night or some sort of vibration caused it to fall. However, what's oddly intriguing is how the photo appeared to look on the floor. I couldn't believe my eyes when I noticed that the section of Jesus came completely off the mounted cross as it hit the floor. Believing strongly in universal communication, I took this as a message that my grandfather was no longer bound by the unfriendly confines of Alzheimer's. Even at 13 years old, I knew that this was some sort of symbolic message that I needed to pay attention to. In a way, this seemingly uncanny circumstance helped commence my grieving process.

As I grew up and started on my path as a paranormal researcher, I have often sensed both Andrew and Helen when they occasionally visit in spirit form. With my own intuitive senses growing stronger as I work in the field of supernatural research, I consider it a blessing to be able to sense and connect with their ethereal energy. In my heart, I know that they are eternally together in heaven's pastures.

In fact, I believe they communicated with me via a spirit box a few years ago. Ali and I proceeded to ask questions relating to the history of the Rancho Buena Vista Adobe when Andrew's vocalization came through the device. Please note that I did not make out his voice audibly when it came through; it was only during playback a few days later that I unquestionably heard it. I heard him say, "Nicole, I love you." Almost immediately after, my grandmother's spirit said, "Fulvio, go home dear." Now, "Fulvio" is an odd name in and of itself—it's also a nickname for my grandfather, known only to the immediate family.

Needless to say, my heart rate accelerated as tingly sensations went up my spine. I rapidly removed my headphones and sat at my desk in utter shock. Of course, my logical mind tried to interfere, speculating on other possible explanations. However, I intuitively knew these spirited vocalizations were those of my dearly departed grandparents. I had that strong feeling of universal confirmation, that visceral all-knowing sense you get when you know you're right about something. Being quite meticulous and thorough with my research, I will have this portion of the audio file undergo forensic voice analysis.

As I previously mentioned, I am forever blessed to have had opportunities to communicate with my grandparents in spirit form. It's something that I hold near and dear to my heart. It is also very helpful during times when I miss them, as I know their spirited essence will always be alive in my soul.

Healing from the Loss of a Beloved Friend's Son

It's quite suitable that I write this piece during the holidays, an annual time of giving thanks and remembering what's truly significant in life. This time circles around us once a year, almost as a universal reminder that life is about loving, sharing, giving, and helping a fellow person in need. The months of November and December allow golden light to shimmer through the veils of darkness and allow love, peace, and humility to reign above all else—even amidst sorrow and grief.

Before I delve into the nexus of the following experience, I want to offer you some pertinent background information that directly connects to it. Back in 2009, I was invited to speak aboard the RMS *Queen Mary* for Ghost Fest IV, a former annual conference held aboard the docked ship in Long Beach, California. In addition to having my first opportunity to present aboard this legendary liner, I was also introduced to sisters Dawn Gaudette and Sharon

Gaudette-Hieserich, two individuals who have since become dear friends of mine. The three of us share a relationship almost beyond mere friendship; it's as though we have a cosmic, soulful bond that has existed even before we met. With such a strong connection, we have often pondered whether we have known each other in past lives.

I firmly believe that we are destined to meet people throughout our lives. Some of these individuals are meant to stay; others come and go. As mentioned in my books about the *Queen Mary*, one of the iconic vessel's legacies is her ability to bring people together from all over the world. Indeed, she bridged the Old World with the new and continues to do so in modern times. Thus, I owe much gratitude to the ship for bringing Dawn and Sharon into my life.

Even though the three of us reside in San Diego, California, time and busy lives frequently interrupt us from getting together. Thus, we don't get to mingle as often as we would like. With this said, time and separation have no bearing on our friendship; it's authentically preserved regardless of life's recurrent interruptions. Each of us is there for the other in times of need; in fact, isn't that what true friendship is all about? Throughout the ensuing years, we have been there for each other both physically and emotionally through extremely challenging moments.

In the summer months of 2012, I received a call from Dawn regarding her dearly loved son, Kyle. Within seconds, I felt the blood drain from my body as she proceeded to tell me that Kyle was rushed to the hospital after choking on food. Suffering from cerebral hypoxia, or lack of oxygen to the brain, for several arduous minutes, he remained in a coma in the intensive care unit. My mom and I swiftly drove to the hospital to meet up with Dawn and the rest of her family. After we parked in the parking garage, Dawn met us outside the front entrance to the medical facility. With tears streaming down her face, we hugged and embraced each other for several minutes. She then told me that she wanted me to visit Kyle in his hospital room.

As I proceeded down the hallway toward Kyle's quarters, I was overcome with heart-wrenching anxiety as I fought the strong desire not to see him in that condition. However, I knew I had to battle these emotions and momentarily put them to rest, as I didn't want them to carry over to Kyle. Just because someone's on life support and comatose does not mean he or she can't feel, think, or experience. As I entered the room, I saw Kyle peacefully lying in bed with the vital sign monitors displaying his physical signs of life. He was suffering hypoxic brain damage and was most likely not going to pull through. I gently placed my hand over his motionless but warm arm and telepathically spoke to him. I told him how loved he was by so many people. I then gently whispered to him that he is free from the boundaries of physical pain and torment.

For several days, my mom and I met up with Dawn and her family at the hospital as they basically camped out day and night in the waiting room. Amidst the anxiety and unknowing, it was comforting to have everyone together during this difficult time. This was surely an experience that supports the theory that there's strength in numbers. Every day, I visited Kyle as he peacefully slept. I consider it a great honor to have been there for him during his final moments in this life.

A few days passed before the family and Kyle's medical team jointly decided it was time to disconnect him from life support. I went in to see Kyle one last time about an hour before he ventured to the stars. It was surreal, utterly sad, and comforting all at the same time. As I went back out to the waiting room, Kyle's immediate family accompanied him to another room. My heart ached tremendously for what Dawn and the family were about to endure: the tragic loss of a beloved son, brother, nephew, and friend. Time seemed to slow down during these moments with seconds mimicking minutes and minutes mimicking hours.

After about twenty minutes elapsed, I visually witnessed something completely unexpected yet utterly beautiful and spiritual in the hallway directly outside of the waiting room. As I sat facing my mom and another one of our friends, I saw light and movement out of my left peripheral vision. Just so you are aware, the waiting area and outside hallway were separated by a set of large, clear windows. When I turned my head and directly looked out these windows, my eyes met a beach ball-sized, circular orb of self-illuminated light rapidly moving toward us, dipping down and shooting straight up as if it was motioning to go through the roof of the building. This ball of light was so bright, almost as bright as staring into the sun. Its edges were not smooth; it had jagged, plasma-like streaks of light around its exterior. Although it happened at lightning speed, it was one of the most beautiful sights I have ever seen.

I did not immediately tell anyone in the waiting room what I had witnessed. Instead, I had this urge to leave the area and go out in the hallway to have some much-needed moments to myself. I proceeded to go into the restroom, which was right around the corner. While in there, I let go of many tears, almost as if I were releasing trapped emotion. After that, I walked over to this bulletin board of photos of hospital staff that hung on a wall. It was at this point that I heard my name being called from inside the waiting room. When I glanced over, people were gesturing for me to come back inside. Once I entered the door, I was told that Kyle had passed just a few minutes prior.

I then knew exactly what I had seen just moments before. As timing suggests, the glowing yet beaming ball of light I saw occurred at the same time Kyle gained his wings. In my heart and soul, I do believe that I witnessed Kyle's spirit leaving the confines of the hospital as it traveled upward toward the heavens. I knew then that he was completely released from the physical anguish he was experiencing. While he breathed his last breath in mortal form, he breathed his first breath in spirit form. This unforeseen encounter has further educated me on the magnitude of spirit and how our true essence can continue to evolve in the ethereal realm.

A few days elapsed before I told anyone about this personal experience at the hospital in the early evening hours of August 2, 2012. One day, I decided to approach Sharon about this encounter. While on the phone, I descriptively told her what I had witnessed and asked for her opinion on when or if I should share it with Dawn. Sharon relayed to me that I should tell her immediately, as it would help provide comfort in such a grueling time. I concurred and then called Dawn to tell her about this experience. Not surprisingly, my encounter helped provide a foundation of peace and serenity for Dawn, and it signaled the beginning of her healing. She has since told me, "Nicole, I always have in my heart what you experienced with my Kyle, my son. Thank you more than I can say; there are no words."

Kyle, along with his surviving brother Seth, was diagnosed with Autism. Typically, strong intuition and innate psychic abilities correlate with Autism. Individuals with these traits are extremely perceptive and telepathic with natural leadership abilities. They have both right and left-brain alignment with sensitivity beyond their years. Nancy Ann Tappe is widely known for her studies of Indigo children and came up with the term "awe-tistic." Consistently dialed into a higher dimension, Kyle exhibited an astute awareness of life, and I believe it allowed him to transition to spirit quite easily after he passed from the mortal plane. Perhaps this is the main reason why he was called home at such a young age.

It's hard for our analytical minds to contemplate why some people are called home sooner than others. Our creator has plans for each and every one of us, and only He knows what's best for us as individuals. Living as mortals is essentially a stepping stone to our next life, wherever that may be. With his wings ready to fly, Kyle graduated from planet Earth and commenced his expeditions into the beyond.

Being human is to experience joy and sadness, triumph and tragedy. We all know what it's like to experience misfortunes that tear right through our heart's center. Indeed, losing a loved one is perhaps life's most challenging event to endure, especially when our beloved is suddenly taken from us without warning. When our soul is bruised with grief, we may question our faith as the emotions of anger and hopelessness flood our core of existence. Solace starts to overshadow anguish when we can fully honor someone's rite of passage and realize that he or she will always spiritually be with us. Sometimes it's rather difficult to remember that when we mortals pass from this earth, it's only our physical body that ceases functioning; our soul continues to thrive and grow. Love accompanies our soul as it survives physical death, and love will continue to intensify in spirit.

A few years after her son's passing, Dawn began to have visions where she opened her eyes in her room to see a beautiful meadow. Kyle was there, crouched down with a big smile. Dawn remembers hearing the chirping birds as peace enveloped her. It was then that her dad walked up behind her son, and she saw them disappear together. Dawn knows that her beloved son is okay. She thinks that he was ready to transition, and he showed her that he's whole and happy where he is.

Seth often asks Dawn where Kyle is. She tells her surviving son that he's in heaven. Even though he doesn't fully grasp this concept, he points up to the sky and says, "Kyle's up there in heaven." As Dawn says, "Seth's heart knows the truth." Surely Kyle received his wings and danced among the angels. His family and friends unquestionably know that there's an extra brightly lit star whenever they look up at the night sky. Indeed, this is Kyle's star, shining and pulsating bright with love for eternity.

Endless Love: Max Transitions to the Afterlife

There is an unspoken and inherent bond between humans and their animals, an eternal connection that exists forever and even grows stronger when physical death knocks at the door. The relationship between these two parties is unlike any other, as it is purely filled with unconditional love and acceptance. In fact, this amalgamation is the sheer embodiment of what *love* is. Physically saying "goodbye" to a beloved animal is one of life's ultimate cruelties; one can imagine how much a person's soul aches when this day comes. It is, indeed, one of the most painful events to endure. However, the soulful union between humans and animals can never be broken, as it remains for eternity. There are countless beautiful stories of people encountering the beloved spirit(s) of their pets, unsuspecting occurrences that help to allay the sorrow and grief.

We know that even though living beings eventually transition from the physical plane, the true essence of their spirited soul remains. This is a concept that I have known for a long time; however, with the 2016 passing of my cat, Max Montgomery Strickland, I gained a further awareness of its actuality. All animal lovers can relate to and empathize with anyone who is going through the physical loss of a cherished animal. When Max passed away, I thought that my world would completely end forever. After a few days of complete, utter sadness and dejection, something beautiful happened: I started to feel peace enter my soul. This commenced my acceptance of Max's passing. It's extremely hard to put into words, but I started to feel Max alive in my heart and soul. I began to feel him with me at all times, a feeling that slowly but surely overpowered the extreme grief. Of course, I miss his physical self, but I find solace in knowing that his vibrant energy and majestic essence are eternally present.

I do believe that many, if not all, animals can communicate with us when they depart this mortal plane. In the majority of cases, we hear of paranormal incidents with cats, dogs, and horses. It would make sense seeing as though they are among the most popular animals to have. However, I think there is more to the equation. I strongly believe that their innately intuitive ability is due to their expansive intelligence, unconditional love, and psychically inclined nature. We can experience ghostly encounters with our adored animals in the same way we can with our dearly loved friends or family members. Whether it's an apparitional sighting, a disembodied vocalization or footstep, an olfactory sensation, or a cold spot, paranormal occurrences with pets and humans are similar across the board.

I adopted Max and his sister, Kayli Savannah Strickland, after the devastating 2003 San Diego, California Cedar Fires, the firestorm that engulfed the majority of the city in smoke and flames. In many ways, their adoption symbolized a Phoenix rising from the flames, ascending from tragedy to life anew. I fell in love with Max and Kayli the moment I first laid eyes on them, when they were just a tender three months of age. I even remember Kayli reaching out her paw and Max looking at me with intent green eyes when I walked up to their temporary home in a local Petco. In fact, this particular location wasn't on my daily list of stores to visit; however, I linked in with my inner wisdom as it yelled at me to make a stop. Words cannot definitively explain this, but it was the start of that unspeakable and everlasting bond that I mentioned above, an endless union that not even death could interfere with. Intriguingly, when I first adopted Max and Kayli, I created the nickname of "KayliMax," not yet aware of how profound that moniker would be in the years to come.

I grew up with cats in my household; through the years, I developed a solid knowledge of felines. From the time I was introduced to Max and Kayli, I knew that they had special, angelic qualities, unlike those of any other cat that came across my path. As a result of universal planning, the three of us were destined to be together infinitely.

For twelve years, I had resplendent times with Max. Like an old friend, he was always there for me, whether I was enduring an illness or coming home after a stressful, difficult day of work. About a year after I adopted Max and Kayli, I was diagnosed with interstitial cystitis, a painful, inflammatory, and theoretical autoimmune disorder of the bladder. For two years, I endured unrelenting discomfort as I went through various diagnostic and surgical procedures. As you can imagine, both Max and Kayli stood by my side and provided me with endless comfort.

In 2005, Max became ill with what we thought was giardiasis, an intestinal infection caused by the giardia parasite. For days, he exhibited horrendous abdominal pain and diarrhea; thus, we took him to a local specialist who treated him with potent antibiotics. After a couple of weeks, we noticed that his symptoms were not improving, so his veterinarians ordered more diagnostic tests. It was eventually discovered that he had an advanced pilonidal cyst, an abnormal growth filled with hair and skin that forms near the tailbone. Surgical removal and a strong course of specific intravenous antibiotics finally eradicated the problem.

Max's will to live was strong; he could have potentially passed away as a result of this malady. Days went by and thousands of dollars were spent. My mom and I did everything we could in our power to help Max heal; as a result of our efforts, one of his veterinarians referred to us as "stellar owners," an honor I hold dear to my heart. For years after, Max continued on with near-perfect health.

However, in the winter months of 2016, the route changed course. I had to take Max to our community's veterinarian due to an eye infection known as conjunctivitis. While Max was there, his doctor listened to his cardiac and pulmonary functions, and it was then that I received the news that he had a heart murmur. A murmur does not necessarily mean that there is heart disease present; however, it can indicate that something more serious is going on. The following day, I took Max to a specialist to get a cardiac ultrasound or echocardiogram of the heart. Just like the wildfires overwhelming San Diego thirteen years prior, I was then engulfed with the tragic news that no animal lover wants to hear: Max had advanced cardiomyopathy, an acquired and often hereditary physical ailment of the heart. As tears swept down my despondent face, the doctor reassured me that medication could help treat the disease and keep Max comfortably alive for many years to come. Needless to say, I drove home with a mixture of reassurance, anxiety, and anger.

Max was on beta blockers for a few days to help manage his cardiac functions. On the fourth night, I noticed that his heart and breathing rates were extremely high. My mom and I then rushed him to the emergency hospital, perhaps the most terrifying time that I have ever had to experience. After a few minutes, the veterinarian came out to talk to us and told us that Max may have had a reaction to the beta blockers; more seriously, he may be going into heart failure. Thus, he had to undergo some more tests, which took a total time of about an hour.

At about the 60-minute mark, I heard the song "Endless Love" playing on the ceiling's radio speakers. It was no coincidence that this was the moment I saw the doctor's forlorn facial expression as he came out to brief my mom and me. No words needed to be relayed as I knew the dreadful news we were about to hear: Tragically, Max was going into cardiac failure.

Max stayed overnight so he could be monitored and receive the oxygen that he so desperately needed. The following day, my mom and I went to see him, and it was then that his attending doctor conveyed that nothing more could be done. My whole world collapsed, and my soul was stabbed with anger, sadness, and hopelessness. I must say that the veterinarians catering to Max were relentless in their treatment of him, and they tried everything to help prolong his beautiful life. After a 45-minute consultation with the medical staff, I was hit with the decision to either keep him on life support or allow him his rite of passage to a peaceful transition to the stars. Of course, I chose the latter, as it would have been completely selfish to keep him alive in the condition he was in. It was his time, and I did everything I could to honor it.

The registered veterinary technician then took us into a room, a location that I never want to see again in my life. Max was lying on a table with an oxygen mask surrounding his face. Placing my arms around him, I told Max how much I loved him and echoed the following words: "Max, my prince and golden boy, I love you so much, and our bond will last forever. Always and forever. You will always be a part of my heart and soul. Endless love, baby. I love you." As I saw the needle responsible for delivering the medication to commence his transition, I kept telling Max how much I loved him and held him until he breathed his last breath and crossed the Rainbow Bridge. When that time came, he had such a peaceful look on his face and body. They then wrapped a paw-printed blanket around his body and brought him into a serene private room where my mom and I had some time to be alone with him. I must say that this was a very therapeutic experience, as it gave us some time to say goodbye.

With death comes the departure of the physical body, but *only* the physical body. Death cannot touch the soul or energy of our fellow human beings and animals. It is my belief that the bonds we have with our beloved family members, friends, and pets grow even stronger in spirit. In fact, the night I came home from the veterinary emergency hospital after Max's passing, I heard his meow in my bedroom as I was getting ready for much-needed sleep. His vocalization was so loud and clear, as if he was reassuring me that he was at peace in heaven's pastures. It was later that same night when I felt Max breathing underneath my hand as I rested in bed. I couldn't help but think that his ethereal inhalations were representative of a new life beyond the ethers. Then, in one of my often-lucid dreams, I saw Max sitting right in front of me as he wrapped his front legs around me. Needless to say, I woke up with complete serenity.

In the days and months that followed, I have continued to encounter his angelic spirit many times and in many special ways. Almost on a daily basis, I hear Max's meow, sometimes several times in a row. In various areas of my home, I have seen him partially or fully manifest before my eyes. Many nights and mornings, I will tangibly feel him jump up on my bed and curl up beside my warm body. I have even felt his disembodied breath in my face as he spiritually positions himself on my chest, something he often did when he was of body.

Max and Kayli cuddled up together in bed. Author's Private Collection

Now, I have pondered why I haven't had as many of these spiritual experiences with my other fur babies who have crossed the Rainbow Bridge. Perhaps Max, Kayli, and I were destined to have such a close soulful relationship, a woven tapestry of pure cosmic love and connection. Maybe we had past lives together, with fate bringing us together again in this lifetime. My mind can speculate all day, yet there may be elusive reasons why we are so intrinsically connected. Maybe it's something that is not intended to be explained but only to be experienced.

I was utterly devastated when Max transitioned. I felt my soul rip apart; however, it was slowly pieced back together when I accepted his passing and undeniably realized that he further became a part of me. This same sentiment occurred when Kayli transitioned in 2019. I know it's hard to not have our furry babies' physical presence with us, but you will find everlasting solace in knowing that their spirit is always there. Once you come to terms with this, you will feel peace permeate your soul. As always, remember the words "Endless love."

Grief is universal. Every single person has experienced the heartache of losing someone close. Bereavement is an experience that collectively unites all of us. Helping others through their time of mourning can further prepare us for the time when we inevitably experience it. I will share that delving into paranormal research has somehow, some way, granted me the foundation to deal with loss. It is my hope that the shared accounts in this chapter have given you a new perspective on the mourning process and the general strength of spirit. It's a reminder that although our loved ones are no longer physically with us, their essence is—and always will be—with us in spirit.

Epilogue

"For those who seek to understand it, death is a highly creative force. The highest spiritual values of life can originate from the thought and study of death."

ELISABETH KÜBLER-ROSS

As I reminisce about that one summer night in Las Vegas when I encountered the ethereal "draft," I never would have imagined that I would be researching the paranormal in my adulthood. Fast-forward many years later as I type this epilogue, I must say that the last half of my life has been fulfilling with wondrous experiences with the spirit realm. When I first started out as a paranormal researcher, I was mainly intrigued with the aspect of conducting investigations, whether they be at private residences, businesses, or iconic historical locations. Don't get me wrong—I am still devoted to the case study process. However, as I have evolved in my research, I have realized that the connections we make with those residing in the ethereal kingdom are what truly matters. It goes beyond capturing a unique EVP or an anomalous photograph; what's important is the irreplaceable rapport we build, in addition to the teachings and messages exchanged between the living and spirit world.

The afterlife is the next link in the chain of a human soul's progression. In reality, the two worlds are not that far apart; rather, they intermittently enmesh with each other to foster endless relationships. Physical death cannot interfere with the many memories we have of departed loved ones, friends, and furry companions. Healing takes place when we realize that our deceased loved ones still have the capability of being with us in heart and soul once they transition. When you reverse the word "afterlife," you get "life after." In reality, do we ever really die? Since our physical bodies are just a shell that houses our eternal energy, it makes sense that we evolve into the next realm of possibilities when we depart the corporeal domain. This process may be infinite, or it may last until our soul reaches the true divine.

Studying the afterlife and unknown dimensions have not only taught me a lot about myself but have granted me opportunities to become further united with my passion for history and those who walked the land before us. Even though I have always enjoyed history, I have gained a deeper appreciation for and knowledge of historical events through my work as a paranormal researcher. Even though I have researched locations across the United States of America, I have spent much time at landmark locations in San Diego, such as the Whaley House, *Star of India*, Rancho Buena Vista Adobe, Cosmopolitan Hotel, etc. It's mind-blowing to be able to converse with spiritual energies from an earlier time period; when it happens, the hollow space between the past and present completely diminishes.

Indeed, further exploration is needed about the nexus of life, death, and beyond. It is my hope that this book has opened up your heart to see the connection between the living realm and the afterlife. Hopefully, the stories and accounts featured throughout have allowed you to see how both worlds are bonded together through love and how physical death cannot interfere with the eternal connections we have with those in the spirit realm.

We all experience the loss of loved ones. It is also my hope that this book and what is shared in it will bring you some comfort and insight when that day comes. Physical death is as much a part of life as life itself. Embrace it and let the healing magic happen.

Bibliography

Articles

"Automatic Writing." *Psychic Elements: Natural Way to Love and Happiness,* accessed April 25, 2020 at https://psychicelements.com/blog/automatic-writing/

Bell, Vaughn. "Ghost Stories: Visits from the Deceased." *Scientific American,* accessed April 3, 2020 at https://www.scientificamerican.com/article/ghost-stories-visits-from-the-deceased/

Cholle, Francis P. "What is Intuition and How Do We Use It?" *Psychology Today,* accessed December 12, 2019 at https://www.psychologytoday.com/us/blog/the-intuitive-compass/201108/what-is-intuition-and-how-do-we-use-it

Gorkin, Mark. "Loss, Ghosts and the Stages of Grief: Part II." *MentalHelp.net,* accessed April 3, 2020 at https://www.mentalhelp.net/blogs/loss-ghosts-and-the-stages-of-grief-part-ii/

Hameroff, Stuart, and Roger Penrose. "Consciousness in the Universe: A Review of the 'Orch OR' Theory," *Physics of Life Reviews,* accessed May 19, 2020 at https://www.sciencedirect.com/science/article/pii/S1571064513001188

Howell, Cate. "Developing Intuition: An In-Depth Guide to Accessing and Decoding the Language of Your Soul." *Two Spirits One Soul,* accessed March 9, 2020 at https://twospiritsonesoul.com/blog/developing-intuition-an-in-depth-guide-to-accessing-and-decoding-the-language-of-your-soul/

Leafloor, Liz. "Body Snatchers and Tortured Spirits: The Dark History of the South Bridge Vaults of Edinburgh," *Ancient Origins,* accessed February 6, 2020 at https://www.ancient-origins.net/ancient-places-europe/body-snatchers-and-tortured-spirits-dark-history-south-bridge-vaults-edinburgh-020481

Luna, Aletheia. "How to Use a Dowsing Pendulum for Divination: Beginner's Guide." *Lonerwolf,* accessed April 25, 2020 at https://lonerwolf.com/dowsing-pendulum/

Luna, Aletheia. "Scrying: How to Practice the Ancient Art of Second Sight (With Pictures)." *Lonerwolf,* accessed April 25, 2020 at https://lonerwolf.com/scrying/

Marie, Tania. "Working with Pendulums: A Tool to the Heart of You." *Tania Marie: Creating Life as a Work of Art with a Magick Rabbit by My Side,* accessed April 25, 2020 at https://taniamarieartist.wordpress.com/tag/history-of-pendulums/

Martin, Sean. "Life After Death: Shock Claim of Evidence Showing Consciousness May Continue as a Soul," *Express,* accessed December 21, 2019 at https://www.express.co.uk/news/science/728897/LIFE-AFTER-DEATH-consciousness-continue-SOUL

McRobbie Rodriguez, Linda. "The Strange and Mysterious History of the Ouija Board," *Smithsonian Magazine,* accessed April 25, 2020 at https://www.smithsonianmag.com/history/the-strange-and-mysterious-history-of-the-ouija-board-5860627/

Painter, Sally. "What is a Séance?" *Lovetoknow,* accessed April 25, 2020 at https://paranormal.lovetoknow.com/ghosts-hauntings/what-is- seance

Pies, Ronald. "Hallucinations of Loss, Visions of Grief," *PsychCentral,* accessed May 19, 2020 at https://psychcentral.com/blog/hallucinations-of-loss-visions-of-grief/

Senkowski, Ernst. "Analysis of Anomalous Audio and Video Recordings," *World ITC,* accessed June 21, 2019 at http://www.worlditc.org/f_07_senkowski_analysis.htm

Silver, Val. "The Mind Body Spirit Connection." *Holistic MindBody Healing,* accessed March 9, 2020 at https://www.holistic-mindbody- healing.com/mind-body-spirit-connection.html

Solberg, Tanya. "The Spirit World: What Happens When We Die?" *The Aetherius Society – New Zealand Branch,* accessed April 21, 2020 at https://www.aetherius.org.nz/spirit-world/

Taylor, Troy. "Spirit Photography: The Strange and Controversial History." *American Hauntings,* accessed on March 30, 2020 at https://www.americanhauntingsink.com/spirit-photography

Van Praagh, James. "Reach Across the Divide: Connect with Spirit in Your Dreams!" *James Van Praagh,* accessed April 25, 2020 at https://www.vanpraagh.com/reach-across-the-divide-connect-with-spirit-in-your-dreams/

Youngblood, Lloyd. "Dowsing: Ancient History." *The American Society of Dowsers, Inc.,* accessed April 25, 2020 at https://dowsers.org/dowsing-history/

Books

Alighieri, Dante. *The Divine Comedy.* New York: Simon & Schuster, 2016.

Bailey, Lee W., and Jenny Yates. *The Near-Death Experience.* New York: Routledge, 1996.

Bird, Christopher. *The Divining Hand: The 500-Year-Old Mystery of Dowsing.* Pennsylvania: Schiffer Publishing, Ltd., 2000.

Bodine, Echo. *Echoes of the Soul: The Soul's Journey Beyond the Light, Through Life, Death, and Life After Death.* California: New World Library, 1999.

Bodine, Echo. *The Key: Unlock Your Psychic Abilities.* California: New World Library, 2006.

Bradley-Hagerty, Barbara. *Fingerprints of God: The Search for the Science of Spirituality.* New York: Riverhead Books, 2009.

Brown, Sylvia. *Contacting Your Spirit Guide.* Carlsbad: Hay House, 2003.

Burnham, Sophy. *The Art of Intuition: Cultivating Your Inner Wisdom.* New York: The Penguin Group, 2011.

Burpo, Todd. *Heaven is for Real: A Little Boy's Astounding Story of His Trip to Heaven and Back.* Tennessee: Thomas Nelson, 2010.

Day, Laura. *Practical Intuition: How to Harness the Power of Your Instinct and Make it Work for You.* New York: Villard Books, 1996.

Dóminguez, Ivo Jr. *Spirit Speak: Knowing and Understanding Spirit Guides, Ancestors, Ghosts, Angels, and the Divine.* New Jersey: New Page Books, 2008.

Doyle Conan, Arthur Sir. *The New Revelation.* California: Aegypan Press, 2007.

D'Souza, Dinesh. *Life After Death: The Evidence.* Washington, DC: Regnery Publishing, Inc., 2009.

Eason, Cassandra. *The Illustrated Directory of Healing Crystals: A Comprehensive Guide to 150 Crystals and Gemstones.* London: Collins & Brown, 2004.

Edward, John. *Infinite Quest: Develop Your Psychic Intuition to Take Charge of Your Life.* New York: Sterling Publishing Co., Inc., 2010.

Ferdowsi, Abolqasem. *The Shahnameh: The Persian Book of Kings.* England: Penguin Classics, 2007.

Fontana, David. *Is There an Afterlife? A Comprehensive Overview of the Evidence.* Pennsylvania: O Books, 2005.

Fox, Mark. *Religion, Spirituality and the Near-Death Experience.* London: Routledge, 2003.

Frazier, Karen. *Crystals for Healing: The Complete Reference Guide with Over 200 Remedies for Mind, Heart, and Soul.* California: Althea Press, 2015.

Gregg, Susan. *The Encyclopedia of Angels, Spirit Guides and Ascended Masters: A Guide to 200 Celestial Beings to Help, Heal and Assist You in Everyday Life.* Massachusetts: Fair Winds Press, 2008.

Gurney, Edmund. *Phantasms of the Living.* University of California Libraries, 1886.

Hilton, James. *Lost Horizon.* New York: Harper Perennial, 2012.

Holt, Henry. *On the Cosmic Relations.* Vol 1. Charleston: Nabu Press, 2010.

Homer, and Pope, Alexander. *Homer's Odyssey.* New York: Simon & Schuster, 2012.

Houdini, Harry. *A Magician among the Spirits.* Amsterdam: Fredonia Books, 2002.

Kaplan-Spitz, Elie. *Does the Soul Survive? A Jewish Journey to Belief in Afterlife, Past Lives & Living with Purpose.* Vermont: Jewish Lights Publishing, 2000.

Kastenbaum, Robert. *Is There Life After Death? The Latest Evidence Analyzed.* London: Prion, 1995.

Kübler-Ross, Elisabeth, and David Kessler. *On Grief and Grieving: Finding the Meaning of Grief Through the Five Stages of Loss.* Maine: Thorndike Press, 2005.

Lanza, Robert. *Biocentrism: How Life and Consciousness are the Keys to Understanding the True Nature of the Universe.* Texas: BenBella Books, 2010.

Lilly, Simon. *Crystals & Crystal Healing: Harnessing the Unique Power of Crystals and Gemstones for Health and Inner Harmony with Over 200 Beautiful Photographs.* London: Southwater, 1998.

Long, Jeffrey M.D., and Paul Perry. *Evidence of the Afterlife: The Science of Near-Death Experiences.* New York: Harper Collins, 2010.

Moody, Raymond. *Life After Life.* California: HarperOne, 2015.

Okun, Barbara, and Joseph Nowinski. *Saying Goodbye: How Families Can Find Renewal Through Loss*. New York: The Berkeley Publishing Group, 2011.

Parkinson, Troy. *Bridge to the Afterlife: A Medium's Message of Hope and Healing*. Minnesota: Llewellyn Publications, 2009.

Pearson, Patricia. *Opening Heaven's Door: Investigating Stories of Life, Death, and What Comes After*. New York: Atria Books, 2014.

Plato. *The Republic*. California: CreateSpace Independent Publishing Platform, 2019.

Pond, David. *Chakras for Beginners: A Guide to Balancing Your Chakra Energies*. Minnesota: Llewellyn Publications, 2003.

Price, Eugenia. *Getting Through the Night: Finding Your Way After the Loss of a Loved One*. New York: The Dial Press, 1982.

Raudive, Konstantin. *Breakthrough: An Amazing Experiment in Electronic Communication with the Dead*. United Kingdom: Colin Smythe Ltd., 1971.

Schwartz, Gary E., William L. Simon and Linda G. Russek. *The Afterlife Experiments: Breakthrough Scientific Evidence of Life After Death*. New York: Pocket Books, 2002.

Strickland, Nicole. *Spirits of Rancho Buena Vista Adobe*. South Carolina: Haunted America, 2018.

Swedenborg, Emanuel. *Heaven and Hell*. A & D Publishing, 2007.

Van Praagh, James. *Healing Grief: Reclaiming Life After Any Loss*. New York: Dutton, 2000.

Van Praagh, James. *Heaven and Earth: Making the Psychic Connection*. New York: Simon & Schuster Source, 2001.

Wilson, Ian. *The After-Death Experience: The Physics of the Non-Physical*. New York: William Morrow and Company, Inc., 1987.

Videos

"Know Your Spirit Guides with James Van Praagh | James Van Praagh." YouTube video, 14:02. "James Van Praagh," September 16, 2015, https://www.youtube.com/watch?v=EHSgac8yxt4

"Researchers Say There's Evidence that Consciousness Continues after Clinical Death | CBS News." YouTube video, 6:02. "CBS News," October 19, 2017, https://www.youtube.com/watch?v=WnoIf2NwaRY

Websites

Ask Your Pendulum – https://askyourpendulum.com/

San Diego Paranormal Research Society – http://www.sandiegoparanormalresearch.com

Legends of America – https://www.legendsofamerica.com/na-healingstones/

Films

Camp, Brandon, et al. *Dragonfly*. DVD. Directed by Tom Shadyac. Los Angeles: Universal Pictures, 2002.

Oedekerk, Steve. *Patch Adams*. DVD. Directed by Tom Shadyac. Los Angeles: Universal Pictures, 1998.

Music

Ace of Base, "The Sign." Released November 23, 1993. Track 2 on *The Sign*. Arista, 1993, compact disc.

Diana Ross & Richie, Lionel, "Endless Love." Released August 1, 1981. Track 8 on *Endless Love: Motown's Greatest Love Songs*. Motown, 1992, compact disc.

The Righteous Brothers, "Unchained Melody." Released January 19, 1955. Track 2 on *Unchained Melody: The Very Best of the Righteous Brothers*. Polydor (Verve) Records, 1990, compact disc.

About the Author

One of the leading paranormal researchers on the West Coast, Nicole Strickland is the founder and director of the well-respected San Diego Paranormal Research Society (SDPRS). Since 2011, she has co-hosted the "Spirits of the Adobe" tours at the iconic Rancho Buena Vista Adobe. She serves as the California Coordinator for the Ghost Research Society and is also a consultant to various other investigative groups, including the American Spectral Society.

Blending her love of history, paranormal studies, and writing, Nicole has written several books, including *Field Guide to Southern California Hauntings, The Haunted Queen of the Seas: The Living Legend of the RMS Queen Mary, Spirited Queen Mary: Her Haunted Legend, RMS Queen Mary: Voices from Her Voyages, San Diego's Most Haunted: The Historical Legacy and Paranormal Marvels of America's Finest City, Spirits of Rancho Buena Vista Adobe,* and *Max and Kayli: Two Remarkable Felines Forever Imprinted on My Heart.* Her books about the *Queen Mary* continue to be best sellers. She is also a writer and contributor to *Paranormal Underground Magazine.*

Nicole is known nationally and internationally for her research on the RMS *Queen Mary* in Long Beach, California. In addition to offering several topics related to the supernatural, she gives presentations about the ship at paranormal conferences, events, and libraries. She has presented at some of the best-known conventions, such as the Oregon Ghost Conference, Port Gamble Ghost Conference, Troy Taylor's Haunted America Conference, Maritime Ghost Conference of San Diego, Preston Castle Benefit Paracon, Ghost Fest IV aboard the *Queen Mary*, and Strange Escapes, among others. Nicole is represented non-exclusively by RK Entertainment.

Nicole has been featured in a myriad of media outlets discussing her work as a paranormal researcher. These include several local San Diego news programs, such as *Good Morning San Diego*, *San Diego Living*, KPBS Evening Edition, and Channel 8 Evening Edition. Nicole has been interviewed for nationally televised programs, including *My Ghost Story: Caught on Camera*, Travel Channel's *Ghost Stories*, and *Famously Afraid*. She has been interviewed on hundreds of radio shows and podcasts and has appeared in many San Diego newspapers and magazines.

Nicole co-hosts *Haunted Voices Radio*, one of the longest-running radio programs featuring a plethora of guests from all areas of the supernatural. In 2020, she debuted her radio show *The Afterlife Chronicles*, which was selected by Feedspot as one of the top 25 programs on the afterlife. In 2023, she will be debuting *The Inspiration Project*, a program featuring inspiring people with inspirational stories.

In addition, Nicole enjoys cooking, reading, traveling, and spending valuable time with family and friends. She enjoys working with other paranormal researchers as she believes that through diligent research, teamwork, and collaboration we will all better understand the vast field of the unknown.